SUSTAINABLE MANAGEMENT PRACTICES IN TOURISM

About the Editors

Professor (Dr.) M.R. Biju, currently working as Dean, School of Social Sciences and Professor of Public Administration and Policy Studies, Central University of Kerala, Kasaragod. He has served the full term as Dean, School of Social Sciences (2017-20), School of Legal Studies (2019-22) and also a short span as Dean, Academic (2020). Prof. M.R. Biju is one of the widely cited writers in the field of Social Sciences with 161 citations and H-index of 6 and i10 index of 3.

Prof. Biju is the Editor of *South Asian Journal of Socio-Political Studies* (*SAJOSPS*), a UGC listed journal (No. 34425 dated 11.01.2017 with an impact factor of 3.1028). He is also serving as Editor-in-Chief of *International Journal of Political Science* (*IJOPS*). He is a prolific writer on socio-political and developmental issues.

He has published thirty three (33) books, one hundred and seventy-five (175) research papers, seventeen (17) book chapters and eleven (11) seminar proceedings. All the books were published by leading publishing houses in New Dehi. He has delivered seventy-eight (78) invited lectures, sixteen (16) Keynote addresses and reviewed over nine hundred books for (*SAJOSPS*).

His teaching and research experience, spanning over three decades, includes several achievements such as completion of three major research projects funded by Ministry of Panchayati Raj, Government of India and University Grants Commission, New Delhi and the post-doctoral fellowship awarded by the UGC in 2004-07. He has also successfully guided doctoral students of the University of Kerala. Seven students are currently pursuing their doctoral studies under his supervision at CUK. He is consistently making professional academic contributions in the capacity of an Associate Board Member of *Economics and Management*, a prestigious journal published by the Technical University of Liberce, Czech Republic; as the Director and Member Secretary of the Asian Institute of Development Research (AIDR); and as a life Member of several Academic and Professional Bodies.

M.R.B. Anantha Padmanabha is currently serving as Deputy Editor of *South Asian Journal of Socio-Political Studies*. He has to his credit a sizeable number of publications in reputed research journals and he has presented papers in national seminars and conferences. He is a Doctoral Student in International Relations and Politics of Central University of Kerala, Kasaragod.

SUSTAINABLE MANAGEMENT PRACTICES IN TOURISM

Edited by
M.R. Biju
M.R.B. Anantha Padmanabha

CONCEPT PUBLISHING COMPANY PVT. LTD.
NEW DELHI - 110059

ISBN: 978-93-5594-671-3

First Published 2025

Published and Printed by

Concept Since 1974

Concept Publishing Company Pvt. Ltd.
A/15-16, Commercial Block, Mohan Garden
New Delhi-110059 (India)
T: +91-11-41101460
E: publishing@conceptpub.com, *W*: www.conceptpub.com

Cataloging in Publication--Courtesy: D.K. Agencies (P) Ltd. <docinfo@dkagencies.com>

Sustainable management practices in tourism / edited by M.R. Biju, M.R.B. Anantha Padmanabha.

pages cm
Contributed articles.
Includes bibliographical references and index.
ISBN 9789355946713

1. Sustainable tourism--India--Management. 2. Sustainable tourism--India--Kerala--Management. 3. Ecotourism--India--Management. 4. Ecotourism--India--Kerala Management. I. Biju, M. R., 1965- editor. II. Anantha Padmanabha, M. R. B., editor.

LCC G156.5.S87S87 2025 | DDC 338.479154 23

Preface and Acknowledgements

Tourism in India is a vibrant and diverse industry, showcasing the country's rich cultural heritage, breathtaking natural landscapes, and spiritual traditions. It is an integral part of the country's economy and cultural identity. With its vast geographical and cultural diversity, India offers a plethora of attractions, experiences, and opportunities for travellers seeking unique encounters.The COVID-19 pandemic, no doubt, has had a profound impact on the tourism industry in India, as it has globally. To curb the spread of the virus, the Indian government imposed strict travel restrictions, including the suspension of international and domestic flights and the closure of tourist attractions. Lockdown measures were implemented in various parts of the country, severely limiting travel and tourism activities. Economically, the tourism sector in India, which employs millions of people directly and indirectly, has been hit hard by the pandemic. The closure of hotels, restaurants, and other tourism-related businesses has led to job losses, reduced incomes, and economic hardships for individuals and communities dependent on tourism. The travel restrictions and fear of contracting the virus have resulted in a sharp decline in tourist arrivals. International tourists were unable to visit India due to travel bans and advisories, while domestic tourists faced limitations on interstate travel. The uncertainty surrounding the pandemic and its evolving nature have significantly affected consumer behaviour. Travellers are now more cautious, prioritizing safety and hygiene measures when choosing their destinations. The preference for offbeat and secluded locations, as well as personalized and sustainable travel experiences, has increased.

The pandemic has also accelerated the digital transformation of the tourism industry in India. Online bookings, contactless services, and virtual experiences have gained prominence. The use of technology, such as virtual tours, augmented reality, and social media engagement, has provided alternative ways for tourists to explore destinations and engage with the local culture. The challenges posed by the pandemic have highlighted the need for resilience and collaboration within the tourism industry. Stakeholders, including government bodies, tourism boards, tour operators, and local communities, must work together to devise innovative strategies and protocols to ensure the safe and sustainable revival of tourism.

Tourism in India, known for its cultural richness, natural beauty, and spiritual experiences, has been significantly impacted by the COVID-19 pandemic. The travel restrictions, closure of tourist attractions, economic repercussions, and changing consumer behaviour have posed unprecedented challenges. However, as the world moves towards recovery, there is an opportunity to rebuild and reshape the tourism sector in a more sustainable and resilient manner. Adopting safety protocols, promoting responsible tourism practices, leveraging technology for enhanced visitor experiences, and supporting local communities are crucial steps to ensure the revival of tourism. Collaboration among stakeholders, including the government, industry players, and communities, will be vital in developing innovative strategies and creating a conducive environment for tourism to flourish once again. As the situation evolves and travel restrictions are gradually eased, it is important for travellers to stay informed about the latest guidelines and regulations provided by official sources. By adhering to safety measures and being considerate towards local communities, tourists can contribute to the recovery of the tourism industry while experiencing the wonders of India in a responsible and sustainable manner.

Keeping this background, this handy volume presents a dozen chapters on varied aspects and issues connected with tourism, viz. responsible tourism, digital marketing, sustainable management practices, ecotourism, environmental management, leisure travel during pandemic days, ill effects of pandemics on tourism sector, ARDL approach for investigating tourism growth and factors affecting sustainable ecotourism in Brazil. Before conclude, the volume editors, would like to add that through these research papers and articles from the academics, researchers and tourism practitioners, they have tried to explore and examine a few fundamental issues confronted with hospitality sector in India. The contributors have presented solid and practical suggestions to revitalise the sector which may be useful for the students, researchers, practitioners and policy makers in the field. These prefatory remarks remain incomplete without expressing our gratitude to those who have been kind enough to help us in the preparation of this volume. First of all, we would like to thank our esteemed contributors to this anthology of articles. Similarly, we are extremely thankful to Sri Ashok Kumar Mittal, Managing Director of Concept Publishing Company Pvt. Ltd., New Delhi who brought out the volume in an elegant form.

M.R. Biju
M.R.B. Anantha Padmanabha

Introduction

Tourism in India is a vibrant and diverse industry, showcasing the country's rich cultural heritage, breathtaking natural landscapes, and spiritual traditions. It is an integral part of the country's economy and cultural identity. With its vast geographical and cultural diversity, India offers a plethora of attractions, experiences, and opportunities for travellers seeking unique encounters.

- **Popular Tourist Destinations:** India boasts numerous popular tourist destinations, each with its distinctive charm. The iconic Taj Mahal in Agra, the historical forts and palaces of Rajasthan, the serene backwaters of Kerala, and the spiritual aura of Varanasi are just a few examples. These sites represent India's rich history, architectural marvels, and scenic beauty.
- **Cultural and Historical Significance:** India's cultural and historical heritage is a cornerstone of its tourism industry. The country is home to numerous UNESCO World Heritage Sites, including ancient cave temples, palaces, and ruins that reflect the legacy of diverse dynasties. Exploring these sites provides visitors with glimpses into India's vibrant past and the evolution of its art, architecture, and culture.
- **Spiritual Tourism:** India is widely recognized as a spiritual destination, attracting seekers from various religious and philosophical backgrounds. Cities like Varanasi, Rishikesh,

and Amritsar hold immense spiritual significance, offering pilgrims and spiritual enthusiasts opportunities for meditation, *yoga*, and participation in sacred rituals. The exploration of India's spiritual traditions facilitates personal introspection and cultural exchange.

- **Wildlife and Nature Experiences:** India's diverse topography encompasses breathtaking natural landscapes and a wide array of wildlife. National parks and sanctuaries, such as Ranthambore, Jim Corbett, and Periyar, provide a chance to witness the majesty of tigers, elephants, and other unique species. Nature enthusiasts can indulge in trekking, birdwatching, and exploring the verdant beauty of hill stations, forests, and coastal regions.
- **Adventure Tourism:** India offers thrilling adventures for adrenaline junkies. From trekking in the Himalayas and skiing in the snow-clad slopes to river rafting in the Ganges and paragliding in the scenic valleys, adventure enthusiasts can find a multitude of activities to satiate their appetite for excitement.
- **Festivals and Cultural Experiences:** India's rich tapestry of festivals and cultural celebrations showcases its vibrant diversity. Diwali, Holi, Navaratri, Eid, and Christmas are just a few of the festivals that provide visitors with the opportunity to immerse themselves in the country's music, dance, traditional arts, and culinary delights. These celebrations foster cultural understanding and create lasting memories.
- **Medical and Wellness Tourism:** India has emerged as a prominent destination for medical treatments and wellness retreats. With state-of-the-art facilities, highly skilled medical professionals, and the ancient healing system of Ayurveda, the country attracts international patients seeking affordable and high-quality health care. Ayurvedic treatments, *yoga* retreats, and meditation centres cater to the growing trend of wellness tourism.

The Impact of COVID-19

The COVID-19 pandemic has had a profound impact on the tourism industry in India, as it has globally. The following are some of the significant challenges faced:

- **Travel Restrictions and Lockdowns:** To curb the spread of the virus, the Indian government imposed strict travel restrictions, including the suspension of international and domestic flights and the closure of tourist attractions. Lockdown measures were implemented in various parts of the country, severely limiting travel and tourism activities.
- **Economic Consequences:** The tourism sector in India, which employs millions of people directly and indirectly, has been hit hard by the pandemic. The closure of hotels, restaurants, and other tourism-related businesses has led to job losses, reduced incomes, and economic hardships for individuals and communities dependent on tourism.
- **Decline in Tourist Arrivals:** The travel restrictions and fear of contracting the virus have resulted in a sharp decline in tourist arrivals. International tourists were unable to visit India due to travel bans and advisories, while domestic tourists faced limitations on interstate travel. This decline has had a ripple effect on the entire tourism value chain, impacting tour operators, hotels, transport services, local artisans, and small businesses.
- **Uncertainty and Consumer Behaviour:** The uncertainty surrounding the pandemic and its evolving nature have significantly affected consumer behaviour. Travellers are now more cautious, prioritizing safety and hygiene measures when choosing their destinations. The preference for offbeat and secluded locations, as well as personalized and sustainable travel experiences, has increased.
- **Digital Transformation:** The pandemic has accelerated the digital transformation of the tourism industry in India. Online bookings, contactless services, and virtual

experiences have gained prominence. The use of technology, such as virtual tours, augmented reality, and social media engagement, has provided alternative ways for tourists to explore destinations and engage with the local culture.

- **Need for Resilience and Collaboration:** The challenges posed by the pandemic have highlighted the need for resilience and collaboration within the tourism industry. Stakeholders, including government bodies, tourism boards, tour operators, and local communities, must work together to devise innovative strategies and protocols to ensure the safe and sustainable revival of tourism.

Tourism in India, known for its cultural richness, natural beauty, and spiritual experiences, has been significantly impacted by the COVID-19 pandemic. The travel restrictions, closure of tourist attractions, economic repercussions, and changing consumer behaviour have posed unprecedented challenges. However, as the world moves towards recovery, there is an opportunity to rebuild and reshape the tourism sector in a more sustainable and resilient manner. Adopting safety protocols, promoting responsible tourism practices, leveraging technology for enhanced visitor experiences, and supporting local communities are crucial steps to ensure the revival of tourism. Collaboration among stakeholders, including the government, industry players, and communities, will be vital in developing innovative strategies and creating a conducive environment for tourism to flourish once again. As the situation evolves and travel restrictions are gradually eased, it is important for travellers to stay informed about the latest guidelines and regulations provided by official sources. By adhering to safety measures and being considerate towards local communities, tourists can contribute to the recovery of the tourism industry while experiencing the wonders of India in a responsible and sustainable manner.

Content of the Volume

Keeping this background, this handy volume presents a dozen

chapters on varied aspects and issues connected with tourism, viz. responsible tourism, digital marketing, sustainable management practices, ecotourism, environmental management, leisure travel during pandemic days, ill effects of pandemics on tourism sector, ARDL approach for investigating tourism growth and factors affecting sustainable ecotourism in Brazil.

In the **Chapter 1**, **Parvathy Mohan** and **Gireesh Kumar G.S.** examines the impact of responsible tourism on host-community in the State of Kerala. According to them, the philosophy of Responsible Tourism revolves around the background of localism and host communities. Local communities play a pivotal role in Responsible Tourism discourses (participation and equal access) as places where actions of empowerment happens. Further, they opine that the Cape Town Declaration highlights the relevance of involving the host communities in decision making that affect their lives. Responsible Tourism basically aims to benefit the host communities in their socio-economic and sociocultural spheres along with reducing the negative effects by conserving the biophysical environment. Moreover, according to the researchers, the varied perspectives around which Responsible Tourism revolves round are its production-consumption relations, tourism sector-host population relations, worker-employer relations, collective moral responsibility and responses of individuals towards Responsible Tourism and the so-called political assumptions behind the implementation of Responsible Tourism in selected destinations. The local population, according to the contributors, is the ultimate beneficiaries of Responsible Tourism as it creates better tourism destinations and enjoyable ambience to the tourists as well as creates utmost respect to the local culture, customs and traditions, thereby creating better quality of life among host population.

In **Chapter 2**, **Anitha R., Ameeshmon S.** and **Smitha S.,** explores the synergies between performing arts and hospitality units. It is a case study based on Kumarakom in Kottayam district of Kerala. To them, the early stages of tourism in India showcase the country's ancient art, architecture, crafts, food, drinks, music, dance, religion, traditions, customs, heritages, museums, and more. Those elements contribute to the cultural identity of each destination and create opportunities for cultural exchange with visitors. However, changes over time can pose challenges to the sustainability of indigenous culture. In Kerala, where hospitality and the resultant industry is a major component of tourism, there is an emerging trend of representing indigenous culture through Performing Arts. Linking hospitality with cultural performances can improve responsible tourism practices as seen in Kumarakom, where fifteen Responsible Tourism (RT) hotels under study benefit around thirty performers of indigenous performing art forms. The study aims to analyse the implications of these cultural and community linkages in the hospitality sector, given the emergence of RT as a global tourism movement through an exploratory survey method using a Questionnaire.

The focus of attention in **Chapter 3** is on the influence of digital marketing in the tourism industry of Kerala with special emphasis on the accommodation sector. The chapter is contributed by **Thansiya N.** According to her, tourism, one of the most emerging economic contributors to every nation, has immense capabilities for overall development. It is a sum of many supporting services like accommodation, attractions and amenities, activities, accessibility, and the like. One of the most influencing elements among these is the accommodation sector. In the modern era of technological upliftment, digital marketing has a storm-like revolution in all industries. As tourism is a globally connected activity, it has a severe impact on the digital world. Digital Marketing platforms generally adopted by the accommodation sector of Kerala include websites, social media marketing, content marketing, blogs, chatbots, VRN, MTA, etc. As cited earlier, the present study focuses on the impact of Digital Marketing methods on the perception level of accommodation managers and the satisfaction level of tourists and how this affects the promotion of tourism in the accommodation sector. The study analyses the digital marketing methods adopted by the classified hotels to promote tourism and its impact on business performance considering the accommodation managers and tourists. The findings of the study reveal that there exists a difference in the opinion of accommodation managers regarding the adoption of DMMs for the promotion of the tourism business and no significant difference in the perception of accommodation managers considering the satisfaction level of tourists concerning the application of these digital platforms.

The central theme of discussion in **Chapter 4**, which is contributed by **Anu Chandran** and **Reena Esther Rani**, is on the sustainable management practices for mitigating ecological pressures in a protected area. The study is an enquiry into the ecotourism ventures of Pichavaram in Tamil Nadu. This investigation probes the role of ecotourism in adding teeth to sustainable practices, thereby ensuring the perpetuation of ecological values in Pichavaram, which is a fragile destination owing to the presence of much endangered flora and fauna. The practices initiated for ensuring sustainability at the destination were examined by way of an ethnographic study conducted through in-depth fieldwork and also interface with visitors, staff of tourism enterprises, and local people. The research revolved around a qualitative micro-level study that reflects the concerns of the local community as to how capitalisation-driven eco ventures act as a quagmire that adds ecological pressures to their homelands. It also assesses and maps the attitudes of tourists and local communities towards the conservation of mangrove wetlands. Conducted in the qualitative research design mode, the case study method was adopted for processing and presentation of study results drawn by applying thematic content analysis based on the data collected from the field. This is in tandem with the ecotourism principles propounded by premier organisations such as the International Ecotourism Society. The findings confirm gaps in the efficacy of sustainability practices stipulated in consonance with the ecotourism ideals in Pichavaram. It was inferred during the course of the study that *real* ecotourism ventures are scant and the prevailing eco-based business model has only accentuated the pressure on the mangrove wetland ecosystem and also the eco-cultural manifestations. Consequently, tourists and the local community recognize that sustainability is an important issue for the future of the area.

Asha T. Rajan and **Ajitha S.** in **Chapter 5**, highlights the marketing and branding devices of tourism in the state of Kerala. According to contributors, tourism development in national and international levels had attracted the "public policy makers" attention. Tourism development and marketing process are closely tied together and can affect each other in different aspects. But tourism industry does not attain considerable progress, due to lack of attention to marketing of the tourism (WTO, 1997). A country that has enough facilities and possess potential of tourism, but does not consider marketing techniques, will not be successful in growing and developing its tourism industry. Thus, in order to gain progress in tourism, giving attention to retrieval look is essential. Recently, in tourism industry, the concept of destination marketing and branding has attracted considerable attention and interest of researchers, government and practising marketeers all over the world. The emerging concept of destination marketing and branding, even though is not widespread, carries important potential for tourism destinations. The process of developing an understanding of the destination branding process as well as the factors influencing its applicability is of great importance in the marketing of tourism. In short, the authors, through their study, tried to analyse the significance of marketing and branding strategies adopted by Government of Kerala in the promotion of tourism. The study analyses the marketing strategies of the Kerala tourism sector, perception of the tourists about the promotional activities of tourism in Kerala and the strategies adopted by the supporting organisations. The findings of the study reveal that the marketing and branding strategies in tourism industry leads to the overall development of tourism sector in Kerala.

Anitha R. and **Ambeeshmon S.**, in their study captioned "Adherence to Environmental Management Criteria in the Responsible Tourism (RT) Classified Resorts of Kumarakom

Tourist Destination and the Post-Covid Scenario" **(Chapter 6)**, states that the implementation of the Responsible Tourism classification criteria in the accommodation units of Kumarakom has been a landmark today. Based on the Global Sustainable tourism criteria; these criteria are developed for ensuring the sustainability of the tourist destinations, and to contribute significantly to the indigenous populations of the destinations. The triple bottom approaches of responsible tourism are the environmental sustainability approach, sociocultural approach, and economic responsibility approach and they form the basis of the classification criteria. Among these, the criteria of both the economic sustainability criteria and sociocultural criteria have been effectively adhered to by the hospitality industry in Kumarakom. Here, the researcher analyses the fourth section of the open-ended criteria which are subjected to the binomial test, and its adherence to the hospitality sector of Kumarakom tourist destination in detail. The responses are collected from the tourists who stayed in the RT classified resorts at Kumarakom. The contributors conclude their study, by stating that the global pandemic is drastically hit by the entire tourism segment. Almost all resorts are forced to reduce their workforce by 50 per cent or to reduce the salary by 50 per cent. No foreign tourist arrivals are recorded for the last eight months.

Bhuwan Chandra Melkani and **Anil Kumar,** in their study **(Chapter 7)** dwells into the issues, challenges and scope for sustainable development in the Kumaon region of the State of Uttarakhand. According to the contributors, tourism industry in the modern era is emerging one of the largest service-sector industry which is contributing in many ways towards economies through generating national income as well as by creating job opportunities especially for local population and thus become an avenue of socio-economic development and cultural exchange. Travel and tourism is not only an activity for leisure and entertainment but it is also enriching and energizing activity. Uttarakhand one of the most beautiful state in the northern belt known as "Devbhoomi" or "Abode of Gods" is a site of temples and pilgrimage, endowed with salubrious climate, exotic greenery, rich flora besides its rich culture. "Kumaon" one of the two region of the State of Uttarakhand attracts large numbers of tourists and is becoming as one of the preferred choice of visit among travellers. Besides all this, the tourism industry in the Kumaon region is facing some issues and challenges which need to be considered to capitalize the potential of tourism in the Kumaon region. Through this study, the authors tried to examine, the challenges and scope of tourism development in the Kumaon region of the Uttarakhand state, the nature of the research is qualitative and employs the secondary sources of data. The results of the study reveals that there are challenges for tourism development, but with certain improvements and proper planning the region can be developed as one of the best tourist destinations because there is vast scope in new forms of tourism and which can be capitalized with proper and efficient planning and execution.

In **Chapter 8**, **Nilanjan Sengupta** and **Mousumi Sengupta,** focus on the issues in leisure travel decisions during the COVID pandemic. The study is exploratory in nature. According to them, the COVID-19 pandemic has had an unmatched influence on people's mobility. Consequently, leisure tourism faces a multidimensional challenge since, people's willingness to travel, concerns during the leisure travels, and resultant leisure travel decisions, have been drastically changed. On investigating certain issues in the context of leisure travel decision, prevailing among the residents of cities of Bangalore (now Bengaluru) and Mysore, in India, the present study revealed that, the respondents' willingness for taking decision to go on leisure travel would be changed significantly, in case improvement in the COVID-19 situation. The respondents' agreement level in leisure travel decision varied significantly only for the health-related and work-related issues, and not for the other issues, such as social, economic, and psychological. The study also revealed that respondents' leisure travel decision was significantly different, based on their level of education, and not on their age, gender, income, and occupation.

Shan Eugene Palakkal has presented a study titled "Pandemics and Its Repercussions on Travel and Tourism Industry" (**Chapter 9**). According to Shan, an invisible foe has swept the globe, catching countries by surprise with its deadly virulence. Travellers who spent time in countries where the novel Coronavirus, SARS-CoV-2, was present, unwittingly took it with them far and wide. Many countries, some faster than others, threw a shield around their travel points when the transmission of the virus that causes the COVID-19 disease became clear. The US, most European countries, Canada and Japan, among others, imposed various levels of curbs on the entry of foreigners and non-essential travel. The frantic effort was to halt the virus on its tracks. As the virus rages on, the challenge of containing the pandemic within national borders looms. Public places are sanitized and people are stopped from gathering in large numbers. Cities everywhere are powerhouses of the economy, but they have become the focus points of risk overnight. Already some global outcomes have started to emerge. Among the sectors worst affected by the prevailing situation is the tourism and hospitality industry. It is in this context that the chapter examines how pandemics affect the global economy, global lifestyle, and global tourism. No doubt, the chapter gives a brief overview of the history of pandemics and the effects of COVID-19 on tourism and economy on a global context and with special reference to Kerala too. Diseases don't care for race or class. But whenever there is a pandemic, deep-rooted social prejudices resurface. The chapter, also highlights how to manage such situations and ways to explore the world without leaving home and how countries can learn lessons from the past.

In **Chapter 10**, **Mallika A. Nair**, submitted a presentation on "Terra Incognita: The Itineraries of Theyyam and its Impact on Ecotourism in Kerala". Through this chapter, the author seeks to map new ways of perception and thought through an extensive enquiry into the ritualistic art form of Theyyam and its evolution into its present status as the most vibrant façade of Cultural Tourism in North Malabar. After, a detailed presentation, Mallika A. Nair concludes her study by stating that although recent trends in tourism industry believes in the demystification of rituals associated with folk art forms like Theyyam, it could indeed contribute towards a more meaningful communication between a culture and its people by emphatically rooting the performer and his performance in its natural space. Rather, in more simple terms, to try not to remove Theyyam from its original locales and move it to the sophisticated quadrangles of theatrical performance. Theyyam has from time immemorial been the façade of North Malabar and its identity to the world. Ecotourism and exercises that indulge in nature treks as well as measures such as documentary/film festivals to showcase and spread profound awareness of the biodiversity of the Western Ghats will, no doubt, help one of the most vibrant natural resources of the Indian subcontinent from being extinct. Demarcating areas close to the sacred groves as plastic free zones and preservation of natural water bodies will also go a long way in preserving the environment. Tourism can definitely help in the economic as well as ecological sustenance of the local community. And a regeneration of ritualistic art forms like Theyyam can indeed, return man to a more pristine future. Environmental policies of the world are best implemented locally and in short span of time. It is indeed the need of the hour that the Western Ghats and its signature of Sacred Groves be preserved as a model on how local measures for the conservation of ecology can be applied globally to curb environmental issues like global warming. An icon like the young environmentalist Greta Thunberg reminds us that the end is not far. The Western Ghats needs us to preserve it even as we need the Western Ghats for our own survival. Theyyam and tourism might as well be the means of charting a route map to attain this sublime goal.

In **Chapter 11, Bijith George Abraham, Glen T. Hvenegaard, Varghese Manaloor** and **Hugo Narumiya**, highlight the factors affecting the sustainable ecotourism developments. It is an innovative study about the tourism service providers in Sao Paulo (Brazil). According to the researchers, Brazilian ecotourism industry is often connected with conservation and sustainability discussions. Though the web-based tourism providers are significant in promoting the tourism network of the country, one of the challenges pertained in the industry focuses on sustainable development practices. The purpose of the study is to highlight the role of certification, conservation goals and sustainable practices amongst the service providers. The study considered 110 web-based ecotourism operators in the state of Sao Paulo, Brazil. The content analysis approach is used in the service provider's website to maintain texts as units. Factor analysis is used to identify the underlying factors that nurture the ecotourism goals and a logistic regression model is applied to ascertain the certification criteria of the ecotourism operators. The study proves that the sustainability of the ecotourism activities offered by service providers is affected by certification. Preserving the environment is the leading goal of the service providers, followed by sociocultural impacts, conduct and ethics, economic contributions, and education. The study designed a model for certification criteria that gives more importance to the sustainability of ecotourism rather than profit from the industry. The chapter unveils the sustainable ecotourism development practices of the service providers and the importance of ecotourism certification.

In the **Chapter 12**, **A. Sankaran**, examines ARDL approach for investigating the tourism driven growth in the context of South Asia. To A. Sankaran, tourism is a modern industry, which promotes socio-economic development in many ways. The positive and significant role played by the tourism industry in different corners of the economy & society was well documented in the literature. To examine the causal relationship between tourism and economic development in the South Asian region is a value addition to the existing body of knowledge. Against this empirical issue, the present study attempts to estimate the functional relationship between tourism and economic development and also the role of tourism in employment generation. To pursue this research, secondary data on the total number of tourist arrivals, the total amount of revenue earned from tourism, total employment have been collected from various sources such as World Development Indicators, World Travel and Tourism Council, World Tourism Organisation, the Statistics and Facts of Global Travel and Tourism Industry and OECD for the period from 2000 to 2020 for South Asian countries. The collected data have been processed using PMG method in the umbrella of Panel ARDL approach of cointegration followed by causality to capture the multidimensional causal relationship among the variables. In general, the result gives evidence for the existence of the tourism-led growth hypothesis enhancing economic progress in South Asia. The result of the exercise revealed some interesting insights for policymaking. As tourism activities like tourist arrival and tourism expenditure positively influence GDP, the policymakers should focus on these activities to tape the potential of tourism. Thereby we can employ unemployed youth, thus enhancing growth.

Before conclude, the volume editors, would like to add that through these research papers and articles from the academics, researchers and tourism practitioners, they have tried to explore and examine a few fundamental issues confronted with hospitality sector in India. The contributors have presented solid and practical suggestions to revitalise the sector which may be useful for the students, researchers, practitioners and policymakers in the field.

M.R. Biju
M.R.B. Anantha Padmanabha

Contents

List of Contributors

A. Sankaran (Dr.), Associate Professor, Department of Economics, School of Management, Pondicherry Central University, Puducherry. **Email:** sankaran_2002@yahoo.co.in sankaranccopu@gmail.com

Ajitha, S. (Dr.), Assistant Professor, Faculty of Public Administration, SDE, University of Kerala, Palayam, Thiruvananthapuram, Kerala. **Email:** dr.ajithas@gmail.com

Ambeeshmon, S. (Dr.), Assistant Professor, Institute of Management in Kerala, University of Kerala, Palayam, Thiruvananthapuram, Kerala. **Email:** ambeeshs@gmail.com

Anil Kumar, Research Scholar, Department of Commerce, M.B. Government P.G. College, Haldwani, Nainital. **Email:** anilbahuguna123@gmail.com

Anitha, R. (Dr.), Assistant Professor, Sree Narayana Arts and Science College, Kumarakom. **Email:** anithasalil@yahoo.com

Anu Chandran (Dr.), Associate Professor, Department of Tourism Studies, Pondicherry University, Puducherry. **Email:** anu.chandran48@gmail.com

Asha T. Rajan (Dr.), Assistant Professor Government College, Attappady, Palakkad. **Email:** ahsatrajan1@gmail.com

Bhuwan Chandra Melkani (Dr.), Assistant Professor, Department of Commerce, M.B. Government P.G. College, Haldwani, Nainital. **Email:** bhuwanmelkani1980@gmail.com

Bijith George Abraham (Dr.), Associate Professor, Marian International Institute of Management (MIIM), Kuttikkanam, Idukki, Kerala. **Email:** beithabraham@gmail.com

Gireesh Kumar, G.S. (Dr.), Principal, Henry Baker College, Melukavu, Kerala. **Email:** gireeshkartha@gmail.com

Glen T. Hvenegaard (Dr.), Professor, University of Alberta, Augustana Campus, Camrose, Alberta, Canada.
Email: gireeshkartha@gmail.com

Hugo Narumiya (Dr.), Summer Research Intern, University of Alberta, Augustana Campus, Camrose, Alberta, Canada.
Email: gireeshkartha@gmail.com

Mallika A. Nair (Dr.), Assistant Professor, Department of English, Vimala College (Autonomous), Thrissur.
Email: mallikanair102@gmail.com

Mousumi Sengupta (Dr.), Professor, HRM & OB, SDM Institute for Management Development, Mysore.
Email: mousumi88@gmail.com

Nilanjan Sengupta (Dr.), Professor, HRM & OB, SDM Institute for Management Development, Mysore.
Email: nilanjan@sdmimd.ac.in

Parvathy Mohan (Dr.), Assistant Professor, Baselius College, Kottayam. **Email:** gireeshkartha@gmail.com

Reena Esther Rani (Dr.), Ad-hoc Faculty, Department of Tourism Studies, Pondicherry University, Puducherry.
Email: rani_reena.ttedu@gmail.com

Shan Eugene Palakkal (Dr.), Assistant Professor, Department of History and Tourism, Stella Maris College (Autonomous), Chennai. **Email:** shan.eugene@gmail.com

Smitha, S. (Dr.), Assistant Professor, School of Pedagogical Sciences, Mahatma Gandhi University, Kottayam.
Email: anithasalil@yahoo.com

Thansiya, N. (Dr.), Assistant Professor, CHMM College for Advanced Studies, Chavarcode, Palayamkunnu P.O., Varkala.
Email: hajithmm@gmail.com

Varghese Manaloor (Dr.), Associate Professor, University of Alberta, Augustana Campus, Camrose, Alberta, Canada.
Email: beithabraham@gmail.com

1
Impact of Responsible Tourism on Host Community in Kerala

Parvathy Mohan and *Gireesh Kumar G.S.*

Introduction

The drastic changes in consumer demand along with the consequences of mass tourism, as well as the criticism on the vagueness and non-operational character of sustainable tourism lead to the evolution of Responsible Tourism. Responsible Tourism can be considered as a response to the drawbacks of Sustainable Tourism and it is often interpreted as a practice-based application of the concept of sustainability (Harold Goodwin, 2011, p. 31). The ideology of Responsible Tourism is linked to the psychoanalytical processes, both at individual and collective levels about the acceptance and the enjoyment of ethical travelling. Responsible Tourism deals with inculcating sustainability in tourism activity by creating willingness among individuals to take up the responsibility for making tourism activity more sustainable both from production and consumption side by involving all the stakeholders. Responsible Tourism is the key to provide benefits to local community by enhancing their ways of living via industry-community rapport. The Triple Bottom Line (TBL) concept of Responsible Tourism envisages Economic Responsibility, Social Responsibility and

Environmental Responsibility. The focal point of Responsible Tourism lies in optimum utilisation of available local resources, providing employment opportunities to local people and thereby getting involved with the decision making processes of their area in connection with tourism promotion. Responsible Tourism do have an immense effect in the quality of life of local population in the tourism destinations (P.V. Mathew & Sreejesh, 2017).

Literature Review

Morrison, A. Saunders, M. Hughes, J. Pope *et al.* (2019); Camilleri, Mark Anthony (2018) and Yu, Chia Pin, Cole, *et al.* (2018) studied the expectations for Responsible Tourism initiatives in tourism destinations. A comparative analysis is made with respect to the expectations of South African visitors and other international visitors. They studied the positive and significant association between the perceived ease of use and perceived usefulness of digital media, which explores the perceived impact of tourism on the host community. Local residents play a crucial role in the development of Sustainable Tourism practices in a destination. They reveal that both sociocultural and environmental benefits contribute to the living experience of the host community. Rezhen Harun, Gabriela O. Chiciudean, Kawan Sirwan, Felix H. Arion and Iulia C. Muresan (2018); Vikneswaran Nair (2018); Yu, Chia Pin, Cole, *et al.* (2018); Ottilie Geiger (2017), tries to analyse the relationship between sustainable tourism developments in a destination with the stakeholder expectations of that destination. Local residents play a crucial role in the development of Sustainable Tourism practices in a destination. Resident support is inevitable for the better health of tourism industry and for the successful community development. The results showed that the local residents are encouraging tourism prospects in their area as it leads to various positive impacts regardless of some negative effects like pollution. Paul V. Mathew, Sreejesh, S. (2017); Joobi V.P. and Dr. Satheesh E.K. (2016); M. Jeon, M. Kang, E. Desmerais (2016); Wantanee Suntikul, Stephen Pratt, Wallace, I. Kuan *et al.* (2016); Athula, C. Ganapala,

Thusara Pradeep Karunathilaka (2016); Muhammed Hafiz Hanafiah, Inoormaziah Azman, Norliza Aminuddin, Muhammed Raziff Jamaluddin (2016); Tanja Mihalic (2016); Yaping Liu, Linlin Nie, Fuqiang Wang and Zhulan Nie (2015) tries to link the quality of life of local people with the responsible tourism initiatives of their respective regions. They try to connect the term "Responsible Tourism" with "Sustainable Tourism" and accordingly a new term called "Responsustable Tourism" has been suggested. They try to explore community perception and their involvement in tourism development activities. They also studied the influence of seasonal attributes on residents' perception of tourism impacts.

Materials and Methods

The term "Responsible Tourism" itself has the implied meaning that growth and development can be "irresponsible" too. The term "irresponsible" can take varied shapes like exploiting available natural resources in a destination, ignoring local community, their cultures, traditions and customs, betrayed attention to HIV/AIDS in the workplace and failure to protect and prevent the environment and pollution. All these kinds of irresponsible tourism practices give weight to the need for a Responsible Tourism Policy and policy instruments (Responsible, 2011). As far as Kerala is concerned, Responsible Tourism is an inspiring concept which was put forward by the Tourism Department; to be at par with the Global Tourism Market. Ever since its inception in the year 2008, so many responsible activities have been initiated by the department and many of them were a huge success. Responsible Tourism always provides a hassle-free travel and tourism experience to tourists and improves tourism benefits to the locals. Kerala has the potential to receive a high rank in the attainment of the globally accepted Sustainable Development Goals (SDGs) by 2030 via Responsible Tourism initiatives. The RT Mission in Kerala is performing exceptionally well that the local population is equipped to earn an additional livelihood, along with what they were already engaged in (Harold Goodwin, 2019).

The study uses both primary and secondary data and is both descriptive and analytical in nature. Primary data is collected through direct interviews with Tourism Department officials, tour operators, hotel staffs, home stay operators, tourists and local community in the selected Responsible Tourism destinations. Secondary data is collected from various published and unpublished sources, websites of Tourism Departments, like, Department of Tourism (DoT), Government of Kerala, District Tourism Promotion Councils (DTPCs), United Nations World Tourism Organisation (UNWTO), International Centre for Responsible Tourism (ICRT), Department of Environmental Affairs and Tourism (DEAT), Pacific Asia Travel Association (PATA), World Travel Mart (WTM), World Travel and Tourism Council (WTTC), etc. As the study requires in-depth information from the sample respondents, a structured interview schedule is prepared after going through various stages. As the first step, the variables for the interview schedule are identified by thoroughly reviewing the available literatures, both printed and online sources. A closed-ended interview schedule is developed to collect data as it is easier for the researcher to get the responses.

The redrafted interview schedules are pre-tested in Kumarakom, one of the famous Responsible Tourism destinations in Kerala. Before going for a Pilot survey, a method is adopted to identify whether the instrument is self-explanatory or not. In light of the above, the instrument is again redrafted for pilot testing. A sample of 100 respondents of local people are selected for pre-testing the interview schedule. The collected data are tested for reliability and validity.

The Sampling Area for the study includes Kovalam (beach destination), Kumarakom (backwater destination), Wayanad (wildlife destination) and Thekkady (hill station destination) in Kerala. The population consists of host population, which comprises of all those people who are residing in the selected destinations for more than ten years and are directly or indirectly involved in Responsible Tourism activities. Here it is not possible to arrive at the exact number of people as the number is difficult to find out. In cases where a strict probability approach is inappropriate or the cost is greatly outweighing the advantages, non-probability sampling techniques can be employed (Maitland-Smith, 2000). Hence, Snow ball sampling method (exponential non-discriminative snowball sampling) is opted for collecting samples from host community as the researcher finds it difficult to find the samples with requisite features and it is hard to select subjects to assemble them as samples for research.

The most difficult task for the researcher is to have a face to face conversation with local residents as different people have varied approaches towards research and researchers. One thousand interview schedules are prepared for local people in the selected destination, 250 each for each of the four destinations. The questions for the schedule are arrived at after closely watching and constantly interacting with the residents. The responses of certain people sound to be biased, some others give only partial information, few are reluctant to give their details and the researcher herself finds certain schedules inappropriate as it gives unbiased details. All these resulted in rejection of certain interview schedules and received final data from 75 respondents in Kovalam, 75 respondents in Kumarakom, 79 respondents in Wayanad and 76 respondents in Thekkady. Hence, a sample of 305 local population are selected for the study. The collected data are analysed through appropriate mathematical and statistical tools like, percentages, averages, standard deviation, one-sample t-test and One-way Analysis of Variance (ANOVA). Data reliability is tested using Cronbach's Alpha. An Exploratory Factor Analysis (EFA) with a principal component method is conducted to identify the scale dimensionality. Correlation Analysis, Factor Analysis, Multiple Regression Analysis and Structural Equation Modelling (SEM) is used to attain the stated objectives.

The study intends to realise the following specific objective:

- To study the effect of Economic, Sociocultural and Environmental impact on various dimensions of Overall

Impact of Responsible tourism in selected destinations using SEM approach.

Results

In this section, the researcher tries to measure the effects of Economic, Sociocultural and Environmental Impact on Overall Impact of Responsible Tourism in the selected destinations of Kerala. The role of Overall Impact constructs is also measured in this segment in a single model. Structural Equation Modelling (SEM) is the only tool which can be used to measure and analyse the direct and indirect effect emanating from the constructs of Economic, Sociocultural and Environmental Impact upon the Overall Impact constructs. The positive economic, sociocultural and environmental impact of tourism makes the local people to be involved in tourism related activities and thus leads to better tourism development in the area (Nunkoo, R. & Ramkisson, H. 2007). The model developed for validation based on review and researchers own qualitative judgement is shown in Fig. 1.1.

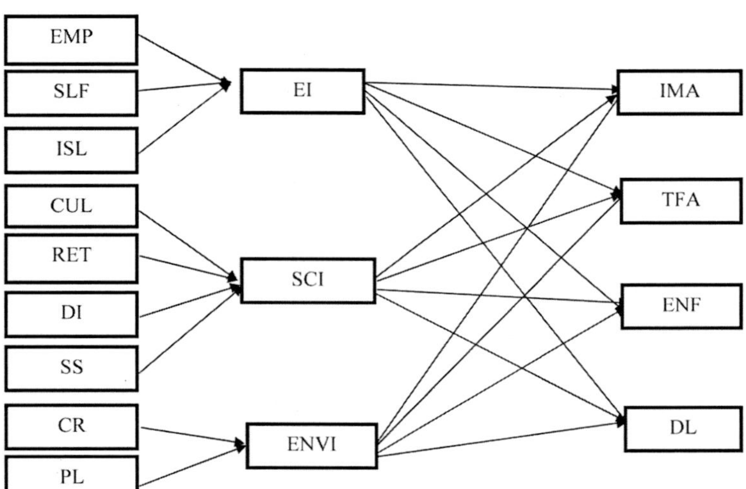

Fig. 1.1: Model for Validation: EI, SCI, ENVI and OI.

The EI, SCI, ENVI and OI Model hypothesized is validated through Structural Equation Model (SEM) using AMOS (Analysis of Moment Structure). Besides using the relative/normed Chi-square (Chi-square/df; df=degrees of freedom) for the assessment of the model fit, the following additional indices from the literature are also considered for assessing the model fit.

Table 1.1: Goodness of Fit Indices: Eco, Socio Env effect on Overall Impact Model

Goodness of Fit Indices	Fit Criteria	Measurement Model
χ^2/df (Normed Chi-square) χ^2–12.84, df-4	<5	3.21
GFI (Goodness of Fit Index)	>0.90	.921
AGFI (Adjusted Goodness of Fit Index)	>0.80	.863
CFI (Comparative Fit Index)	>0.95	.958
NFI (Normed Fit Index)	>0.90	.911
Standardized Root Mean Square Residual (SRMR)	<0.08	.032
RMSEA (Root Mean Square Error of Approximation)	<0.08	.029

Table 1.2 shows the results of the SEM conducted. The direct effects of the independent variable on dependent variables are shown in Table 1.2 with the R^2 values.

Table 1.2: Decomposition of Direct Effect for the Hypothesized Model

Independent Variable	Dependent Variable	Direct Effect	R^2
Employment Generation	Economic Impact	0.272***	0.487
Sustenance and Layoff		0.147**	
Improved Standard of Living		0.362***	
Cultural Identity	Sociocultural Impact	0.349***	0.571
Social Stigma		0.369***	
Revival of Traditions		0.168***	
Destination Image		0.082	

(*Contd.*)

Independent Variable	Dependent Variable	Direct Effect	R^2
Conservation of Resources	Environmental Impact	0.374***	0.563
Pollution and Littering		0.478***	
Economic Impact	Improved Amenities	0.225**	0.348
Sociocultural Impact		0.328**	
Environmental Impact		0.107***	
Economic Impact	Tourist Friendly Ambience	0.171***	0.546
Sociocultural Impact		0.404**	
Environmental Impact		0.199***	
Economic Impact	Environment Friendliness	0.053**	0.425
Sociocultural Impact		0.501***	
Environmental Impact		0.258**	
Economic Impact	Destination Lacunae	0.093	0.389
Sociocultural Impact		0.534*	
Environmental Impact		0.293**	

Standard path coefficients are reported.
***p<.001, **p<.01.

Direct Effect of Constructs in EI, SCI, ENVI and OI Model

Table 1.2 clearly shows SEM analysis in AMOS, which clearly emphasizes the statistically validated paths in the model. The R^2 value denoted shows, how the dependent construct variance is explained by the significant independent variables. Each hypothesis set is being explained individually in Table 1.3.

Table 1.3: Direct effect of EI, SCI, ENVI and OI Model

Path	Hypothesis	SRW	Significance	Inference	R^2
EMP→EI	Ho: Employment Generation has no significant effect on Economic Impact of RT in selected destinations.	0.272***	***p<.001	**Reject H_0**	**0.487**

(*Contd.*)

Path	Hypothesis	SRW	Significance	Inference	R^2
SLF→EI	H_o: Sustenance & Layoff has no significant effect on Economic Impact of RT in selected destinations.	0.147**	**p<.01	**Reject H_o**	**0.487**
ISL→EI	H_o: Improved standard of living has no significant effect on Economic Impact of RT in selected destinations.	0.362***	***p<.001	**Reject H_o**	
CUL→SCI	H_o: Cultural Identity has no significant effect on Sociocultural Impact of RT in selected destinations.	0.349***	***p<.001	**Reject H_o**	**0.571**
RET→SCI	H_o: Revival of Traditions has no significant effect on Sociocultural Impact of RT in selected destinations.	0.168***	***p<.001	**Reject H_o**	
DI→SCI	H_o: Destination Image has no significant effect on Sociocultural Impact of RT in selected destinations.	0.082	-	**Accept H_o**	
SS→SCI	H_o: Social Stigma has no significant effect on Sociocultural Impact of RT in selected destinations.	0.369***	***p<.001	**Reject H_o**	

(Contd.)

Path	Hypothesis	SRW	Significance	Inference	R^2
CR→ENVI	H_o: Conservation of resources has no significant effect on Environmental Impact of RT in selected destinations.	0.374***	***p<.001	**Reject H_o**	**0.563**
PL→ENVI	H_o: Pollution & Littering has no significant effect on Environmental Impact of RT in selected destinations.	0.478***	***p<.001	**Reject H_o**	
EI→IMA	H_o: Economic Impact of RT has no significant effect on Improved amenities.	0.225**	**p<.01	**Reject H_o**	**0.348**
SCI→IMA	H_o: Sociocultural Impact of RT has no significant effect on Improved amenities.	0.328**	**p<.01	**Reject H_o**	
ENVI→IMA	H_o: Environmental Impact of RT has no significant effect on Improved amenities.	0.107***	***p<.001	**Reject H_o**	
EI→TFA	H_o: Economic Impact of RT has no significant effect on Tourist Friendly Ambience.	0.171***	***p<.001	**Reject H_o**	**0.546**
SCI→TFA	H_o: Sociocultural Impact of RT has no significant effect on Tourist Friendly Ambience.	0.404**	**p<.01	**Reject H_o**	

(*Contd.*)

Path	Hypothesis	SRW	Significance	Inference	R^2
ENVI→TFA	H_o: Environmental Impact of RT has no significant effect on Tourist Friendly Ambience.	0.199***	***p<.001	**Reject H_O**	**0.546**
EI→ENF	H_o: Economic Impact of RT has no significant effect on Environment Friendliness.	0.053**	**p<.01	**Reject H_O**	
SCI→ENF	H_o: Sociocultural Impact of RT has no significant effect on Environment Friendliness.	0.501***	***p<.001	**Reject H_O**	**0.425**
ENVI→ENF	H_o: Environmental Impact of RT has no significant effect on Environment Friendliness.	0.258**	**p<.01	**Reject H_O**	
EI→DL	H_o: Economic Impact of RT has no significant effect on Destination Lacunae.	0.093	-	**Accept H_O**	
SCI→DL	H_o: Sociocultural Impact of RT has no significant effect on Destination Lacunae.	0.534*	*p<.05	**Reject H_O**	**0.389**
ENVI→DL	H_o: Environmental Impact of RT has no significant effect on Destination Lacunae.	0.293**	**p<.01	**Reject H_O**	

Source: Compiled by the researcher.
***p<.001, **p<.01, *p<.05

Discussions

In this part, the researcher explains the direct effect of Employment Generation (EMP), Sustenance and Layoff (SLF) and Improved Standard of Living (ISL) upon the Economic Impact (EI) of RT. The R^2 value denoted is 0.487 which shows Economic Impact of RT varies on account of the three constructs, and the variation is found to be 48.7 per cent. Here based on the significance of regression weight it can be found that **EMP, SLF and ISL** has a significant effect upon Economic Impact of RT in the selected destinations.

Also, the researcher explains the direct effect of Cultural Identity (CUL), Revival of Traditions (RET), Destination Image (DI) and Social Stigma (SS) upon the Sociocultural Impact (SCI) of RT. R^2 is the per cent of the variance in the dependent explained jointly by the independents. The R^2 value denoted is 0.571 which shows Sociocultural Impact of RT varies on account of the four constructs, and the variation is found to be 57.1 per cent. Here based on the significance of regression weight it can be found that **CUL, RET, DI and SS** has a significant effect upon Sociocultural Impact of RT in the selected destinations.

The researcher also is delighted to explain the direct effect of Conservation of Resources (CR) and Pollution & Littering (PL) upon the Environmental Impact (ENVI) of RT, as shown in the hypothesized model. R^2 is the per cent of the variance in the dependent explained jointly by the independents. The R^2 value denoted is 0.563 which shows Environmental Impact of RT varies on account of the two constructs, and the variation is found to be 56.3 per cent. Here based on the significance of regression weight it can be found that CR and PL have a significant effect upon Environmental Impact of RT in the selected destinations.

The researcher explains the direct effect of Economic Impact (EI), Sociocultural Impact (SCI) and Environmental Impact (ENVI) upon Improved Amenities (IMA) of RT. R^2 is the per cent of the variance in the dependent explained jointly by the independents. The R^2 value denoted is 0.348 which shows Improved Amenities (IMA) in the destination varies on account of the three constructs, and the variation is found to be 34.8 per cent. Here based on the significance of regression weight it can be found that **EI, SCI** and **ENVI** have a significant effect upon Improved Amenities of RT in the selected destinations.

In this part, the researcher explains the direct effect of Economic Impact (EI), Sociocultural Impact (SCI) and Environmental Impact (ENVI) upon Tourist Friendly Ambience (TFA) of RT. R^2 is the per cent of the variance in the dependent explained jointly by the independents. The R^2 value denoted is 0.546 which shows Tourist Friendly Ambience (TFA) in the destination varies on account of the three constructs, and the variation is found to be 54.6 per cent. Here based on the significance of regression weight it can be found that **EI, SCI** and **ENVI** have a significant effect upon Tourist Friendly Ambience (TFA) of RT in the selected destinations.

In this part, the researcher explains the direct effect of Economic Impact (EI), Sociocultural Impact (SCI) and Environmental Impact (ENVI) upon Environment Friendliness (ENF) of RT, as shown in the hypothesized model. R^2 is the per cent of the variance in the dependent explained jointly by the independents. The R^2 value denoted is 0.425 which shows Environment Friendliness (ENF) in the destination varies on account of the three constructs, and the variation is found to be 42.5 per cent. Here based on the significance of regression weight it can be found that **EI, SCI and ENVI** has a significant effect upon Environment Friendliness (ENF) of RT in the selected destinations.

In this part, the researcher explains the direct effect of Economic Impact (EI), Sociocultural Impact (SCI) and Environmental Impact (ENVI) upon Destination Lacunae (DL) of RT, as shown in the hypothesized model. R^2 is the per cent of the variance in the dependent explained jointly by the independents. The R^2 value denoted is 0.389 which shows Destination Lacunae (DL) in the destination varies on account of the three constructs, and the variation is found to be 38.9 per cent. Here based on the significance of regression weight it can be found that **SCI and ENVI** have a significant effect upon Destination Lacunae (DL) in the selected destinations, whereas it is found that **EI** does not have any significant effect on DL.

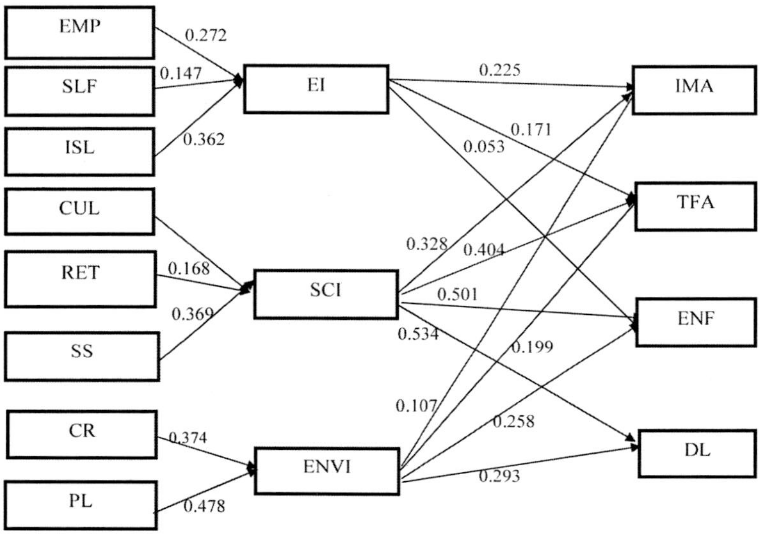

Fig. 1.2: Validated Model: EI, SCI, ENVI and OI.

Source: Compiled by the researcher based on SEM results.

Conclusion

The effect of Economic Impact, Sociocultural Impact and Environmental Impact of RT upon the Overall RT impact is measured by using Structural Equation Model (SEM). The EI, SCI, ENVI and OI Model hypothesised is validated through SEM using Analysis of Moment Structure (AMOS). The model has both direct and indirect effects of independent variables on the dependent variable. The independent variables are the constructs of Economic, Sociocultural and Environmental Impact of RT in the selected destinations, all of which have a direct effect upon Overall Economic, Sociocultural and Environmental Impacts. The EI, SCI and ENVI of RT is found have a direct effect upon the dependent variable of Overall Impact (OI) constructs, except EI to

Destination Lacunae (DL). Therefore, it is proved that, Economic Impact of Responsible Tourism in selected destinations is not having a direct effect upon Destination Lacunae. Thus, the null hypothesis Economic Impact of RT does not have any significant effect upon Destination Lacunae (DL) gets accepted. All the constructs of EI, SCI and ENVI had statistically significant indirect effect upon Improved Amenities (IMA), Tourist Friendly Ambience (TFA), Environment Friendliness (ENF) and Destination Lacunae (DL). The indirect effect of the constructs of EI, SCI and ENVI of Responsible Tourism shows that all the constructs except Destination Image (DI) and Conservation of Resources (CR) has significant indirect effect upon the construct Improved Amenities (IMA) of Overall Impact (OI). The results corroborate with the study made by (Androitis, K., 2004) that the economic, sociocultural and environmental impact of tourism ultimately leads to the overall impact and this overall impact is the determining force behind tourism support initiatives of the public.

References

Amin, R.M. (2016). Domestic Tourists' Mindset towards Responsible Tourism Management: A Case Study on Cox's Bazar, Bangladesh. *International Journal of Tourism Cities.*

Andreck, K.L., Valentine, K.M., & Vogt, C.A. (2005). Residents Perceptions of Community Tourism Impacts. *Annals of Tourism Research, 32*, 1056-76.

Androitis, K. (2004). The Perceived Impact of Tourism Development by Cretan Residents. *Tourism and Hospitality Planning and Development,* Routledge Publications, *1*(2), 123-44.

Anter, M. & Attia, M.A. (2017). Layoff Policies in Egyptian Tourism Sector: The Relation between Economic Benefit and Employees' Loyalty. *Journal of Faculty of Tourism and Hotels,* Research Gate Publications, *8*(2).

Archer, B., Cooper, C., & Ruhanen, L. (2005). The Positive and Negative Impacts of Tourism. *Global Tourism.*

Ardahaey, F.T. (2011). Economic Impacts of Tourism Industry. *International Journal of Business and Management.* Published by Canadian Center of Science and Educatuion, *6* (8).

Broderick, J. (2012). *Understanding Carbon Budgets and the Safe Climate Space for Responsible Tourism.* New Delhi: Ashish Publishing House.

Brougham, J.E., & Butler, R.W. (2002). A Segmentation Analysis of Resident Attitudes to the Social Impact of Tourism. *Annals of Tourism Research, 8*(4), 569-90.

Broun, T., Churchil, G., & Peter, P. (1993). Improving the Measurement of Service Quality. *Journal of Retailing, 69*(1), 127-39.

Budeanu, A., Miller, G., Moscardo, G. *et al.* (2016). Sustainable Tourism, Progress, Challenges and Opportunities: An Introduction. *Journal of Cleaner Production,* Vol. III.

Elizabeth, O. (2013). The Impact of Economic Growth on Employment in Nigeria. *International Business and Management,* Research Gate Publications, *6*(1), pp. 113-19.

Eraqui, I.M. (2007). Local Communities' Attitude towards Impacts of Tourism Development in Egypt. *Tourism Analysis, 12,* 191-200.

Feruzi, K.J. (2012). *An Evaluation of Responsible Tourism Practices in the Tanzanian Tourism Industry.* Peninsula University of Technology.

Filosofova, T. & Apostolov, D. (2016). Effects of Tourist Satisfaction: Influence on the Touristic Flows of Bulgeria in Russia. *Tourism Highlights,* pp. 1-10.

Forsyth, T. (2018). Environmental Responsibility and Business Regulations: the Case of Sustainable Tourism. *The Geographical Journal, 163,* 270-80.

Goodwin, H. (2017). The Challenge of Overtourism. *Responsible Tourism Partnership.*

Goodwin, H., & Font, X. (2012). *Progress in Responsible Tourism.* United Kingdom: Goodfellow Publishers.

Joobi V.P., & Satheesh E.K. (2017). Local Community Participation in Responsible Tourism: A Case Study of Kumarakom Grama Panchayath. *International Journal of Current Research in Multidisciplinary (IJCRM), 2*(11), 5-11.

Jurdana, D.S & Frleta, D.S. (2016). Satisfaction as a Determinant of Tourist Expenditure. *Current Issues in Tourism,* Routledge Publishers.

Jurdana, D.S & Frleta, D.S. (2016). Factors Affecting the Expenditure of Domestic and Foreign Tourists: The Evidence from Rijeka and Opatija, Croatia. *Tourism and Hospitality Industry, Congress proceedings,* pp. 418-31.

Keat, W.K., & Musa, N. (2014). Responsible Tourism System Dynamic Planning Model for Rural Area. *Journal of Hospitality and Tourism.*

Kencana, E.N. & Darmayanti, T. (2017). Causality between Frequency of visit with Tourist Satisfaction: A Multi-group Analysis. *Udayana Journal of Social Sciences and Humanities,* Research Gate Publications, *1*(2).

Musavengane, R. (2019). Small Hotels and Responsible Tourism Practices: Holeliers' Perspectives. *Journal of Cleaner Production,* Vol. 220.

Mustelier-Puig, L.C., Anjum, A. & Ming, X. (2018). Interaction Quality and Satisfaction: An Empirical Study of International Tourists When Buying Shanghai Tourist Attraction Services. *Cogent Business & Management,* pp. 1-20.

Thett, K.K. (2012). Responsible Tourism in Myanmar: Current Situation and Challenges. *Ministry of Foreign Affairs of the Czech Republic Within Its Transition Promotion Programme.* Burma Centre Prague Publishers.

Venu, V., & Goodwin, H. (2008). *The Kerala Declaration on Responsible Tourism, Thiruvananthapuram.* Department of Tourism, Government of Kerala.

Wang, Chang, Zhang, Jinhe, Cao, Jingjing, *et al.* (2019). The Impact of Behavioural Reference on Tourists' Responsible Environmental Behaviour. *Science of the Total Environment.*

Zhuang, X., Yao, Y. & Li, J.J. (2019). Sociocultural Impacts of Tourism on Residents' of World Cultural Heritage Sites in China. *Sustainability.* pp. 2-19.

2

Responsible Tourism: Exploring the Synergies Between Performing Arts and Hospitality Units

The Case of Kumarakom

Anitha R., Ambeeshmon S. and *Smitha, S.*

Introduction

Music, Dance, Art and Folk dances are an integral part of any region's culture. Kerala has its own indigenous folk and classical dances. According to Kerala tourism, there are nearly fifty different dance forms performed in Kerala. The prominent ones are Thiruvathirakali, Theyyam, Koodiyattam, Chakiyar Kuthu, Ottamthullal, etc. The classical dances are *Kathakali & Mohiniyattam*. By linking the dance performances with the hospitality sector by the Responsible Tourism (RT) cell of Kumarakom, the local community can preserve and conserve the art forms while maintaining its sustainability and hence sustain through such performances the well-being of local community.

Objectives of the Study

- To study the impact of linking the cultural performance of local community with the RT hotels in Kumarakom.

- To analyse the role of RT hotels in the promotion of indigenous performances.
- To collect the opinion of local community before and after linking the cultural programmes by RT Cell with the RT hotels.

Literature Review

According to Robinson and Smith (2009)

> "destinations, their people and cultures are experienced by the tourists and not just gazed upon. Observing the tourists reveals that they actually spend considerably less time than we think in formalized cultural settings such as galleries, museums and historical buildings. Rather more time is spend in restaurants, cafes, bars, shops, the airport and the hotel."

He found that

> "For the increasing number of tourists roaming the surface of the planet it creates an ever-expanding number of experiences and possibilities. All tourism is "cultural" in this sense. As tourists, and as people in a globalizing world we are increasingly in contact with other "cultures" able to experience the consequences of each and the commonalities of all."

Tourism is one of the so-called culture industries of post-modernity, is heavily involved not only in the economy but also in the cultural transformation of places (Urry, 1995 cited by Uta Papen). According to Duim, Peter and Akama,

> "their study illustrates the various complex ways in which tourism enters communities and how communities become entangled in the global tourism industry".

Their studies on "Village Life Experiences in Northern Tanzania" a concept for the cultural tourism project (CTP) has been developed, propagated and implemented by a six-member project team in close cooperation with the national Tanzanian Tourist Board (TTB) and with the local population, until it reached the present stage, which now involves eighteen projects. Every village offers a package of different possible visits. A half day trip in the IIKding a village, for instance typically begins with the provision of lunch consisting of local cuisine, a walk through the village, a visit to the traditional craftsman and/or the traditional medicine man, buying of local souvenirs, sightseeing at the local waterfall and finally a traditional dance performed by local dancers. In 1995, the tourism project attracted fifty tourists, and five years later the number had increased to over 5,000 tourists (Jaworski and Richard, 2009). In many of the hotel's cultural programmes are specially arranged by hotel people. Gupta (2002) opined that

> "such ventures could certainly also be extremely useful for many struggling singers and dancers since while they do get some encouragement by way of appreciation, they also earn substantial amounts to sustain themselves in otherwise non-lucrative hobbies and performances."

A carefully managed tourism industry can help poor rural women to become increasingly empowered, and improve their status in their families and within society.

Research Gap

With respect to India, responsible tourism is an emerging sector and as a test case, it is implemented in the State of Kerala. Among the selected four destinations, Kumarakom was only found successful due to its unique implementation approach. Initially, the responsible tourism cell of Kumarakom identified the performers and later by a registration process they constructed a linkage with the hospitality sector. This linkage is found as the key success of this project.

Research Problem

The responsible tourism practices at Kumarakom are one of the most sought-after responsible tourism models in India. Cultural performances of the local performers with the branded responsible tourism hotels by the responsible tourism cell of the Department of Tourism, Kerala are an excellent initiative. But on the other hand, the benefit should trickle down to the community. It is observed that the cultural group created with the participation of local community is one of the most significant contributor of RT initiative at Kumarakom.

Research Methodology

The study is analytical and descriptive in nature. A survey method is used for data collection. The tool used is a structured questionnaire. At the inception stage, there were only 30 performers. Out of these 30 performers, 27 were given the questionnaire. The primary data collected were analysed using a descriptive statistical technique like simple percentage analysis.

Responsible Tourism

An early definition of responsible tourism used by the South African Department of Environmental Affairs and Tourism (DEAT), 1996 considers responsible tourism as tourism that promoted responsibility to the environment, through its sustainable use, responsibility to involve local communities in the tourism industry; responsibility for the safety and security of visitors and responsible government, employees, employers, unions and local communities. The three pillars of responsible tourism are economic responsibility, social responsibility and environmental responsibility. The present study highlights the cultural responsibility of RT practices at Kumarakom.

Cultural Group

At its inception, a women's cultural group was constituted to perform indigenous and traditional art forms of Kerala. Women and children were included in this group. A Singari Melam, Thiruvathira & Kolkali group were established initially. This cultural group was linked with hotels which became a success. Today more than 500 performers are part of this venture at Kumarakom tourist destination alone.

Responsible Tourism Hotels

A hotel/resort/heritage home/ayurveda resort/serviced villas/ house boat/home stay is classified as a responsible tourism hotel by gaining a minimum of 500 points out of 1,000 points in the four major classification criteria namely sustainable management (200), sociocultural responsibility (250), economic responsibility (250) & environmental responsibility (300). Hotels of Kumarakom have a prominent role in promoting RT practices with the support of local community. Recently, the Government of Kerala has decided to extend this classification all over Kerala, identifying its sustainable agenda.

Cultural Programmes

Some of the indigenous dance forms performed in the RT hotels are the following.

Kathakali: Kathakali is the classical dance drama of Kerala. In this performing art the actors do not speak. The songs are recited by the background singers. The movements are rhythmic and graceful. Through facial expressions, gestures and postures and in fine tune with the background music, the expressions are represented through *mudras*.

Mohiniyattam (Dance of the Temptress): It is an old temple art of Kerala. It is a solo dance performed by a woman. The music is classical Carnatic.

Thullal: The origin of this solo dance exposition is attributed to Kunchan Nambiar a well-known genius poet of Kerala. His songs were written in Simple Malayalam. Three types of Thullal are there. Ottan, Seethankan, and Parayan based on the difference in the rhyme of the Thullal songs, costume and dance. Due to its satirical touch this art form is very popular among common man. Based on mythological stories, the performers musically narrate the story.

Thiruvathirakali: This dance form is performed by women during the Onam season. The women rhythmically move in a circular way based on the tune of Thiruvathira songs.

Kolkali: It uses the wooden sticks. Beating the wooden sticks, the dancers rhythmically move in a circular shape.

Kerala Nadanam: This art form is evolved from Kathakali. Guru Gopinath (Kathakali masetro) and his wife Thankamani Gopinath (well-known dance performer) developed this dance form. Even though he created this dance it was named Kerala Nadanam only after his death. The costume and facial make up of this dance style is in fine tune with the role.

Result and Discussions

The major observation from five major demographic characteristics of the performers which are used as demographic variable. Almost all the performers were surveyed for this study. Out of 27 respondents 23 (85.00%) respondents were woman and 4 (15.00%) men 16 (59.00%) of the respondents belong to the age group between 14-20 followed by 03 (11.00%). It is also observed that between respondents between the age group of 21-25, followed by 2 (7.00%) between 26-30, 04 (15.00%) between 31-35 and the rest 2 (7.00%) greater than 36. The Job status of the respondents revealed that 17 (63.00%) of the performers are students studying in ninth standard followed by 05 (19.00%) graduation. It is also observed from the result that 02 (7.00%) of the respondents are doing labour work. Finally, 2 (7.00%) engaged in other work. Educational qualification of the respondents shows that respondents from standard nine to graduation constitutes 20 (74.00%). Followed by 05 (19.00%) of the respondents have educational qualification up to SSLC. Finally it is observed that 02 (07.00%) of the respondents have qualification <10th. The monthly income of the respondents shows that 05 (19.00%) of the respondents have a monthly income between 1,000-2,000.

Followed by 05 (19.00%) of the respondents have a monthly income of 2,500-5,000. It is also observed that 10 (37.00%) of the respondents from Kumarakom has monthly income between 10,000-8,000. 04 (15.00%) of the respondents have a monthly income between 10,000-25,000. Finally, only 3 (11.00%) of the respondents have a monthly income between 30,000-50,000. From the variable on dance performances, it is highlighted that dance performance 13 (48.00%) perform group items such as Kolkali and Thiruvathirakali. 9 (33.00%) of the engaged individual items such as Kerlanadanam, Mohiniyattam, Kathakali, Thullal and rest 05 (19.00%) perform both items. In addition to the above-mentioned traditional Kerala art forms, Kuchipudi and Bharatanatyam was also performed. 15 (56.00%) of the dancers were trained by masters and 12 (44.00%) are self trained. 23 (85.00%) responded that the cultural linkage was benefited and the remaining 4 (15.00%) were not benefited. It is observed from the individual impacts. 27 (100.00%) of the performers opined that changes have occurred in their routine life. Among them 11 (41.00%) opined their food habits also changed. 22 (81.00%) were found to be satisfied with the present income and the rest 19 per cent not satisfied. It is also observed that 18 (67.00%) joined with the RT programme of two year duration, followed by 07 (26.00%) of the respondents joined for one year time and 26 (7.00%) are of 02 (6.00%) months duration only. The output regarding extent of support from stakeholders such as hotels, domestic tourists, foreign tourists and the family was found to be 27 (100.00%). 13 (48.00%) are engaged in other jobs too and the rest 52 per cent are not engaged. The output regarding highlights that the attitude of the superiors were excellent by 26 (96.00%), very good by 4 per cent, also the attitude of the domestic tourists and foreign tourists were excellent by 96 per cent, very good by 4 per cent; the attitude of the co-workers and family were excellent by 24 (89.00%) and very good by 11 per cent respectively. From the output regarding opinion of performers before and after linking cultural programmes with the hospitality sector by RT cell highlights that 8 (30.00%) of the performers own a vehicle before linking and after the linkage it is increased to 11 (41.00%). 24 (89.00%) have owned a house and property before linkage. After it increased to 25 (93.00%). The lifestyle before linkage was found to be 8 (30.00%). Later it changed to 27 (100.00%). The extra income also increased from 5 (19.00%) to 23 (85.00%). Before linkage, the performers those who joined saving scheme were 7 (26.00%). It increased to 26 (96.00%). Before linkage nobody responded regarding the purchase of gold. After linkage 17 (63.00%) were able to invest in gold. Observation regarding extent of economic impact, it was observed that the majority of the agreements were strongly accepted by the respondents. 14 (52.00%) of the of the performers strongly agreed with the statement and "could settle their debts" while 5 (19.00%) agreed and 5 (19.00%) neutral, 3 (15.00%) disagreed with the statement. 20 (74.00%) of them feel there is a "peaceful atmosphere than in the past", the rest 7 (26.00%) agrees with this view. From this opinion one could assume that their performances were accepted by all stakeholders of tourism sector. The statement "I could earn a fixed amount every month" was strongly agreed by 12 (52.00%), agreed by 8 (30.00%), neutral by 5 (27.00%), disagreed by 2 (11.00%). around 44% of the respondents opined that the "income helps to meet daily expenses", 13 (30.00%) agreed, 21 (9.00%) neutral and 10 (7.00%). Disagreed with the "statement, it is possible to engage in other works too" is strongly agreed by 1948 per cent, agreed by 77 per cent, neutral by 17 per cent and disagreed by 37 per cent. "The linkage of cultural programmes with the hotels could preserve various art forms" without change was strongly agreed by 70 per cent of the respondents, 26 per cent agreed with this statement and 4 per cent neutral about it. Nobody responded to disagree or strongly disagree with the statement.

Major Findings and Suggestions

- From the research output, it is clearly observed that 23 (85.00%) of the respondents were female compared to 04 (15.00%) male.

- Looking at the age group of the respondents it is observed that age group between 14-20 is more involved in performing arts.
- From the result it is also observed that 17 (63.00%) of the respondents are students.
- It is also observed that 20 (74.00%) of the respondents are students qualified between Standard IX to bachelors.
- It is observed that 10 (37.00%) of the respondents get a monthly income between 6,000-8,000.
- 13 (48.00%) of the respondents perform in group items.
- It is also observed that 15 (56.00%) of the total respondents are trained by masters.
- It is observed that 23 (85.00%) of the respondents have given positive opinion about RT linkage.
- It is surprising to observe that 27 (100.00%) of the respondents agreed that changes occur in their routine life.
- 11 (41.00%) of the respondents agreed that there food habits have changed a lot.
- 22 (81.00%) of the respondents agreed that they are happy with the present income.
- It is also observed that 18 (67.00%) of the respondents have completed two years joining with RT Cell.
- It is observed that 27 (100.00%) of the respondents agreed that they have wholehearted support from family, hotels, tourist and other stakeholders.
- It is also observed that 26 (96.00%) of the respondents agreed that attitude of the supervisor, domestic tourist and foreign tourist as well as co-workers and family members 24 (94.00%) has changed.
- All the respondents have irrespectively agreed 27 (100.00%) that the lifestyle has changed drastically.
- Finally 20 respondents have given their view that there is a peaceful atmosphere now.
- The before-after linkage of cultural programmes with the hospitality sector reveals that there is considerable change

occur in the entire living standard including income, employment, earning and food habit of performers.

Major Recommendations

Empowerment of women is one of the major initiatives of the responsible tourism programme. Thus, more and more women's involvement can give more economic gain to the family as a whole.

- Teenagers need to be motivated for taking up and studying cultural art form. As many of the art forms are at the brink of extinction.
- There should be proper emoluments' for the performance performed by the performing artist.
- Dance and native arts need to be strengthened by opening new training centres to give proper training for the upcoming budding artist.
- There should be a holistic approach rather that making performing art as a business.
- Community interaction needs to be strengthened by meetings and talks and listening to their grievances seriously.
- Through the RT initiative performing arts and native indigenous arts from the need to be revived.

Conclusion

In this chapter, the impact of the linkage of cultural programmes by the local community with the hospitality sector was found to be a great success. The younger generations benefited the most. Kathakali performers always have high demand than any other performers. Many non-RT hotels were also promoting cultural performances. Within a short span of time, the performers as well as the RT cell and hotel people could make a change in society. The authenticity of performance is a question in many destinations. In the case of Kathakali programmes, one should be careful about it. Most of the studies revealed that responsible tourists are high-ended tourists and spend a considerable amount to experience the diverse culture of the visited destinations. Since the hospitality industry is the backbone of the tourism industry, the newly branded RT hotels are a unique attraction in our country. The classification scheme introduced by the Department of Tourism gave an impetus to RT practices. The cultural linkage with hospitality sector added a golden feather in the cap of RT practices at Kumarakom. Since MICE (Meetings, Incentives, Conferences, and Exhibitions) tourism has emerged as a growing segment in the tourism arena, sky is the limit for indigenous cultural performances. It enhances dance as a career choice as well.

References

DEAT (1996). *Whitepaper on the Development and Promotion of Tourism in South Africa.* Department of Environmental Affairs in Tourism, Government of South Africa.

Gupta, *et al.* (2002).*Cultural Tourism in India: Museums, Monuments & Arts (Theory and Practice)*, Indraprastha Museum of Art and Archaeology, New Delhi, p. 87.

Jaworski, A. & Ritchard, A. (Ed.) (2009). *Tourism and Cultural Change: Discourse, Communication and Tourism;* cited by Uta Papen, pp. 79 & 104-20. CBS Publishers, New Delhi.

Robinson, M. and Smith, M. (2009). *Cultural Tourism in the Changing World-Politics, Participation and (RE) Presentation.* Tourism and Cultural Change—Discourse, Communication and Tourism, p. 79.

Web References

The facets of Cultural Tourism in Kerala and Tamil Nadu accessed on15/02/17 (Sodhganga.inflibinet.ac.in/bitstream/10603/12807/10/10_chapter%204.pdf)

https://en.wikipedia.org/wiki/Kerala_Natanam. Accessed on 15/2/17.

www.kerala-tourism.org/dances of Kerala. Accessed on 14/2/17.

3
The Influence of Digital Marketing in the Tourism Industry of Kerala with Special Emphasis on the Accommodation Sector

Thansiya N.

Introduction

Digital marketing focuses on marketing all possible goods and services via a virtual platform. It is the modern trend of the marketing strategy adopted all-over the countries irrespective of the industries they belong to. The Internet has upended how consumers engage with brands. It is transforming the economics of marketing and making obsolete many of the function's traditional strategies and structures. For marketers, the old way of doing business is unsustainable (Edelman, 2010). Tourism always stands as a significant promoter of the economic, social and cultural development bondage of every nation, even after recovering from the COVID pandemic situation. The influence of technology is unavoidable everywhere, especially considering the recent demands of customers who lie on easy accessibility with easiness at their fingertips. In the tourism sector where customers are scattered worldwide must depend on modern technological upgrades to get the best offers at the best possible prices. God's own country, Kerala, is elegant with its natural and cultural beauty and is placed in the top positions on the world tourism map. The tourism industry depends on the core sectors like accommodation, accessibility, attraction, and activities and amenities. So, it's always crucial to look after the changes taking place in these sectors. Through these digital platforms, authorized brands, once which was not accessible to the ultimate customers, made it possible to directly communicate regarding the services by eliminating the role of intermediaries. The necessity to include digital marketing in the overall marketing strategy of the tourism industry in Kerala contributes to the better achievement of overall marketing excellence in different components constituting the industry and business goals by enabling brands to gain insights about consumer behaviour and better satisfy their expectations.

Review of Literature

Kasim, A. (2007) identifies hotels as an important sector in tourism. Although generally considered a smokeless sector, hotels interact with the environment, particularly in terms of resource consumption. This chapter establishes a link between the hotel sector and sustainable development. Safak Sahin (2013) analyses whether green advertising is more effective in hotel advertising and varies in effectiveness according to hotel categories. Various strategies for greening are also examined to understand their comparative effectiveness. This study aims to expand knowledge about the effectiveness of environmentally responsible print advertising in the hotel industry context. Sunny Ham, *et al.* (2011) investigate the digital marketing practices in the restaurant industry and links those practices to financial performance. The results show that restaurant companies without digital marketing practices show higher risk-adjusted returns than other restaurant companies.

Significance of the Study

Digital marketing platforms have a concrete base for the functioning of new-era business cocoons. Tourism, as it lies its roots in nature has a significant impact on the promotion through digital platforms as it is spread all over the world. Recent trends show that communication through social media acts as a source of information regarding tourism destinations at the tourists' fingertips. The customers, the king of every market have their own changing attitudes towards the platforms they are going through. The accommodation sector constitutes a major role in the promotion of the tourism industry everywhere, in Kerala also. As the accommodation sector is considered the most influencing sector of the tourism industry, the application, and impact of digital marketing platforms for the promotion of the tourism industry, and the performance of the accommodation sector are crucial in these times.

Scope of the Study

The study is focused on the impact of digital marketing in the tourism industry of Kerala with special reference to the accommodation sector in general. As the accommodation sector of Kerala includes a large number of classifications, for the convenience of the study, the registered number of classified hotels is considered which has been published by the Department of Tourism in their latest Annual Statistical Report of 2019.

Statement of the Problem

The accommodation sector of Kerala is a wide concept for the tourism industry. The tourists' preference changes according to the accessibility and affordance of the facilities they are expecting and available to them. Keeping the economic and expectation-wise balancing, the customers prefer the accommodation units. The modern era focused on digital and virtual platforms influences the tourism sector like influences in all other industries. The industry, as it covers a worldwide chain has to cross-check whether it can access and gain the entire benefits of digital marketing platforms, especially the most economically influencing sector of the tourism industry, the accommodation sector.

Research Questions

1. What are the digital marketing platforms generally followed by the tourism industry in Kerala?
2. What are the expectations of the accommodation managers regarding the promotion through digital marketing networks?
3. What is the impact of this digital marketing platform on their business?

Objectives

The major objectives of the study are listed below:

1. To analyse the digital marketing platforms contributing to the tourism industry of Kerala.
2. To examine the impact of digital marketing in the promotion of tourism considering the accommodation sector.
3. To evaluate the perception of accommodation managers regarding the satisfaction level of tourists with tourism promotion through digital platforms.

Hypotheses of the Study

1. There is a significant difference in the opinion of accommodation managers regarding the impact of digital marketing on the tourism promotion
2. There is a difference in the opinion of accommodation managers regarding the satisfaction level of tourists with the digital marketing.

Methodology

Research Design

The study is descriptive and analytical and attempts to describe the influence of digital marketing in the promotion of the tourism industry of Kerala. It also focuses on the perception of tourists regarding the satisfaction level of using digital platforms.

Data Source

The study uses both primary and secondary data, where primary data are collected by using a structured interview schedule constituted for accommodation managers and secondary data includes books, newspaper reports, articles in journals, theses, websites, etc.

Sampling Design

The Population

As per the data from the Ministry of Tourism, Government of India, in Kerala, the total number of classified hotels and the number of rooms available as on 31 December 2019 are 505 and 12,593 respectively.

Table 3.1: Population of Classified Hotels in Kerala

Sl. No.	Hotel	Number
1	Heritage Hotel—Classic	3
2	Heritage Hotel—Basic	13
3	3-star	263
4	4-Star with alcohol	82
5	5-Star Deluxe	8
6	5-Star with Alcohol	8
7	5-Star without Alcohol	16
Total		**393**

Source: Annual Reports, Department of Tourism, Govt. of Kerala (2019).

Figure 1.1 exhibits the population of classified hotels in Kerala.

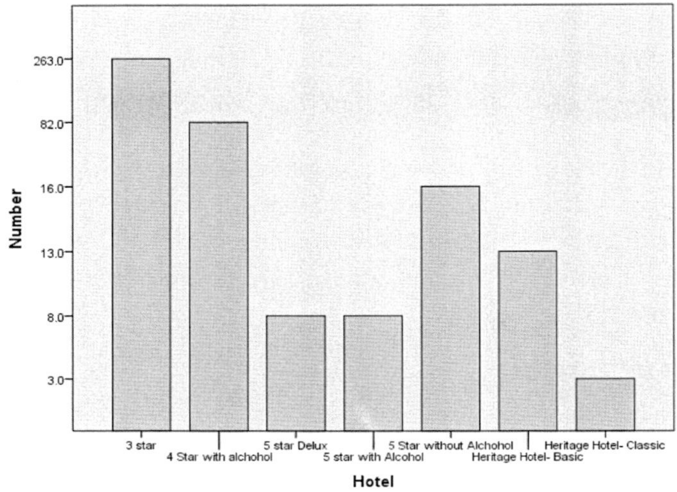

Fig. 3.1: Population of Classified Hotels in Kerala.

Source: Primary data.

Sample Size

A sample consisting of 150 accommodation units is considered for the study.

Sampling Method

A proportionate stratified sampling method has been used by drawing a sample from each stratum in proportion to the latter's share of the total population.

Result and Discussions

Digital Marketing Platforms in Tourism Industry

Technology has changed the way of advertising (Magano & Cunha, 2020) and the way it is broadcast (Jiménez-Barreto, Rubio, Campo & Molinillo, 2020). Because the tourist industry is characterized by a different spectrum of online channels, the challenge lies with tourist marketing consultants to be aware of how tourists access information (Almeida-Santana & Moreno-Gil, 2017) and to find efficient marketing tools and strategies that contribute to maximizing profits (Angeloni & Rossi, 2020). The digital marketing tools for the tourism accommodation sector generally includes websites of the accommodation sector, tourism blogs, social media platforms, virtual reality networks, mobile travel applications, email or newsletter, content marketing, chatbots, influencer marketing, and so on.

Table 3.2: Digital Media Platforms and Applications by the Classified Hotels

Sl. No.	Digital Platform	Frequency
1	Own Website	150
2	Blogs	140
3	Social Media Platforms	150
4	Virtual Reality Network	65
5	Mobile Travel Application	72
6	Influencer Marketing	73
7	Chatbots	105
8	Content Marketing	119

Source: Primary data.

Figure 3.2 shows the graphical representation of digital media platforms adopted by the accommodation units.

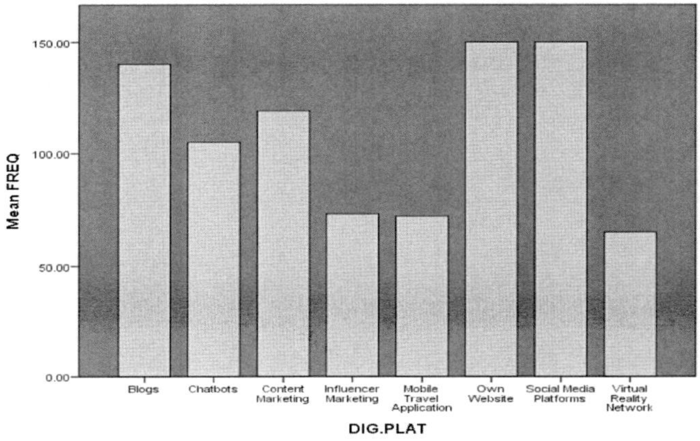

Fig. 3.2: Digital Media Platforms and Applications by the Classified Hotels.

Source: Primary Data.

It is clear from Table 3.2 that classified hotels use digital media platforms for the promotion of their business in an effective manner. Considering the websites, social media platforms, and blogs of accommodation units stand at the top level in its application while the influencer marketing technique is least followed by the classified hotels considering the frequency distribution.

Table 3.3: Descriptive statistics of Digital Marketing methods

N	Mean	Std. Deviation
8	109.25	35.9355

Source: Primary Data.

It also indicates the mean value of these elements of digital marketing is 109.25 and the Standard Deviation is 35.9355, which indicates the classified hotels apply the digital marketing platforms for their business promotion to a good extent.

The Impact of Digital Marketing Methods in the Promotion of Tourism in Accommodation

Considering the opinion on the impact of Digital Marketing Methods in the promotion of tourism in the accommodation sector, the Chi-square test has been applied and the result is shown in Table 3.4.

Table 3.4: Impact of DMM on the Promotion of Tourism

	Observed N
Highly Positive Impact	34
Positive Impact	70
No Impact	23
Negative Impact	23
Total	**150**

Source: Primary Data.

It is evident that out of 150 classified hotels, 70 accommodation managers believe that they have a positive impact from the application of Digital Marketing Methods in the promotion of the tourism business; 34 respondents have a high positive impact on their business; 23 each opinioned they have no impact and negative impact respectively towards the application of digital marketing tools in the business.

Hypotheses

H_0—There is no significant difference in the opinion of accommodation managers regarding the impact of digital marketing on tourism promotion.

H_1—There is a significant difference in the opinion of accommodation managers regarding the impact of digital marketing on tourism promotion.

Table 3.5 gives the test statistics according to the chi-square test.

Table 3.5: Test Statistics

	Impact of DMM on the Promotion of Tourism
Chi-Square	39.707
df	3
Asymp. Sig.	.000

Source: Primary Data.

The chi-square statistic provides a value of 39.707, which is significant at the 5 per cent level. There exist differences in the opinion of accommodation managers regarding the impact of Digital Marketing Methods. Therefore, the null hypothesis is rejected. It may be concluded that there is a significant difference in the opinion of accommodation managers regarding the impact of Digital Marketing Methods on the promotion of business in the accommodation sector.

The Perception of Accommodation Managers regarding the Satisfaction Level of Tourists with the Application of Digital Marketing Methods

The generally followed Digital Marketing Methods for the promotion of tourism by the accommodation sectors include own websites, blogs, social media, VRR, MTA, influencer marketing, chatbots, and content marketing. In this part of the analysis, an attempt is made to assess the DMMs and their effect on tourists.

Table 3.6: Descriptive Statistics

	Mean	Std. Deviation
Own Websites	2.17	.972
Blogs	1.75	.768
Social Media	2.61	.982
Virtual Reality Network	2.67	.901
Mobile Travel Application	2.03	.870
Influencer Marketing	2.43	.900
Chatbots	1.61	.850
Content Marketing	1.61	.850

Source: Primary Data.

Considering the perception of accommodation managers, it is identified that the highest mean values are assigned to VRN and social media. The least demanding with chatbots and content marketing. From the group statistics given above, it is observed that the mean scores indicating the satisfaction level of tourists with Digital Marketing Methods show differences in variables under consideration. To explain the possible variations observed in these variables, the test of chi-square has been applied. The hypotheses to be considered are:

Hypotheses

H_0—There is no difference in the opinion of accommodation managers regarding the satisfaction level of tourists with the digital marketing methods.

H_1—There is a difference in the opinion of accommodation managers regarding the satisfaction level of tourists with the digital marketing methods

The test result of the chi-square is shown in Table 3.7.

Table 3.7: Chi-square Test

Chi-Square	**.750[a]**
df	6
Asymp. Sig.	.993

The chi-square statistic provides a value of 0.750 with the degree of freedom 6 which is not significant at the 5 per cent level. It is found that there is no significant difference in the opinion of accommodation managers regarding the satisfaction level of tourists towards Digital Marketing Methods for tourism promotion in the accommodation sector. Thus, the null hypothesis failed to reject.

Summary of Findings

1. Considering the classified hotels which are considered for the study, among the 150 units, the majority are three-star hotels.
2. All the sample units under study have social media and their websites as their digital media platforms.
3. The majority of the accommodation managers believe that the DMMs have a positive impact on the promotion of the tourism business in the accommodation units.
4. There is a significant difference in the opinion of accommodation managers regarding the impact of digital marketing on tourism promotion.
5. It is found that there is no significant difference in the opinion of accommodation managers regarding the satisfaction level of tourists towards Digital Marketing Methods for tourism promotion in the accommodation sector.

Conclusion

The accommodation sector maintains a prominent role in the tourism industry as it serves as a fundamental part of the tourism sector. There is a great diversity in the nature, type, and size of accommodation units, so it is categorized under various heads. Considering the influence of Digital Marketing Methods in the tourism promotion of the accommodation sector, it is evident from the study that it has a positive impact on tourism promotion as tourism services are spread across the globe. It is also considered that tourists are also satisfied with the adoption of such digital platforms in their accommodation choice.

References

Akbaba, A. (2012). "Understanding Small Tourism Businesses: A Perspective from Turkey". *Journal of Hospitality and Tourism Management*, 19.

Annual Report 2018-2019, Ministry of Tourism, Government of India.

Annual Report of Department of Tourism, Government of Kerala, 2019.

Batinié, (2015). "Role and Importance of Internet Marketing in the Modern Hotel Industry". *Journal of Process Management: New Technologies, International*, *3*(3), 34-38.

Chaffey, D., Ellis-Chadwick, F., Mayer, R., Johnston, K. (2009). *Internet Marketing: Strategy, Implementation and Practice*. 4th Edition. Prentice Hall.

Judy (2003). "E-Marketing, 3rd edition", ND-AMA: School of Marketing.

Kerdpitak, C. (2022). "The Effects of Innovative Management, Digital Marketing, Service Quality, and Supply Chain Management on Performance in the Cultural Tourism Business". *Uncertain Supply Chain Management, 10*(3), 771-78.

Lilien, G.L., Rangaswamy, A., De Bruyn, A. (2007). *Principles of Marketing Engineering*.

Miller, M. (2011). *The Ultimate Web Marketing Guide*, Pearson Education.

Strauss, J., Frost, R. (2009). *E-Marketing*. 5th Edition. Pearson Prentice Hall.

UNWTO Annual Reports 2019.

4

Sustainable Management Practices for Mitigating Ecological Pressures in a Protected Area

Inquiry on Ecotourism Ventures at Pichavaram in Tamil Nadu

Anu Chandran and *Reena Esther Rani*

Introduction

Ecotourism is among the most significant game-changers in the realm of tourism in the past two decades. It is realized that local communities can do a world of good to advance the ideals of ecotourism in almost all types of destinations. Thus emerged the concept of Community-Based Ecotourism (CBE). The local community can become change agents and usher in proper mechanisms for the conservation of habitats and its species. They can turn out to be effective nature guides and conservationists. Furthermore, the synergy between host populations, non-governmental organisations (NGOs), scientific and research institutes, public sector agencies and cooperatives, and private enterprises would galvanize the ecotourism practices in hill/mountain, coastal, forest, cave, island, and desert destinations; all of them dotted with fragile landscapes and natural manifests. The idea of ecotourism entails sensitivity to the ecological as well as cultural resources. All the stakeholders are required to abide by a set of guidelines to invigorate ecotourism, whereby global biodiversity shall be sustained in its verve and vitality. Ecotourists need to realize and respect the ecological value of the environment. The sector of ecotourism is growing at a fast pace with an estimated yearly growth rate of 20-34 per cent since the 1990s (The International Ecotourism Society, 2006). Pichavaram Mangrove Forest, thriving by the Bay of Bengal in the State of Tamil Nadu, is the second largest mangrove forest in the world and also one of the unique ecotourism spots in south India. Pichavaram, known for its backwater attractions and dense mangrove forest woos hordes of tourists at national and international scales. The development of ecotourism as a revenue earner by formulating a business model has accentuated the pressure on the mangrove wetland ecosystem and also the cultural manifestations. The effects of tourism development at Pichavaram have brought unprecedented changes to the ecological resources. Tourism activities in different ways increasingly put stress on natural resources resulting in irreparable loss to environmental treasures which necessitate the realisation of sustainable ecotourism development at this destination.

Ecotourism is a powerful means for supporting conservation as well as providing income for communities in and around protected areas. It can contribute to economic development and conservation of protected areas by: (a) generating revenues that can be used to sustainably manage protected areas; (b) providing local employment, and (c) inculcating a sense of community ownership. However, careful planning and management are central to attaining a balance between the ecological, social, and economic objectives without which ecotourism activities would have tampered that can possibly lead to environmental damages and ecological hazards. Furthermore, envisioned as a positive approach towards sustainable development, unplanned or poorly planned and implemented tourism ventures can have serious negative effects, offsetting the benefits it was designed to provide, Rome and Abigail (1999).

Scope and Study Zone

Pichavaram is one of the major ecotourism spots of Tamil Nadu. About 500-1,000 tourists visit Pichavaram every day (Ministry of Environment & Forests). Tourism activities at this destination have brought about many irreversible changes to the proliferation of the species of mangroves and shallow waterways over the years. Even though the destination entices a large number of tourists, the practices for sustainable development are sparse at the destination. The studies about sustainable ecotourism development and the importance of conserving and protecting natural resources are very limited and therefore no comprehensive report of the engagements of local community and stakeholders towards conservation of mangrove wetlands is prepared and the matter is not accorded due thrust. In this backdrop, the present study examines the importance of sustainable ecotourism development of the destination and brings forth certain enablers for devising a new roadmap of involving more residents in environmental protection and ecotourism development that could eventually facilitate local natural resource management and achieve sustainable ecotourism. The study zone encompasses the tourism spots of Pichavaram. Data has been collected from the local community members of Pichavaram, ecologists, environment activists, nature-buffs, the visitors as well as the staff members of tourism operatives in the destination. The scope of this work posits streamlining of *real* ecotourism in destination Pichavaram.

Research Objectives

This study has been conducted with the broad objective of analysing the role of ecotourism in fostering sustainable development in Pichavaram without compromising the innate charm of the ecological features and verdant landscapes of the habitat.

The specific objectives are:

1. To examine the ecotourism practices and ventures which are in vogue at destination Pichavaram vis-à-vis underpinning the ecological values of the species of the wetlands.

2. To assess the attitude of stakeholders towards conservation of the Mangrove Wetlands for enhanced efficacy in destination marketing.
3. To identify the prevailing gaps in the sustainable management propositions of ecotourism ventures in Pichavaram and suggest ways to address them.

Literature Review

Ecotourism Development and Its Potential

Ecotourism represents a segment of nature-tourism, that is, travel to relatively undisturbed or uncontaminated natural areas (Gössling, 1999). The term "ecotourism" can be described with the following five concepts: nature conservation, low impact, sustainability, meaningful community involvement and environmental education, Mojca Stubelj Ars *et al.* (2010). Ecotourism is considered as successful when it reduces the environmental impacts of tourism activities while delivering benefits for local community culturally and economically as well as fostering environmental education, M. Sivakumar *et al.* (2014).

Ceballos-Lascurain (1987, p. 13) provided one of the first definitions of ecotourism as

> "travelling to relatively undisturbed or uncontaminated natural areas with the specific objective of study, admiring, and enjoying the scenery and its wild plants and animals, as well as any existing cultural manifestations (both past and present) found in these areas".

More recent definitions cover benefits to the local economy, ethical management, environmental education and conservation and preservation of the area (Fennell, 1999). Although a contested concept, the International Ecotourism Society's definition (2010) of ecotourism as "responsible travel to natural areas which conserves the environment and improves the well-being of local people" is often cited.

Ecotourism represents a small but growing proportion of the world's tourism (Schulte, 2003; TIES, 2006). Given its close relation to nature, ecotourism has the potential to become an important ally of conservation and to contribute to the long-term preservation of Natural Protected Areas (NPAs) and their biodiversity. Moreover, due to their close link with local people, ecotourism enterprises that incorporate a social dimension may become powerful tools for local development. In this way, ecotourism may fight poverty and rural exclusion in NPAs and their surroundings (Gössling, 1999; Krüger, 2005; Stronza, 2000). Holden (2008) notes that strains between the economic benefits of tourism and environmental pressures can be addressed through a stronger commitment to environment and related ethics from the governments.

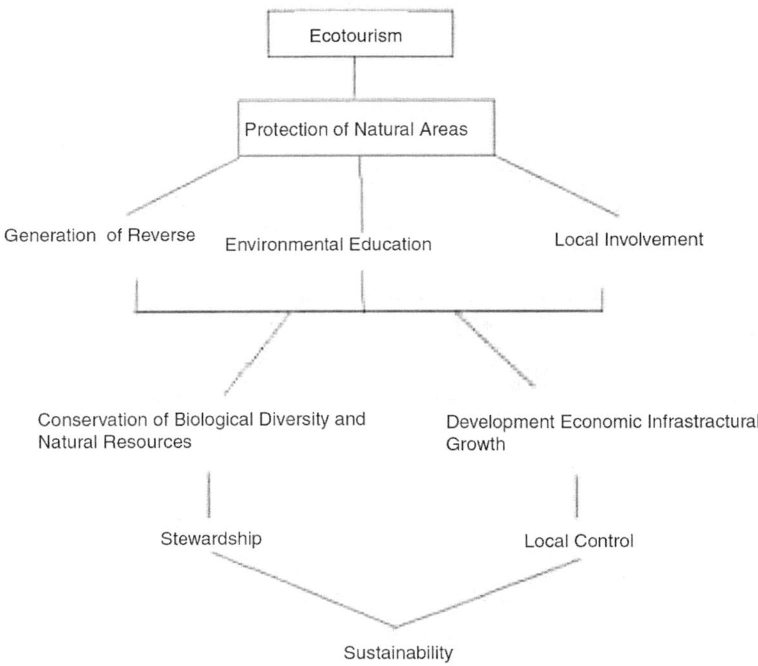

Fig. 4.1: Links between ecotourism and sustainability
Source: Ross and Wall (1999, p. 124).

Wetlands and the Attitude of Stakeholders Towards Conservation of Mangrove Wetlands

Sustainability has been represented as 'an edifice supported by the "three pillars" of economic growth, environmental protection, and social progress' (Schoolman, Guest, Bush, & Bell, 2011, p. 68) and sustainability research therefore incorporates concepts from multiple disciplines and reflects broader social and political thinking. Sustainable tourism is predicated in the belief that economic growth and environmental quality are not mutually exclusive and research is grounded predominantly in the areas of tourism impact, sustainability assessment, development, planning and visitor attitudes and behaviour (Lu & Nepal, 2009).

The National Ecotourism Development Plan (CNTA 2008, cited in Wang *et al.* 2009, p. 263) presents the mission of ecotourism as: advocating the harmony of the environment and the economy, strengthening construction of ecological environment, improving education, constantly meeting the demand of ecotourism, and ensure sustainable tourism development.

The increasing importance of the concept of sustainable development has led tourism researchers to posit the latest phase of tourism as rooted in the paradigm of sustainability (Macbeth, 2005). Sustainable development attempts to negotiate between three tropes of economic growth, ecological sustainability and empowerment or participation which, according to the Johannesburg Summit, are its three interdependent, mutually reinforcing pillars (Clive, 2007). Local people may be sensitized through effective campaigns (Anu Chandran, R.C., 2010).

The geographical resource of wetland has been distinguished thus: "A wetland is a land which is wet". But not all wetland results in a wetland. Why is this so? A wetland is found where the land is wet enough (i.e., saturated or flooded) for long enough to be unfavourable to most plants, but are favourable to plants adapted to anaerobic soil conditions. As soil becomes increasingly wet, the water starts to fill the space; between the soil particles. When all the spaces are filled with water, the soil is said to be saturated. In areas which are not wetlands, water drains away quickly and the soil does not remain saturated. However, in wetlands the water persists or drains away very slowly and the soil remains saturated or flooded for long periods. Soil in these conditions is said to be waterlogged. Depending on factors such as temperature, it usually takes a week or so for the plant roots and other living organisms in the soil to use up the oxygen, causing anaerobic conditions to develop in the waterlogged soil. The importance of wetlands got a global visibility after the famous Ramsar Convention which was held in Iran in the year 1971. The Ramsar Convention (1971) Article 1(1) defines Wetland as

> "area of marsh, fen, peat land or water, whether natural or artificial, permanent or temporary, with water that is static or flowing, fresh, brackish or salty including areas of marine water, the depth of which at low tide do not exceed six meters. It may also incorporate riparian and coastal zones adjacent to wetlands and islands or bodies of marine water deeper than 6 meters at low tide lying within the wetlands. A Ramsar Site, or Wetland of International Importance, is a wetland area designated under the Ramsar Convention by the national government of a Member State. Currently there are over 2,000 such sites covering over 192 million hectares: an impressive global network of wetlands that meet criteria related to their biodiversity and uniqueness."

Researchers often refer to wetland as "kidneys" of the earth and forest as the "green lungs" of the earth. The same concept has also been adopted by the European Commission, which groups the wetlands in Europe broadly as marine and coastal wetlands, estuaries and deltas, rivers and flood plains, lakes, freshwater marshes, peat lands and manmade wetlands (CEC, 1995). Cowardin *et al.* (1979) defines wetlands as "the lands transitional between terrestrial land aquatic systems where the water table is usually at or near the surface, or the land is covered by shallow water". It includes three attributes that help to delineate a wetland: (i) the area must be permanently or periodically inundated or water must be present for at least seven successive days during the growing season; (ii) the area must support hydrophytic vegetation; and (iii) the substrate is predominantly hydric soils that are saturated or flooded for a sufficiently long period to become anaerobic in their upper layers. The following is a brief description of the major classes of wetlands under the Cowardin (1979) system. Marine—Open Ocean overlying the continental shelf and coastline exposed to waves and currents of the open ocean shoreward to (1) extreme high water of spring tides; (2) seaward limit of wetland emergent's, trees, or shrubs; or (3) the seaward limit of the estuarine system, other than vegetation. Salinities exceed 30 parts per thousand. Estuarine—Deepwater tidal habitats and adjacent tidal wetlands that are usually semi-enclosed by land but have open, partly obstructed, or sporadic access to the ocean, with ocean-derived water at least occasionally diluted by freshwater runoff from the land. The upstream and landward limit is where ocean-derived salts measure less relatively than during the period of average annual low flow. The seaward limit is (1) an imaginary line closing the mouth of a river, bay, or sound; and (2) the seaward limit of wetland shrubs, or trees when not included in, (i) Riverine—all wetlands and deepwater habitats contained within a channel except those wetlands (a) dominated by trees, shrubs, persistent emergents, emergent mosses, or lichens, and (ii) which have habitats with ocean-derived salinities in excess of Lacustrine-Wetlands and deepwater habitats; (3) situated in a topographic depression or dammed river channel; (4) lacking trees, shrubs, persistent emergents, emergent mosses, or lichens with greater than 30 per cent aerial coverage; and (5) whose total area exceeds 8 hectares (20 acres); or area less than 8 hectares if the boundary is active wave-formed or bedrock or if water depth in the deepest part of the basin exceeds 2 m (6.6 ft) at low water. According to Bacon (1987), recreational use of wetlands need not conflict with their conservation objectives. However, decisions concerning the protection of wetlands should precede recreational planning. From the utilitarian point, wetlands can be defined as transitional areas between permanently flooded deep water environments and well drained uplands that contribute a wide array of biological, social, and economic benefits (Watzin & Gozzelink, 1992). Orams (1995) argued that ecotourism management strategies should attempt to move ecotourism experiences beyond mere enjoyment to a more active role which incorporates learning, attitude, and behavioural change. Through these desired objectives, the activities of visitors would actually contribute to the health and viability of the natural environment. The Boondall Wetlands Reserve has adopted such management strategies through the facilitation of education at the Visitor Centre. By providing financial support and/or labour through community involvement, visitors are assisting directly in the maintenance and protection of the natural environment. The behavioural objective is more complex and difficult to measure and is recognized as being a somewhat idealistic objective, wetland ecosystems are such a complex resource. They account for about 6 per cent of the global land area and are among the most threatened of all natural resources. Wetlands found in temperate climate zones in developed economies have long suffered significant losses and continue to face an ongoing conversion threat from industrial, agricultural, and residential developments, as well as from hydrological perturbation, pollution, and pollution-related effects (Turner, 1991). Pursuits in the realm of ecotourism can be a gamechanger in aspects such as lifestyle modifications with more sensitivity and traditional occupations. The social livelihood transformation of the local community through ecotourism ventures can be detected with respect to the lifestyle; as to how they have access to basic necessities like having bathrooms and having their own modes of transportation. All these means were created by twitching their traditional occupation roles like fishing, to operating in ecotourism ventures like operating homestays (Kunjuraman *et al.*, 2022).

Methodology

Devised in the fact-finding mode, both primary and secondary data were compiled, analysed, and processed for this study. By way of pursuing ethnographic study during March 2022 to April 2022, field notes were prepared and secondary data were gathered. In May 2022, interviews were conducted with host community, tourists, and other stakeholders. Views and statements were gathered from local residents, planning and promotional stakeholders, tourism authorities and tourists visiting Pichavaram; adopting qualitative method through focus group interviews, direct interviews, and schedules. Content analysis method was chosen to infer from the responses. Secondary data was collected from the field comprising study reports, surveys, consultancy works, dossiers, tourism promotional literature and also from books, journals, government reports, websites, magazines, publications of Tamil Nadu Tourism Development Corporation (TTDC), and other scholarly works.

Content Analysis: Study Leads and Cues

Officials and Promoters' Views on Ecotourism Management in Pichavaram by way of Incepting Sustainable Practices, and Providing Accent to Ecological Values

The responses of focus group interviews with (a) tourism officials, (b) practitioners from private sector tourism enterprises, and (c) local community representatives have been coded in consonance with the study objectives and depicted below:

Ecotourism has been recognized as a cardinal segment of Tamil Nadu's tourism industry which has embarked on a mercurial curve in the past two decades owing to the enamouring natural resources and sustainable activities. Though there was consensus in some aspects among the participants of focus group interviews (tourism officials and private enterprises) like "Pichavaram is an ideal spot for city-bugged and pollution-fatigued tourists; mangroves have tremendous ecological value, and wetland ecosystem of Pichavaram is fragile, the views pertaining to Ecotourism Policy implications for Pichavaram, the efficacy of resource stewardship, and benefits to local population" were divergent.

Ecotourism is being raised as an engine for achieving balanced regional development in Pichavaram. This is keeping in view the tourist generating markets, viz., both foreign and domestic and also the revenue generated by the influx. Tourism industry practitioners, especially from the neighbouring hubs such as Puducherry, Chidambaram, Thanjavur, Chennai, and Cuddalore expressed the lack of avenues for tourist spending in Pichavaram. Concerns were mostly raised from the perspective of consistently maintaining the physical environment without in any way compromising on its fragility. All the stakeholders converged on the aspect of indiscriminate sanction of outlets and viewed that it could lead to tampering of the natural ambience. Furthermore, it was categorically stated that distortions in the landscape can lead to ecological disruption. Many interviewees noted that proper control over commercial exploitation of ecotourism resources lacks the requisite fervour. The group laid stress on the fact that badly planned components of tourism in the destination such as board walk, eco-friendly boating, food outlets, and solid waste management mechanism will deteriorate the ecological value of the place. Albeit, this view had divergences too as certain participants observed that nature-based tourism activities would sensitise the ecotourists as regards the protection of the resources; provided the visitors possess and displays the attributes of *real ecotourists*. Moreover, the promotion needs to be in tune with the ideals of *real ecotourism*.

It was argued that the design of tourism facilities is not in sync with the local architecture features and dimensions and leads to visual pollution. Continuous monitoring of tourism properties and evaluation of their Environmental Management Systems (EMS) on a periodic basis were mentioned to be not up to the mark and a factor of high concern. The mangrove swamps of Pichavaram provide basic outlets for flood control and also the ingredients for local fishing industry. The experts opined that setting up of tourist ventures at the cost of depletion of mangroves and farming lands poses danger to the habitats. The pointers of experts underscored strengthening of the current efforts of preservation of mangroves and the fact that the area should not be allowed to shrink.

As a matter of fact, no comprehensive and lucid study on the physical economic, social, and psychological carrying capacity has been conducted without which it cannot be ratified whether the sustainable practices devised are in consonance with the destination dynamics. Matters such as trampling of vegetation and flora, littering of non-biodegradable wastes, issues associated with overcrowding and congestion, pollution of water bodies, and depreciation of mangrove cover are cases pronounced as of great concern. Local community members are rarely consulted in matters related to tourism. It is ironical that they are not party to the decision-making process even in cases where the inputs could be drawn from traditional wisdom at the local level. Though insufficient representation in tourism trade is found, the host community can be the driving force of ecotourism by integrating the indigenous elements.

The educative value of ecotourism, according to all the experts who were interviewed, was surprisingly deficient in Pichavaram. Interpretation and education of eco-sites are at the crux of ecotourism. It was underpinned that sustainable practices turn out to be meaningful and effective when all the stakeholders are enabled with the provisions for learning more about biodiversity and cultural ecology. The opinion leaders from the host community indicated that the planting of exotic species even for beautification purposes in the backwater zone will be detrimental to the floral species and also the ecosystem *in toto*.

The Prevailing Gaps in the Practice of Ecotourism Ideals in Pichavaram vis-à-vis Study-based Solution Driven Recommendations

The Chinese words for ecotourism, viz., Sheng Tai Nu You

translates as "tourism that is not based on exploiting or harming the local environment, ecology or society". As pointed out by Wang—there is no generally accepted definition (Wang *et al.*, 2009), rather, "ecotourism" has been used loosely; often as a marketing ploy to attract visitors (Nianyong and Zhuge, 2001; Wang *et al.*, 2009).

In spite of the lack of an agreed definition, there is broad consensus that ecotourism comprises a number of key features (Epler Wood *et al.*, 1991; Wight, 1994; Ross and Wall, 1999; Blamey, 2001; Weaver, 2001a). Primarily, it is nature based; involving "deliberate or purposeful responsible" travel to see, experience and enjoy the natural environment. Second, it involves some form of cultural and environmental education with the implicit assumption that this will promote environmental and cultural understanding and conservation of natural resources. Third, it is sustainably managed and includes the generation of income to support conservation efforts and enhance the broader development of the host community who are actively involved through local participation (Fennell, 1999; Weaver, 2001b).

Registered conservancies can formulate tourism plans and drive sustainable development in Pichavaram. Furthermore, for livestock management and prevention of water pollution, local community members can take the role of key actors, though the incorporation of tourism into community life has to be exercised meticulously. Pichavaram do not offer any special provision for women to engage with ecotourism, say for instance, sale of indigenous handicrafts or any traditional souvenir article. Yet, the community cultural life could be promoted through women. The host population needs to be wary of the fact that unsustainable exploitation of natural resources or cultural degradation adversely affects the destination image. One aspect which should be carefully considered is maintaining acceptable levels of visitor use. The Board Walk facility in Pichavaram has certain grey areas to be rectified. Site sensitive design for the local infrastructure and superstructure is a dire necessity. Environment-friendly waste management and energy systems have to be tapped. Site-specific operators from the local population must be identified and trained in ecologically sustainable practices. Ecotourism planners could possibly plan for deploying field guides who can disseminate know-how on sustainable tourism lucidly and engagingly. A well-stacked ecotourism interpretation entre will leverage the nature-friendly agenda for the destination. No tourism property worth being a certified entity has been incepted in Pichavaram.

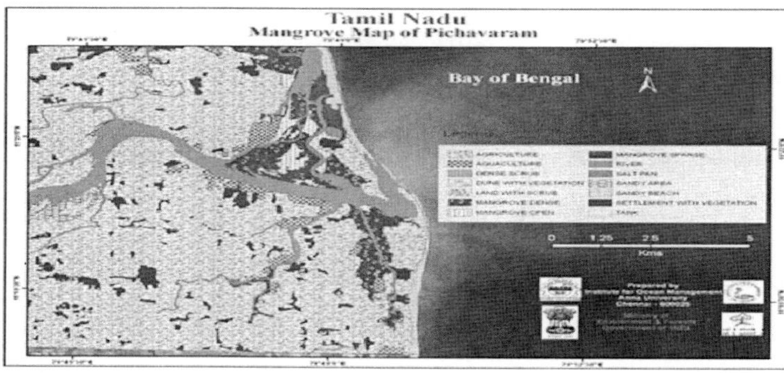

Fig. 4.2: Mangrove Map of Pichavaram.

Fig. 4.3: Mangrove Map of Pichavaram.

Source: Centre for Coastal Zone Management and Coastal Shelter Belt, Ministry of Environment, Forests & Climate Change, Govt. of India. **Prepared by:** Institute for Ocean Management, Anna University, Chennai.

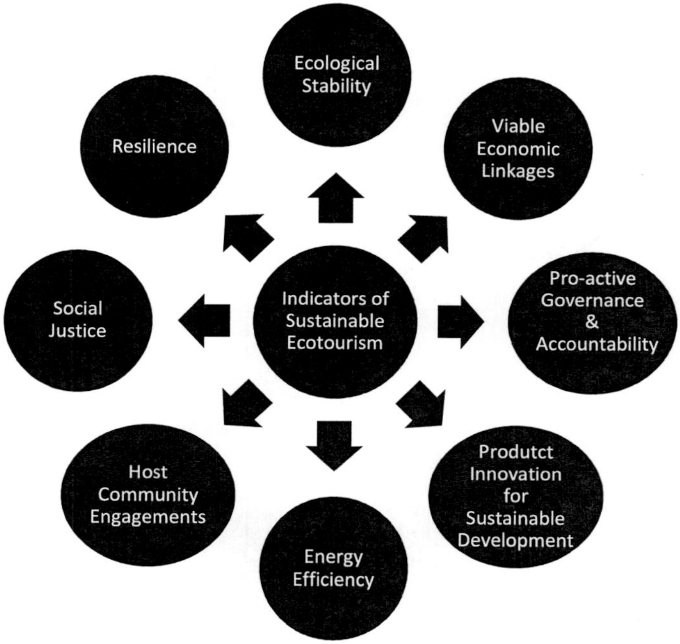

Fig. 4.4: Model Featuring Indicators of Sustainable Ecotourism in Pichavaram (Research Output).

Table 4.1: Checklist for Ecotourism Potential of Pichavaram

S. No.	Checklist	Particulars	Opinion	Remarks
1.	Is the protected area	Close to an International airport?		It is in proximity to the Chennai International Airport 208 km.
		Moderately close?	Yes	
		Remote?		
2.	Is the journey to the area	Easy (short) and comfortable?	Yes	It is well connected by National Highway 32 and Grand Southern Trunk Road.
		A bit of an effort?		
		Arduous or dangerous?		

(*Contd.*)

S. No.	Checklist	Particulars	Opinion	Remarks
3.	Does the area offer the following	Star species attractions?	Yes	The Pichavaram swamps, sprawled across 11,000 ha. of backwaters, are a labyrinth of 4,000 canals and 1,700 islands. It is the home to at least 23 recorded species of mangroves, including Avicenna and Rhizophora.
		Other interesting wildlife?	Yes	Fish and molluscs to crabs and other crustaceans.
		Representative wildlife?	Yes	There are around 177 species of birds which are varied in 15 orders and 41 families. Indigenous and migratory avian fauna can be viewed.
		Distinctive wildlife viewing (on feet, by boat, from hides)?		
4.	Is successful wildlife viewing	Guaranteed?	Yes	
		Usual?		
		With luck or highly seasonal?		
5.	Does the area offer	Several distinct features of interest?	Yes	Apart from Ecotourism, Sustainable tourism, people also enjoy bird watching and exploring Chidambaram City for its rich cultural heritage.
		More than one feature of interest?		
		One main feature of interest?		
6.	What standards of food and accommodation are offered?	High standards		There is a Diaspora of south Indian and Indo-Chinese Cuisines offered by TTDC-Tamil Nadu Tourism Development Corporation. For a decent resting place, one has to travel to Chidambaram which is just 14.5 km from Pichavaram.
		Adequate standards	Yes	
		Rough standards		

(*Contd.*)

S. No.	Checklist	Particulars	Opinion	Remarks
7.	Does the area have additional	High cultural interest?	Yes	Chidambaram is the nearest cultural hub. It is called as the temple town. It houses the famous Nataraja Temple.
		Some cultural attractions?		
		Few cultural attractions?		
8.	Is the area:	Unique in its appeal?	Yes	It is the world's second largest Mangrove forest.
		A little bit different?		
		Similar to other visitor reserves?		
9.	Does the area have	A beach or lakeside recreational facility?	Yes	The nearby towns Cuddalore and Pondicherry have beaches and other Recreational facilities like scuba diving and surfing.
		River, falls, or swimming pools?		
		Any other recreation possibilities?		
10.	Is the area close enough to other sites of tourist interest to be part of a tourist circuit?	Yes, other attractive sites	Yes	An ideal circuit will be Chennai City Pickup to Pichavaram via Pondicherry Route and Stay in Chidambaram.
		Moderate potential		
		Low or no such potential		
11.	Is the surrounding area	Or high scenic beauty or intrinsic interest?	Yes	
		Quite attractive?		
		Rather ordinary?		

(*Contd.*)

S. No.	Checklist	Particulars	Opinion	Remarks
12.	Is the cost of the visit	High		The cost of the entire circuit trip will cost roughly around USD 200 including accommodation, boat ride in Pichavaram Mangrove forest and food.
		Moderate		
		Low	Yes	

Source: Mackinnon *et al.,* 1987.

Major Inferences and Ways Forward

- Government machinery must focus on improving the coverage and efficacy of the Environment Impact Assessment (EIA) and other feasibility studies including Limits of Acceptable Change (LAC) and subsequent decision-making process. Soft tourism is the order of modern day ecotourism and experts in environmental affairs can enhance the vibes of environment based resource stewardship in Pichavaram.
- Ecotourism in Pichavaram must lay emphasis on meaningful travel. The destination is a fertile ground for promoting slow and conscious travel.
- Unique projects such as Eco-tels, Eco-lodges, Eco-resorts and Eco-parks can be established in proximity to the destination; in tandem with the feasibility reports. Accreditations and green certifications for ecotourism projects are concrete steps in ensuring sustainable development. Tourism planning in Pichavaram can turn the spotlight on *plantation tourism* taking into account the floral backdrop and it will also propel the principles of SD.
- Eco-development Committees may be constituted by enjoining host community members to ensure pro-active participation and to enable dynamic engagements for better preservation.
- Visitor management strategies are utmost essential for sustainable ecotourism development. Scientific knowledge of visitor impacts will add strength to SD ventures. Continuous

evaluation and monitoring will also give impetus to sustainable development of the eco-site.

- The *sense of place* of Pichavaram is the natural heritage mainly the mangroves. Branding efforts pertaining to the ecotourism haven need to lay stress on all the ecological delights around the backwater for effective *place-making.*
- Land use planning can never compromise on the exactitude in Pichavaram which is an ecologically fragile destination.
- Xeriscape-planting flora that requires less water for beautification—can be an ideal venture for the destination in the present day.
- Water resources required by local farmers and villagers must not be indiscriminately diverted for tourism uses. This may in future lead to host-guest conflict.
- Cultural ecology can be a paradigm as regards the efforts for protection of mangroves. When the preservation is connected to the cultural mores, beliefs, and rites, the efforts become committed as well as voluntary.
- Self Help Groups (SHGs) can promote garbage reduction and cleanliness enhancement.
- Interpretation centres are found wanting and need to be set-up.
- Community-based tourism by way of project initiatives and indigenous cultural expressions can play a vital role in bringing sustainable solutions to the eco-destination.
- Environmental education through knowledgeable tour guides has the potential in mitigating the ill effects of tourism as well as promoting sustainable practices.
- Ecotourists and hosts need to have genuine exchange of ecological values and attempt to revive the traditions.
- Continuous management of the ecotourism spots is a dire necessity and the policy framework needs to cover the key aspects of evaluation and monitoring.
- Experiential holidays, especially camping, birding, and soft trekking have ample prospects in Pichavaram.

- A sculpture garden in the eco-destination is in line with the ideals and therefore would add tremendous value.
- Environmentally responsible marketing is the need of the hour in the destination.
- Positive checks can go a long way in establishing the ideals of sustainable ecotourism.
- Tourists should be sensitized not to bestrew large quantities of garbage in the pristine countryside of Pichavaram.
- Revenue management by way of channelizing the finance from visitor entry fees, boating, etc., towards conservation and enhancement of natural heritage of Pichavaram is to be given due thrust.
- Care must be taken not to introduce alien forms of plant life into the delicate ecosystem of the mangrove wetland through the footwears and clothes of the tourists.
- Apply best biodiversity conservation actions.
- The demerits could be offset by high quality planning, design, and management.
- Ecologically Sustainable Development (ESD) must be the major aim of this destination to meet the needs of local community and to protect the natural environment.
- Develop and manage the tourism industry in a way which conserves its natural resources and minimizes its environmental impacts.
- Developing a source of long-term financial sustainability for the conservation of the biological site is very mush essential.
- Ensure that tourism strategies developed at all levels of government are based on ESD principles and provide effective mechanisms for industry and community input.
- Encourage environmentally appropriate tourist behaviour and adopt codes of environmental behaviour and practices and improve tourist awareness of ESD principles.

Conclusion

Ecotourism is indeed a sustainable development option in Pichavaram. It can offer ample opportunities for mitigating pressure on the wetland ecosystems, though it is not the ultimate solution. This study reinforces the fact that there is a cost of unplanned and uncontrolled development and the authorities and destination designers must see to it that the adverse effects are mitigated to the best possible extent. Site integrity, both cultural and biological integrity, is to be preserved not only for future tourists but also for the local population. This work provides insights into the challenges associated with sustainable development of the destination and the prospects of ecotourism development in the protected areas. Sustainable ecotourism is necessary for conservation of nature, economic development, and promotion of culture. Pichavaram needs diversified tourism products that benefit conservation of mangrove ecosystem and rural communities. Environmental awareness of local ecotourism businesses would make tourism a sustainable development tool. Without this reorientation, efforts to achieve sustainable development at Pichavaram will be a difficult proposition. Imbibing balance of nature and sustainable ecotourism development at Pichavaram would not only benefit the local people but also enable tourists to experience the virtues of the exotic scenic beauty of the mangrove ecosystem. It was quite evident during the course of the study that community-based tourism can play a vital role in bringing sustainable solutions.

Scope for Further Research

Pichavaram attracts hordes of migratory birds. The destination has immense prospects for promoting Avian Tourism. Thus a study to unveil sustainable activity-based ecotourism through bird spotting and avian trails will be a paradigm shift, whereby the destination can uphold the ideals of sustainable development.

References

Anu Chandran, R.C. (2010). "Eco-consciousness and Tourism Promotion: A Study on Pichavaram, Tamil Nadu, with Special Emphasis on Mangrove Ecosystems". *Tourism Theory and Practice*, ISSN 0973-6611.

Bacon, P.R. (1987). "Use of Wetlands for Tourism in the Insular Caribbean". *Annals of Tourism Research, 14*: 104-17.

Bakkes, J. (1997). "Conclusion". In Moldan, B., Billharz, S. and Matravers, R. (Eds). *Sustainability Indicators: A Report on the Project on Indicators of Sustainable Development*. Chichester: John Wiley and Sons.

Blamey, R.K., 2001. "Principles of Ecotourism". In D. Weaver (Ed.) *The Encyclopedia of Ecotourism*. New York: CABI Publishing, 5-22.

Brinson, M.M., Rheinhardt, R.D., Hauer, R.F., Lee, C.L., Nutter, W.L., D.R. Smith, Whigham, D. (1995). A Guidebook for Application of Hydrogeomorphic Assessments to Riverine Wetlands, Wetlands Research Programme Technical Report WRP-DE-11.

Ceballos-Lascurain, H. (1987). "The Future of Ecotourism". *Mexico Journal*, 13-14.

CEC (1995). Wise Use and Conservation of Wetlands, COM (95) 18 a Final. Office for Official Publications of the European Communities, Luxembourg.

Clive, George (2007). "Sustainable Development and Global Governance", *The Journal of Environment Development, 16*(1): 102-25.

Cooper, C. and S. Wanhill (1998). Tourism Development: Environmental and Community Issues. Developing Indicators of Sustainable Tourism. Report for visit forum. Chichester, U.K.: John Wiley and Sons.

Costanza, R., Darge, R., De Groot, R., Farber, S., Grasso, M., Hannon, B., Limburg, K., Naeem, S., O'Neill, R.V., Paruelo, J., Raskin, R.G., Sutton, P. & Van Den Belt, M. (1997). "The Value of the World's Ecosystem Services and Natural Capital". *Nature, 387*: 253-260.

Cowardin, L.M., Carter, V., Golet, F.C. and LaRoe, E.T. (1979). Classification of Wetlands and Deepwater Habitats of the United States. US Fish and Wildlife Service Pub FsW/OBS-79/31, Washington DC. Department of Water Affairs and Forestry, 1995. Procedures to Assess Effluent Discharge Impacts. WRC Report No. TT64/94, Water Research Commission, Pretoria.

Cowardin, L.M., V. Carter, F.C. Golet, E.T. LaRoe (1979). Classification of Wetlands and Deepwater Habitats of the United States. U.S. Department of the Interior, Fish and Wildlife Service, Washington, DC. Jamestown, ND: Northern Prairie Wildlife Research Center Online. http://www.npwrc.usgs.gov/resource/wetlands/classwet/index.htm (Version 04DEC1998).

Eber, S. (1992). "Beyond the Green Horizon: A Discussion Paper on Principles for Sustainable Tourism". *Worldwide Fund for Nature*. UK: Godalming.

Edward Maltby (1991). "Wetlands and their Values", In Max Finlayson and Michael Moser (eds.), *Wetlands* (Oxford/New York: Facts on File), 8.

Epler Wood, M., Gatz, F., and Lindberg, K. (1991). "The Ecotourism Society: An Action Agenda". In J. Kusler (ed.), *Ecotourism and Resource Conservation*. Selected papers from the 2nd international symposium. Ecotourism and Resource Conservation Madison: Omnipress, 75-79.

Fennell, D. (1999). *Ecotourism: An Introduction*. London: Routledge.

Frissel, S.S., J. Stankey and G.H., (1972). "Wilderness Environmental Quality: Search for Social and Ecological Harmony". In: *Proceedings of the 1972 National Convention*; Hot Springs, AR. Washington, DC: Society of American Foresters Geographer.

Garg, K. (1983). "Vertical Distribution of Fungi in Sunderban Mangrove Mud". *Indian Journal of Marine Sciences, 12*: 48-51.

George, I. & Kuriakose, S. (2012). "A Study to Analyse the Satisfaction Level of Tourist Relating to Facility Available in the Back Water Tourism in Alleppey", *IJEMR*, Vol. 2, Issue 3.

Gössling, S. (1999). "Ecotourism: A Means to Safeguard Biodiversity and Ecosystem Functions?", *Ecological Economics, 29*: 303-20.

Holden, A. (2008). *Environment and Tourism*. London: Routledge.

Honey, M. (1999). *Ecotourism and Sustainable Development*. Washington, DC: Island.

James, E.J. (2007). "Hydrologic Consideration in the Management of Wetlands of Kerala", *Proceedings of Kerala Environment Congress 2007*, Trivandrum, Kerala.

Karlaganis, C. and Narayanan, N.C. (2014). "Governance Challenges in Linking Environmental Sustainability to Tourism: Where is the House Boat Industry in Kerala", India Headed? *Working Paper* No. 2013/09.

Kerry Black and Baba, M. (2001). *Developing a Management Plan for Ashtamudi Estuary*, Kollam, India, p. 546.

Krüger, O. (2005). "The Role of Ecotourism in Conservation: Panacea or Pandora's Box". *Biodiversity and Conservation, 14*: 579-600.

Kunjuraman, V., Hussin, R., & Aziz, R.C. (2022). "Community-based Ecotourism as a Social Transformation Tool for Rural Community: A Victory or a Quagmire?" *Journal of Outdoor Recreation and Tourism, 39.* https://doi.org/10.1016/j.jort.2022.100524

Kusler, J.A. (2006a). *Common Questions: Wetlands and Ecotourism.* Association of State Wetland Managers, Inc., USA.

Kusler, J.A. (2006b). Common Questions: Definition of the Terms Wetland "Function" and "Value", Association of State Wetland Managers, Inc., USA.

Lili, P., Lijuan, C.U.I., Ming, W.U. (2010). "Tourist Behaviour in Wetland Park: A Preliminary study in XiXi National Wetlands, Hangzhou, China", *Chin. Geogra. Sci.*, *20*(1): 66-73.

Lim., C. & McAleer, Use of Wetlands for Sustainable Tourism Management.

Lu, J., & Nepal, S.K. (2009). "Sustainable Tourism Research: An Analysis of Papers Published in the Journal of Sustainable Tourism". *Journal of Sustainable Tourism, 17*(1): 5-16.

Macbeth, Jim (2005). "Towards an Ethics Platform for Tourism", *Annals of Tourism Research, 32*: 962-84.

MacKinnon, J. & MacKinnon, K. (1986). *Review of the Protected Areas System in the Indo-Malayan Realm.* Gland & Cambridge: IUCN.

MacKinnon, J.K., G. Child and J. Thorsell (1987). *Managing Protected Areas in the Tropics.* Gland, Switzerland: International Union for the Conservation of Nature.

Manning, R.E. and D.W. Lime (2000). "Defining and Managing the Quality of Wilderness Recreation Experiences". In *Wilderness Science in a Time of Change Conference: Wilderness Ecosystems, Threats and Management*, 4.

Mathieson, A. and G. Wall (1982). *Tourism: Economic, Physical and Social Impacts*, New York: John Wiley & Sons.

McArthur, S., (2000). "Beyond Carrying Capacity: Introducing A Model to Monitor and Manage Visitor Activity in Forests". In *Forest Tourism and Recreation.* CAB International, pp. 259-66.

McCoy, K.L., E.E. Krumpe and S. Allen (1995). "Limits of Acceptable Change Planning: Evaluating Implementation by the US. Forest Service", *International Journal of Wilderness Press, 1*(2): 18-22.

MoEF (1990). *Wetlands of India: A Directory.* Ministry of Environment and Forests, Govt. of India, New Delhi.

Mojca Stubelj Ars *et al.* (2010). "Towards the Ecotourism: A Decision Support Model for the Assessment of Sustainability of Mountain Huts in the Alps." *Journal of Environmental Management, 91*: 2554-64.

Nair, A.S.K., Sanker, G. and Mathew, K.J. (2001). "Estimation of Wetlands in Kerala using IRS data". Pro. 13th Kerala Science Congress KSCSTE, Govt. of Kerala, pp. 60-61.

National Wetland Inventory and Assessment, Information Brochure, Ministry of Environment and Forests, Government of India, 9 June 2011.

Nianyong, H. and Zhuge, R. (2001). "Ecotourism in China's Nature Reserves: Opportunities and Challenges". *Journal of Sustainable Tourism, 9*(3): 228-42.

Orams, M.B. (1995). "Towards a More Desirable Form of Ecotourism", *Tourism Management, 16*: 3-8.

Rome, Abigail (1999). "Ecotourism Impact Monitoring: A Review of Methodologies and Recommendations for Developing Monitoring Programmes in Latin America". *Ecotourism Technical Report,* Series Number 1, pp. 3-4.

Ross, S. and Wall, G. (1999). "Ecotourism: Towards Congruence between Theory and Practice". *Tourism Management, 20*(1): 123-32.

Schoolman, E.D., Guest, J.S., Bush, K.F. & Bell, A.R. (2011). "How Interdisciplinary is Sustainability Research?: Analysing the Structure of An Emerging Scientific Field". *Sustainability Science, 7*(1): 67-80.

Schulte, S. (2003). *Guía conceptual y metodológica para el desarrollo y planificación del sector turismo.* Santiago de Chile: Naciones Unidas.

Sivakumar, M. and Annadurai, R. (2014). "Impact of Ecotourism in Pichavaram: A Study". *International Research Journal of Management and Humanities,* ISSN 2347-3274.

Stankey, H. George, McCool and F. Stephen (1984). "Carrying Capacity in Recreational Settings: Evolution, Appraisal, and Application". *Leisure Sciences, 6*: 453-73.

Stronza, A. (2000). Because it is Ours: Community-based Ecotourism in the Peruvian Amazon. Ph.D. dissertation, University of Florida, Gainesville.

TIES (2010). The International Ecotourism Society (TIES) [online]. Available from: http://www. ecotourism.org/site/c.orLQKXPCLmF/b.4832143/k.CF7C/The_International_Ecotourism_Society__Uniting_Conservation_Communities_and_Sustainable_Travel.html. Are you aware that Pichavaram Mangrove ecosystem is an protected area?

TIES (2006). The International Ecotourism Society. TIES Global Ecotourism. Available from http://www.ecotourism.org.

Turner R.K., & T. Jones (eds.) (1991). *Wetlands, Market and Intervention Failures,* London: Earth Scan.

Turner, R.K. (1991). "Economics and Wetland Management", *Ambio, 20*(2): 59-63.

UNEP (1999). Mediterranean Action Plan: Tourism and Sustainable Development. Paper prepared by the Mediterranean Commission on Sustainable Development (MCSD), p. 9.

UNEP (2011). Towards a Green Economy: Pathways to Sustainable Development and Poverty Eradication—Tourism: Investing in Energy and Resource Efficiency. PART II: Investing in Energy and Resource Efficiency: Tourism.

Varshney, C.K. (1984). *All-India Wetland Survey: Questionnaire 1984*. Wetland Working Group, Department of Environment, Government of India, New Delhi.

Varshney, C.K. (1987). "Wetlands of India: Economic and Scientific Importance". Paper presented at the Conference on Wetland and Waterfowl Conservation in Asia, Malacca, Malaysia, 23-28 February 1987. IWRB & Interwader.

Vinayachandran, N. & V.S. Joji (2007). "Groundwater Information Booklet of Wayanad District, Kerala State". Central Groundwater Board, Ministry of Water Resources, Government of India, Thiruvananthapuram.

Wall, G. and Mathieson, A. (2006). *Tourism, Change and Opportunities*, Harlow: Pearson Education Limited.

Washburne, R.F. (1982). "Wilderness Recreational Carrying Capacity: Are Numbers Necessary? *Journal of Forestry, Society of American Foresters*, Vol. 80, No. 11, 1, pp. 726-728 (3).

Watzin, M.C. & Gozzelink, J.G. (1992). The Fragile Fringe Coastal Wetlands of the Continental United States. Louisiana Grant College Programme, Louisiana State University, Baton Kange, LA; U.S. Fish and Wildlife Service, Washington, DC and National Oceanic and Atmospheric Administration, Rockville.

Weaver, D. (2001a). *The Encyclopedia of Ecotourism*. Oxon: Cabi Publishing.

Weaver, D. (2001b). *Ecotourism*. Milton: Wiley.

Wight, P. (1994). "Environmentally Responsible Marketing of Tourism". In E. Cater and G. Lowman (Eds.) *Ecotourism: A Sustainable Option*. Chichester: Wiley, 39-53.

World Commission on Environment and Development (WCED) (1987). *Our Common Future*. Oxford University Press, Oxford.

Zacharias, S., Manalel, J., Jose, M.C. & Salan, A. (2008). *Backwater Tourism in Kerala: Challenges and Opportunities, Conference of Tourism in India-Challenges Ahead*, pp. 524-528.

Webliography

http://www.tamilnadutourism.org. Accessed on 28/3/2022

http://www.ttdconline.com. Accessed on 28/3/2022

http://www.forests.tn.nic.in/ecotourism/ecotourism_home.html. Accessed on 25/3/2022

https://www.ecotourism.org. Accessed on 27/3/2022

http://www.incredibleindia.org/en/travel/ecotourism. Accessed on 28/3/2022

http://www.varunvoyages.com/brochure/files/assets/downloads/page0008.pdf

http://www.holidayiq.com/travel-guides/kumarakom.pdf

http://greatbackwaters.com

www.rtkerala.com

https://www.keralatourism.org/rt-kumarakom-firstfield.php

http://www.kittsedu.org/responsible-tourism-initiative.php

http://www.thehindu.com/news/national/kerala/responsible-kerala-tourism-to-spread-wings/article6429268.ece

http://gitpac.com/responsible-tourism/

http://www.ramsar.org/categories

http://wwf.panda.org/about_our_earth/about_freshwater/intro/majorwetlands

http://www.ramsar.org/tourism. Accessed on 10-4-2022

http://www.wetlands.org. Accessed on 10-4-2022

http://www.keralatourism.org. Accessed on 13-4-2022

http://www.wayanadtourism.org. Accessed on 25-4-2022

http://www.wayanadtravel.com/where-to-go/pookot-lake. Accessed on 16-4-2022

http://www.keralatourism.org/destination/sasthamkotta-lake-kollam/40. Accessed on 20-3-2022

http://www.keralatourism.org/destination/vembanad-lake.../111. Accessed on 28-3-2022

http://www.ashtamudilake.com. Accessed on 28-3-2022

http://www.holidayiq.com/travel-guides/kumarakom.pdf

http://greatbackwaters.com

http:// www.rtkerala.com

https://www.keralatourism.org/rt-kumarakom-firstfield.php

http://www.kittsedu.org/responsible-tourism-initiative.php

http://www.thehindu.com/news/national/kerala/responsible-kerala-tourism-to-spread-wings/article6429268.ece

http://gitpac.com/responsible-tourism/
http://www.ramsar.org/categories
http://wwf.panda.org/about_our_earth/about_freshwater/intro/majorwetlands
http://www.unwto.org
http://www.greenpeaceindia.org
http://www.equitabletourism.org
http://www.dhanfoundation.org
http://www.atree.org
http://www.un-documents.net/wced-ocf.htm.

5
Marketing and Branding of Tourism in Kerala
An Analysis

Asha T. Rajan and *Ajitha, S.*

Introduction

In today's highly competitive and dynamic global tourism environment, there arise a need to develop a clear brand identity, reflecting the core strengths and personality of its products. Destination branding is an important marketing strategy adopted by nations to promote tourism. It is widely reported and recognized even in international circles that Kerala Tourism is well known and accepted as a product due to its own unique features. The slogan "God's Own Country" is very catching and it sounds very justifiable, considering the special attributes of the state. Kerala Tourism is even regarded as a model to other lines of industries and other states. It is also a fact that Kerala's tourism industry is growing at a faster pace. The state had reportedly became one of the places with the highest brand recall, with its unique positioning and targeting efforts. Many places of Kerala have great historical importance and now it become one of the branded destinations. In short, Kerala's culture, tradition, diversified natural attractions, climate, people, religious heritages, social development and administrative surroundings are the major determinants of tourism development in Kerala.

Due to industrialisation and urbanisation, our tourism sector needs to move towards a new strategy, where it does not adversely affect the environment. But like any other sectors in Kerala, the chief motto of tourism industry is to maximize profits, using available natural resources. This helps in the sustainable development of tourism in Kerala. However, branding all the features of Kerala will help in the economic development of the state and also leads to tourism promotion. Government of Kerala is focusing to create marketing strategies for the destination with the potential of natural resources. For marketing purpose, destination branding is needed and Kerala had been placed in the tourism industry with a brand image. This helps in the successful promotion of tourism in Kerala as a tourism super brand among the destinations.

Objectives

The major objectives of the study are:

1. To analyse the marketing and branding strategies for the development of tourism in Kerala.
2. To examine the satisfaction level of tourists about the tourism products of Kerala.
3. To study the role of organisations in tourism marketing in Kerala.

Data and Methods

The present study has been designed as descriptive-cum-analytic in nature. For better understanding of various dimensions of tourism marketing and branding of the state, primary data were collected from tourists who are the prime beneficiaries of the strategies adopted and organisations who are the main contributors for the development of tourism industry in Kerala. The data is collected through a structured questionnaire.

Marketing and Branding Strategies of Tourism in Kerala

Kerala model development is a much-debated topic all over the world and it has been regarded as a model for many other developing societies. The potential of tourism sector to stimulate economic and social development, which in turn helps in transforming economies is internationally acknowledged. Today, Kerala Tourism is a global super brand and is regarded as one of the destinations with the highest brand recall. The tag line "Kerala—God's Own Country" was adopted in its tourism promotions and has become synonymous with the state. Tourism is an important economic activity and continues to be the fastest growing sector and hence is included among the top three industries in the country. Although India has progressed a lot since the 1950s, with respect to tourism, the country is still way behind the developed or even the developing countries. In comparison, India earns one seventh of China, one-fourth of Indonesia and less than half of Philippines from tourism. Kerala is the foremost state in India that realized the potential of Ayurvedic /Health tourism and has widely marketed it throughout the state. About two decades back, Kerala started with the task of promoting Ayurveda on a larger scale. It is estimated that about 30 per cent of the foreigners coming to Kerala avail themselves to Ayurvedic care and about 40 per cent of the state's tourism revenue is generated from the same.

Kerala is included in the list of "fifty must see places in the life time to visit" and also bagged the super brand award among 101 strong brands in India. In recent times, tourism is emerged as the major revenue generating business to Government of Kerala. This contributes significantly towards the growth of Kerala in providing employment and contributing to the overall productivity of the state. The most important marketing strategy of tourism taken by Kerala State was the Private-Public-Partnership (PPP) to promote tourism. Kerala had gained a great market position in tourist industry by the promotion of back water tourism, which is the major attraction of Kerala. The other aspects are the ecotourism initiatives and the branding of traditional art forms like Kathakali and Theyyam, the traditions of Kalaripayattu, Kalaritherapy and Ayurveda are also showcased before the tourists. Kerala tourism industry is doing innovative and vibrant advertising campaign for the promotion of the industry. The tourism industry in Kerala can be in the best position by providing innovative branding techniques.

Kerala, as part of its marketing strategy, continuously organizes road shows all-around the world for the promotion of Ayurveda along with modern medicine. The tour operators have also come to realize that delivering quality in service results greater business and increased profits. In international and domestic markets, Kerala Tourism launched innovative marketing campaign for retaining the market supremacy. The Department of Tourism had made many tourism marketing promotions, by being a regular participant in national and international tourism trade fairs. Kerala Tourism had participated in the leading international tourism trade fairs. Community participation in tourism development is successfully implemented in Kerala through Kerala Responsible Tourism (RT) initiative, which supports the development of the natives who are living adjacent to the destinations. Government of Kerala realized that safety, hygiene, quality service, etc. can be achieved through the introduction of quality standards, registration, certification, regulation and legislation. The comprehensive plan also includes guidelines and measures to ensure fair pricing. Beyond a competitive pricing strategy, achieving quality is another key to Kerala's competitiveness. The ability to attain international standards and consistent delivery of high-quality products and services are the critical success factors in the promotion of Kerala products in the global market.

Perspective Analysis of Marketing Strategies in Kerala

Tourism industry is dependent on various factors which are inevitable for operating as an independent industry or generating economy. The well-being of one sector will directly or indirectly impact each other. The marketing mix perspective analysis of tourism consists of product perspective analysis, price perspective analysis, place/distribution perspective analysis, promotion perspective analysis, people perspective analysis, process perspective analysis and physical evidence perspective analysis.

Product Perspective Analysis

Kerala Tourism has the advantage of local resources and is able to attract tourists with the help of tour packages and other offers. It may be according to the seasons, special days and festivals. Some of the important products offered by Kerala Tourism are Cruise and Coast packages, Seasonal packages and Holiday packages including Jungle Holiday packages. Certain other forms of tourism in the state are also identified as the more potential areas or attractions for designing tour packages. These include Nature Tourism, Pilgrimage or Religious Tourism, Health Tourism, Culture and Traditional Tourism, Heritage Tourism, Ecotourism, Adventure Tourism, Sports Tourism and Rural Tourism. The Nature Tourism has always remained as the backbone of tour packages in Kerala. The beautiful backwaters, beaches, waterfalls, hill stations, vegetations with wildlife and an abundance of flora and fauna, etc., make the state an ideal destination for nature lovers. Kerala is popular in the world for Health Tourism. Ayurveda is the main health-conscious tourism product of the state, which brings much foreign exchange to the country and Kerala is the only place in the world, where the ancient form of science and the holistic system of medicine based on nature is being practised. The myriad resource potentials of Kerala tourism industry make the tour operators in the state, capable to develop and market innumerable number of varied tour packages.

Price Perspective Analysis

Even though, Department of Tourism is the regulatory body of tourism in Kerala, the pricing decision in the tourism industry is not limited to that regulatory mechanism. Despite Kerala tourism offers several price related packages to the tourists including value-based pricing, the bargain pricing has become prominent among the Kerala holiday makers. The state tourism has adopted various pricing for its products like tourism packages, accommodation, transportation, etc. Department of Tourism has adopted a differential pricing strategy, i.e., pricing mechanism for domestic tourists who are charged with reasonable pricing policy and international tourists with premium rates. The pricing of tourism products also has to take into account the complexity created by seasonality of demand and the inherent perishability of the product.

Place Perspective Analysis

The place element in marketing mix in the tourism context is highly significant, as it is a form of distribution network. Most of the foreigners arrive from places like United Kingdom (UK), United States of America (USA), France and Australia, as Kerala is equipped with a strong network of international airports, roadways and railways to meet the travel requirements of these tourists. In the place perspective analysis of tourism, tour packages have a vital role to play. A tour package distribution channel usually consists of tour operators, brokers, travel agents and tourists. The tour operators sell a holiday package directly to the clients and sometimes through other channels. These packages are mainly distributed to the DTPCs, tourism reception centres, marketing divisions, sales agents, etc. The Department of Tourism, Kerala had international agents and offices in various countries like UK, USA, UAE, etc., which help in the marketing of the destinations. A number of offices and helpdesks situated in Kerala and other major cities in the country help in the efficient promotion of destinations in Kerala.

Promotion Perspective Analysis

The role played by promotion perspective analysis, has been instrumental to the growth of modern tourism. Promotion of the tourism product is carried out through various means such as advertisement, personal selling, sales promotion, publicity and public relations. All these aspects of the promotional perspective play a vital role in the overall performance of the industry. These aspects are so intermingled with each other, that it is often very difficult to distinguish between them. Kerala tourism has a clear marketing promotional perspective, which includes advertisement, public relations, publicity, sales promotion and personal selling. The eye-catching brand name, "Gods Own Country" and slogans like "one of the Ten Love Nests in India", had helped Kerala in its marketing performance.

People Perspective Analysis

People perspective is an important factor in tourism development process as it requires close cooperation and consensus among various stakeholders. The positive and negative effects of tourism have an impact over the future perceptions of the people. The people element of the marketing mix is significant, because this aspect of the marketing contributes mostly to the variability of the tourism product in respect of service-encounter. Government of Kerala had taken initiatives which will help in the interaction and relationships between visitors or tourists, employees of tourism organisations and the host community or the local residents. The product satisfaction experienced by the visitors, the satisfaction of employees and the degree to which tourism is either accepted or rejected in the host destination are the key factors in the tourism circuit of Kerala, as their views are very important in the destination management.

Process Perspective Analysis

The tourism experience is highly dependent on the quality-of-service delivery as perceived by the user, as it accentuates certain characteristics that have an incorporating effect on the overall tourism marketing planning process. It compiles all the characters in such a manner that their knowledge becomes essential in deciding about the planning process. In fact, the study of the process involved in the tourism promotion of Kerala helped in running the affairs of tourism marketing.

Physical Evidence Perspective Analysis

In the context of tourism marketing, physical evidence refers to the design or layout of the tourism product or the built-in environment owned and controlled by an organisation. Organisations in Kerala play an important part in the promotion of tourism, as the physical evidence aspect is more often used to influence purchasing. As Kerala is a unique destination in the world, more attention has to be given for the promotion of tourism. The destination development alone cannot contribute a lot for the promotion of tourism industry. Constant efforts to promote Kerala as a tourist destination needs more attention.

Communication Strategies of Marketing of Tourism in Kerala

Marketing communication in the management of tourism destinations in Kerala, influence the usage and effectiveness of traditional forms of marketing communication. In Kerala, for tourism destination promotion, new modern trends of marketing communication like Internet marketing, social media, mobile apps and the word-of-mouth marketing helped in the evaluation of usage of modern marketing communication. Social media marketing seems to be an important way for marketing tourism destination to communicate with potential visitors. Some of the marketing communication strategies are analysed below:

Advertisement

Advertising campaigns are predominant in Kerala to promote travel destinations in international market. In the local and international market of tourism in Kerala, advertisement is one of the most important factors that helps to attract the tourists. The destination advertisement is very important in tourism development of Kerala as it gives adequate information to the tourists about its natural resources, culture, heritage and all other things which the tourists need to know about the place. Advertising campaigns are also an effective promotional tool. Advertisement through online marketing or e-marketing are practised in Kerala to promote the marketing of the destinations and tourism services.

Personal Selling

Personal Selling is important in the tourism marketing of Kerala. Well-educated and trained sales personnel help in the marketing of the tourism products and in the development of the tourism industry. The development of tourism business in Kerala has been influenced by the services rendered by the travel agents and travel guides as they are the information carriers and presenters of a tangible product or intangible services or ideas to the customers. In tourism industry, the sales personnel are responsible for dealing the customers for the promotion of their products, when they reach the destination and ensures that the tourism products satisfy the need of the tourists.

Sales Promotion

To promote a product in tourism market of Kerala—the hotels, resorts and other tourism related functions make price discounts, rewards or upgrading of the products supplied to the consumers. To attract the potential customers, the sales promoters offer services such as free night lodging, free breakfast, etc. Product sampling is also done in the sales promotion, to know whether the customers like a new product or willing to order the product. Kerala Tourism Development Corporation (KTDC) often conducts contests by giving the customers a chance to win trips, cash prizes, gifts by lucky draw, etc., and also offers discounted price to attract new guests and increase the sales. Giving premium to the regular customers for products and services like movie tickets, pizzas, bonus offers, gift vouchers, etc., are also part of sales promotion.

Publicity

Kerala Tourism publicity mainly comprises of the publicity leaflet, folder, brochure and poster which are used among others to convey the information or communicating the knowledge about the destinations to the largest possible number of persons. Brochures are important in tourism publicity and it has to be used widely and effectively. The brochure of Kerala Tourism offers greater possibilities than a folder to combine with each other the publicity and service, suggestions and information. Posters are another important publicity medium of tourism. The effectiveness of a poster lies on the psychological factors which expresses the impersonation of Kerala as a tourist destination. Films are also an outstanding publicity medium of Kerala Tourism as it represents potentialities of the major destinations of Kerala.

Public Relations

Public relations play a key role in promoting the organisations of tourism in Kerala, its products and services. For attracting the tourists, public relations act as a bridge towards change, a means for adjusting to the new attitudes triggered by change. Identifying the most efficient ways of promoting tourist products, building a positive image, increasing the visibility of tourist destinations are the major challenges of public relations in tourism. The responsible tourism initiatives of Kerala which provides a real opportunity for promoting local products and services and the tourist potential of Kerala may enhance a positive impact upon the public in terms of tourist destinations.

There are plenty of communication strategies adopted for the enhancement of tourism sector in Kerala. Technological advancement in the state is capable of promoting the tools for marketing in an effective way. The Kerala tourism effectively uses web promotion, event-based campaigns, mass media campaigns, collaborating with private agencies for promoting of tourism, participating in international fairs, MICE initiatives, etc. for marketing its products. Kerala is way ahead in the use of social media marketing strategies, as it is not only using just to advertise the tour packages, but also enables the visitors to gain more information about the culture and tradition of the state. Kerala gains top position in tourism and hospitality sector compared to other states of India. The state had strategic planning and regular monitoring of the activities for improving the marketing strategies and providing more exposure to the tourist destinations.

Role of Destination Marketing and Branding in Tourism Development of Kerala

India is endowed with a naturally beautiful landscape and all vital ingredients that make it a successful tourism product. The vastness of the country offers varied climatic options making India a hotspot round-the-year. A vast geographical spread and a rich historical and cultural heritage add to its charm. Tourism stands as one of the largest foreign exchange earners for India and provides immense job opportunities to the society. Realizing the potential of the tourism industry, Government of India took initiatives to market the destination in a professional manner in the late 1990s. In 1997, an advertising campaign "Eternally Yours" was launched. The "India Changes You" campaign, launched in 1998, promoted the whole of India as one destination, offering a unique experience. Focused marketing, innovative marketing strategies and attractive slogans have made India the most sought-after destination.

The tourism development strategies taken by Kerala enabled it to become one of the leading destinations internationally. A clear branding strategy is essential for the success of tourism industry. Government of Kerala is on the right path in promoting "Brand Kerala", as the state has been one of the most significant tourism success stories in India. Kerala was an unknown entity in the tourism map about three decades ago. Serene backwaters, traditional art forms and Ayurveda of the state had helped to bring out Kerala as a stand-alone destination among others in India, makes the importance of branding the destinations. The tourism policy of Kerala, which declares it as a major industry was a success initiative, which gives a firm footing for Kerala Tourism. Public-Private-Participation, travel marts and online propagandas had helped Kerala to be a global player in the tourism market. The ecotourism projects as well as the tie-ups with airlines and tour operators also helped the image of Kerala to reach new heights. In the early 1990s, advertisements featuring the tagline, "God's Own Country", began to appear in the print and electronic media in India. The campaign was run by Kerala Tourism Development Corporation (KTDC) and was intended to promote the south Indian State of Kerala as a tourist destination.

Kerala Tourism is the only tourism destination "Super Brand in India", a unique status that has catapulted the "God's Own Country" to the pedestal of fame in the world. Tourism in Kerala has emerged as a major revenue spinner and job provider, making it a vital sector for growth and development. It was in 1986 that Kerala declared tourism as an industry which should be given the status and concessions eligible for other industrial projects. It is a reported fact that Kerala Tourism has witnessed a boom especially after the 1990s and now the industry is showing signs of rapid growth both in terms of tourist inflow and earnings. The state authorities first promoted Kerala as the land of lagoons, lakes and backwaters. The focus then shifted to hill stations, waterfalls, the Western Ghats, wildlife sanctuaries and its rich cultural heritage. Traditional art forms like Kathakali, Koodiyattam and Kalarippayattu, Snake boat races and Ayurveda became the new attractions (Sarvani, 2003). Kerala Tourism Development Corporation (KTDC) adopted the slogan "God's Own Country" in its advertising campaigns. This slogan, some opine, was first used by Vipin Mohan when he created the first web page on Kerala in 1993. Others believe that Walter Mendez, the corporate creative director of the national advertising agency Mudra Communications, gave the tagline "God's Own Country" to Kerala Tourism (Parvez, Javed, 2008). However, the state now holds the super brand status, by its effective marketing and branding strategies. An exception to other traditional lines of industries, there exists Public-Private-Participation in the tourism industry in Kerala. All the promotional efforts by Kerala Tourism were supplemented by the private sector. Government is acting as a catalyst in encouraging private sector investment for the development of tourism infrastructure.

At present, in order to sustain competition, Kerala tourism is offering a variety of tourist packages with attractions such as Ayurvedic tourism, Pilgrimage tourism, Heritage tourism, Adventure tourism, Meetings, Incentives, Conferences and Exhibitions (MICE) and Medical tourism. The state also offers special support for the promotion of ecotourism. It is learnt that the state is now taking up more initiatives in the areas of better infrastructure, tourism product development, conservation of nature and heritage, human resource development and professionalism in the tourism sector. Today, the government is planning to mold Kerala into a model of responsible tourism with special focus on conservation and preservation of nature and culture. The state has adopted a long-term, focused marketing and conservation strategy that will position Kerala as a destination for global tourists (Dwibedi *et al.*, 2015).

Satisfaction Level of Tourists on the Marketing Strategies of Tourism in Kerala

Rapid rise of Kerala as a hot tourist destination has attained international focus. The state has clinched as one of the most significant tourism success stories in India, which emerged as a new model for promotion of tourism. Kerala has done well with its strategy to market itself as a multidimensional destination with a variety of attractions such as backwaters, beaches, hill stations, flora and fauna, Ayurvedic rejuvenation centres, pilgrim centres and its cultural heritage. Kerala Tourism's branding has worked at moving away from its association of being a beach-destination to a land of backwaters with lazy, luxury cruising on traditional houseboats and to health treatments in the land of Ayurveda. The clear strategy for tourism growth and sheer marketing efforts had gained a lot of tourists from all over the world.

Tourist arrival of Kerala is increasing over the years. It is essential to record the socio-economic as well as the interest of Kerala Tourism in order to achieve further tourism development. According to Government of Kerala reports, the growth in domestic tourist arrivals in the first quarter of 2019 is a strong reflection of the state government's efforts to repair the damage in double-quick time. During January-March 2019, the total number of tourist arrivals (both domestic and foreign) was 46,12,937 as compared to 43,18,406 during the same period in 2018. The number of domestic tourists arrived in the state was 41,90,468 as against the figures of 38,77,712 during the corresponding period in 2018, registering an increase of 8.07%). Kerala's success as a global destination shows, how the land had taken right steps in the right direction, which can positively and decisively impact the economic and social profile of the state.

This study tries to understand how far Kerala had succeeded in establishing its tourism brand in the international market and tries to analyse how far the impact of marketing and branding had helped in the development of tourism industry.

As a part of primary analysis, the data is collected from the tourists who had visited to the three major tourism destinations of Kerala; Punnamada in Alappuzha, Munnar in Idukki and Kovalam in Trivandrum were selected. (No. of samples collected—Alappuzha-45, Idukki-101 and Trivandrum-227) and their response on the marketing strategies adopted by the Government of Kerala in the promotion of tourism. Table 5.1 depicts the percentage distribution of tourists according to the level of satisfaction for the strategies of tourism in Kerala. For better results and interpretation, satisfaction of the strategies can be scored as highly satisfied, satisfied, average, dissatisfied and highly dissatisfied. With regard to the basic facilities, 16 per cent of people are highly satisfied. 67.6 per cent responded that they are satisfied to somewhat extent and only 1.3 per cent opined that they are not satisfied with the basic facilities in Kerala. With regard to cleanliness, 48.5 per cent are satisfied to somewhat extent and only 1.1 per cent are highly dissatisfied. Average response can be marked in the case of accessibility of road/air/rail networks by the tourists, that is 42.4 per cent each of the respondents scored satisfied and average responses. Around half of the tourists are satisfied with the attitude of locals. Only 2.1 per cent of them are highly dissatisfied with the same. 24.7 per cent of tourists are highly satisfied and 44.8 per cent of tourists are satisfied with the packages available in the Kerala tourism sector. 41 per cent of tourists are satisfied with the accommodation facilities and it is noted that 30.6 per cent are highly satisfied with the same. With regard to tourist information centers 53.6 per cent are satisfied and 3.7 per cent are found to be highly dissatisfied. 45.3 per cent of tourists are satisfied with the services of the guide. Around half of the tourists are satisfied with the support services, i.e., 42.6 percentage of people are satisfied and 31.9 percentage of people have average satisfaction, with the support services like travel agents. 4.8 per cent of tourists are dissatisfied with the same. 44 per cent of tourists are satisfied with the tour operators and 4 per cent found to be highly dissatisfied. Around 40 per cent and 36 per cent of tourists respectively have somewhat and average satisfaction with emergency helpline numbers. Average response can be found in the case of health care facilities of Kerala.

Table 5.1. Percentage Distribution of Tourists According to the Level of Satisfaction of the Strategies of Tourism in Kerala

Variables	Scaling				
	Highly satisfied	Satisfied	Average	Dis-satisfied	Highly Dis-satisfied
Basic facilities	16.0	67.6	13.7	1.3	1.3
Cleanliness	6.7	48.5	38.3	5.4	1.1
Accessibility by road/air/rail networks	3.2	42.4	42.4	6.2	5.8
Attitude of locals	16.9	50.4	27.6	2.9	2.2
Packages available	24.7	44.8	25.5	2.4	2.6
Food/drinking water	22.0	44.2	29.2	1.9	2.7
Accommodation	30.6	41.0	25.5	2.4	0.5
Tourist information centres	10.5	53.6	27.9	4.3	3.7
Service of guides	13.1	45.3	34.0	5.7	1.9

(*Contd.*)

Variables	Scaling				
	Highly satisfied	**Satisfied**	**Average**	**Dis-satisfied**	**Highly Dis-satisfied**
Support Services (travel agents)	16.4	42.6	31.9	4.8	4.3
Tour operators	16.4	44.0	29.0	6.6	4.0
Emergency Helpline	8.9	39.9	35.9	8.8	6.5
Health care facilities	13.7	33.8	34.0	8.6	9.9

Table 5.2 depicts the percentage distribution of tourists according to their perception about the promotional activities of tourism in Kerala. For better understanding of results, responses can be scored as excellent, very good, good, average and poor. While looking the perception of tourists in the case of information brochures regarding tourism, it is observed that, nearly half of them have "very good" perception (49.3%) followed by "good" (25.2%) and "excellent" (17.7%). In case of advertisements, more than 50 per cent of tourists have "very good" perception, followed by "excellent" and "good". Regarding the service of tour operators, 44.2 per cent of tourists have "very good" perception followed by "excellent" and "good". Only 4 per cent of tourists have poor perception on the same. Regarding websites, around 30 per cent perceived as "excellent" and 41.6 per cent have "very good" perception. About the services of District Tourism Promotion Council, it is observed that 13.4 per cent responded as "excellent", 44.2 per cent of people have "very good" perception, followed by "average". The same trend can also be found among the activities of tourist guide, publicity and other activities.

Table 5.2: Percentage Distribution of Tourists According to their Perception about the Promotional Activities of Tourism in Kerala

Promotional Activities	Scaling				
	Excellent	**Very good**	**Good**	**Average**	**Poor**
Information brochure	17.7	49.3	25.2	4.8	3.0
Advertisements	21.7	50.4	20.4	4.0	3.5

(*Contd.*)

Promotional Activities	Scaling				
	Excellent	Very good	Good	Average	Poor
Tour operators	24.4	44.2	19.8	7.5	4.1
Website	28.4	41.6	22.8	4.8	2.4
District Tourism Promotion Councils	13.4	44.2	33.5	5.4	3.5
Tourist Guide	21.4	42.6	27.9	5.9	2.2
Publicity	24.7	42.4	26.3	4.3	2.3
Others	16.4	46.6	27.6	4.6	4.8

The section concluded that, the effective utilisation of marketing strategies was evident from the interaction of tourists in Kerala. More than half of the tourists are the beneficiaries of tourism marketing strategies adopted by Government of Kerala. Hill stations, beaches and backwaters are found to have great demand among the tourists and the study observed the significance of a need-based development of tourism in prioritized destinations.

Tourism Marketing and Branding through Organisations

Organisations in Kerala play a vital role in the tourism marketing and branding. Destination marketing is remarkable in tourism marketing of the state. Organisations made impressive rating of tourism destination as in some places, destinations are branded by the quality of the organisations also. Here, an attempt was made to gather some information regarding the functions of tourism organisations in Kerala. It is noticed that there are so many limitations to collect data from the organisations through direct way by using structured questionnaire. Some basic information were collected from 60 organisations across the three destinations of Kerala which were selected for the analysis. Following section deals with the major strategies of tourism organisations in Kerala.

Table 5.3 depicts the facilities and services of tourism organisations in Kerala. Around 52 percentage of the organisations facilitated with swimming pool, 12 per cent have shopping facilities and 75 percentages of organisations have emergency health care facilities. Fifty percentage of organisations arrange the integration between government agencies/tour operators with customers, especially for foreign tourists. About 73 and 80 percentages of organisations respectively having conference hall and restaurant.

Table 5.3: Facilities and Services of Tourism Organisations in Kerala

Variables	No. of Organisations	Percentage
Swimming pool	31	51.7
Shopping	7	11.7
Emergency health care	45	75
Linkage with Tour operators and Govt. agencies	30	50
Conference Hall	44	73
Restaurant	48	80
Others	48	80

Table 5.4 depicts the promotional strategies of tourism organisations in Kerala. It is observed that 48.3 per cent of organisations made their promotional strategies through advertisement, 65 per cent are through integrated packages and 53.3 per cent went for information brochures. 63.3 percentage of organisations made their promotional activities through publicity. Around 90 per cent are promoted through websites and social media. 43.3 per cent participated in fairs as part of their promotional strategies.

Table 5.4: Promotional Strategies of Tourism Organisations in Kerala

Strategies	No. of Organisations	Percentage
Advertisement	29	48.3
Integrated packages	39	65
Information brochures	32	53.3
Publicity	38	63.3
Website & Social media	54	90
Participation in fairs	26	43.3

This section on marketing and branding through organisation analyses that even though Kerala had strategies on marketing and branding, the number of organisations supporting for the promotion of tourism is limited. Most of the organisations are not up to international standards with regard to the norms fixed for the preservation of the environment for attaining sustainable development.

Tourism industry is a major contributor to the economic and social development of Kerala. The policy effect of tourism marketing and branding will help in perceiving quality of tourism products. The result of the survey will help in adding literature, provide basis for future research in tourism policy and to give an awareness to the Department of Tourism on the importance of marketing and branding of the explored and unexplored destinations of Kerala.

Conclusion

Tourism is considered by the state government with high priority in today's highly competitive and dynamic global tourism environment. Kerala has been branded as the most wanted tourism destination. In the tourism arena, there is a need to develop a clear brand identity, reflecting the core strengths and personality of its products. From the last few years, the development of tourism in Kerala is done by the marketing and promotional measures taken by the government, considering the importance of destination marketing. Planned and sustained development of marketing and infrastructure had made Kerala, the "Green Gate Way" of India, who had found a niche for herself in the tourism map of the world. From the first tourism policy onwards, there was an emphasis on developing new product or new destination every year. This is a part of tourism strategy to develop an image of market in the destination tourism of Kerala to attract high spending discerning travellers who seek unique experiences from the destination. But the performance of Kerala Tourism brand, the only tourism super brand in India does not really justify the inherent potential of Kerala Tourism. The literature reports also admit that Kerala Tourism potentials and products are not yet fruitfully exploited. The performance in tourism development is not at all commendable in tune with the diversified destination features of Kerala. From the analysis of marketing and branding strategies of tourism, it is observed that Kerala's brand, "God's Own Country", has been so cleverly associated with all of Kerala's products, that it is difficult not to describe it otherwise. The study suggests even though the state had adopted various strategies in marketing and branding of its tourism products, for a better development it is essential to adopt new initiatives like short-term strategies and long-term strategies in the development of tourism. Creating framework of policies for the management of tourism industry, for carrying out effective marketing practices and focus on the sustainability aspect of tourism and rural tourism, will help in the overall development and well-being of the local community.

References

Dwibedi, Tama (2015). "An Empirical Analysis on Kerala Tourism." *International Journal of Research in Social Sciences, 5.5*: 518-31.

Manoj, P. K. (2010). "Tourism in Kerala: A Study of the Imperatives and Impediments with Focus on Ecotourism." *Saaransh RKG Journal of Management, 1.2*: 78-82.

Nunkoo, Robin, Dogan Gursoy, and Yogesh K. Dwivedi (2020). "Effects of Social Media on Residents' Attitudes to Tourism: Conceptual Framework and Research Propositions." *Journal of Sustainable Tourism*, 1-17.

Parvez, Shaik Javed, *et al.* (2018). "Digital Marketing in Hotel Industry." *International Journal of Engineering & Technology, 7.2.21*: 288-90.

Sanghvi, Vir (2009). *26/11: The Attack on Mumbai.* Penguin UK.

Sharma, Sukarn, *et al.* (2012). "Should HPTDC Restart its Timeshare Scheme." *Journal of Emerging Technologies and Business Management, 3.1*: 36-56.

World Tourism Organisation (Madrid), *International Tourism: A Global Perspective.* World Tourism Organisation, 1997.

6

Adherence to Environmental Management Criteria in the Responsible Tourism (RT) Classified Resorts of Kumarakom Tourist Destination and the Post-Covid Scenario

Anitha, R. and *Ambeeshmon, S.*

Introduction

As part of the responsible tourism initiative many classification criteria have been introduced by the Department of Tourism, Government of Kerala, for the first time in the hospitality sector of Kumarakom in the year 2013. Out of a total of 1,000 points, a minimum of 500 points is required to become an RT branded hotel, a homestay, and a resort or houseboat. Properties with scores between 750-1,000, 600-749, and 500-599 will be classified as platinum, gold, and silver respectively. The objective of this classification is to minimize the negative impacts and maximize the benefits of the stakeholders, especially the local community through sustainable approaches to tourism. There are four sections for these criteria. In each section, a minimum of 50 per cent point is required for qualifying RT Brand. There are 70 criteria in this scheme. The last section is the environmental management criteria. Under this, there are 27 criteria. Here the researcher explores the major six yes or no statements and their adherences to the RT branded properties at Kumarakom. The other three major criteria are sociocultural RT, Economic RT, and sustainable management RT.

Objectives

- To analyse the adherences to environmental management criteria in the RT branded resorts of Kumarakom tourist destination.
- To study the post-COVID scenario in the tourist destination.

Methodology

The study is descriptive and analytical. The fourth section of the classification criteria introduced by the Department of Tourism, Government of Kerala is used for the study. The survey questionnaire method is adopted. Responses from thirteen RT branded resorts are included as samples. Judgement sampling is used for data collection. The closed-ended questions were only analysed to study the adherence to RT criteria. The primary data have been analysed using Binomial Test.

Review of Literature

The study conducted around 40 hotels in London, Knowels (1998) found that physical and natural environments are assets for attracting tourists to a destination. Hotels are playing crucial roles in mitigating environmental impacts and make a substantial contribution to quality improvement.

According to Kasim (2006), hotel sector is one of the key business segments of tourism which is focused on more environmental obligations than any other business segments.

From the study conducted on 100 hotels in the Cape Town Hotel Sub-Sector Musavengane *et al.* says that in Cape Town the authorities are well informed about the CSR practices and they are well aware of the environmental practices. But they are not aware of the responsible tourism concept and its guidelines.

Jones (2017) in his study examines the challenges of the hospitality industry and how this can be overcome and how the industry can contribute to achieving sustainable development goals.

RT Good Practices at Destination Kumarakom

Organic farming, agriculture, and allied activities, land cultivation, vegetable cultivation, fish farming, dairy development, indigenous art craft development, awareness programmes on various aspects of the tourism industry, training programmes on various entrepreneurial projects, starting of small enterprises, hospitality linkages with RT practices, waste management, waste treatment, promotion of ethnic cruises, afforestation, resource mapping, labour directory, event directory of various fairs and festivals, village life experience package tours, lotus cultivation internalize the services of "Kudumbasree" in cleaning, cooking natural food, cultural events such as *pancharimelam*, etc. are the important good practices implemented as part of the RT practices besides linking all activities with the hospitality sector.

RT Good Practices in the Accommodation units at Kumarakom

The major good practices are the generation of local employment both permanent and part-time, linkage of local produces with the accommodation units, waste management, and waste minimisation, adoption of energy-saving and energy reduction methods, rainwater harvesting, organic farming, species protection, biodiversity conservation, enhancing indigenous food, local souvenirs development, promotion of village life experience (VLE) packages, sewage treatment plant, waste disposal, plastic collection and disposal, awareness campaigns and cultural performances, etc. Some of the case studies below revealed the RT practices implemented and have been followed successfully. As part of the socio-economic responsibility, employment is provided to the local community. The use of plastic is controlled and minimized by enhancing cloth bags. The plastic collection and disposal mechanism is persistent in most resorts. Coconut lagoon, Taj, Club Mahindra, and such premium properties have a good mechanism for reuse. The Coconut lagoon minimized the use of plastic by using refillable water bottles. LED bulbs have been widely used by almost all accommodation units. Rainwater harvesting and recycled water usage are found common. A few have solar-powered vehicles. But people hardly use the solar-powered energy mechanism widely. The premium properties' monthly expenses on energy are around Rs. one lakh. Earth check certification and carbon footprint exist at coconut lagoon. Thus as part of the RT classification scheme, the sustainability indicators have been adopted and followed successfully. The Club Mahendra holidays successfully utilized the Hunar Se Rozgar (HNR) scheme for women empowerment by providing training in mushroom cultivation. The HNR scheme was started by the union ministry in the year 2009 to provide employable skills for the weaker section of the society.

Awareness Programmes

A series of awareness programmes have been organized for various stakeholders in subsequent periods. The major ones are the following.

Energy Management

In association with the Energy Management Centre Kerala, the investigator conducted awareness programmes for Kudumbasree members of 60 numbers for three consecutive years for energy management. In the third year, 70 per cent of the community members could reduce their energy usage by using energy-efficient equipment/measures and by using labelled standard types of equipment. Demonstration classes by the experts from energy management Kerala were conducted to make awareness to all and sundry. The use of CFL and LED has been promoted. The usage of faulty types of equipment will increase the consumption of current. While making use of one unit of power 800 gm carbon dioxide is emitted. Such emission is harmful to the environment. All this knowledge enhanced the awareness of the usage of electric and electronic types of equipment and the reduction of energy consumption.

Plastic Collection and Waste Management

Another one is plastic pollution.The plastic is collected from every house near Kavanatinkara. This collected plastic was sent for recycling through the RT destination cell. The sewage treatment plant located at Kumarakom collected waste from all houseboats at least once a month. The defaulters will be informed and if they failed to report, their license will be cancelled. A register is maintained by the authorities for that. The problem is that many of the houseboats are operating without a license. Such boats do not have any options of disposal rather than getting them dumped into the water bodies and by polluting the backwater in a big way. By the latest reports, only 80 houseboats have registered under the RT classification scheme. But more than 200 houseboats have been operating at Kumarakom. The carrying capacity of the houseboats should be controlled; otherwise, it may affect the ecosystem balance of the area. Many studies revealed that the Lake Vembanudu is a biological desert. The reason may be that fish, clam, and shrimp species have disappeared from these regions. In the nearby Alappuzha backwaters, more than 1,600 houseboats ply across the canals. The licensed ones came around to 1,300. RT practices were started recently. One could guess the pollution rate from tourism development. Awareness programmes for all the stakeholders are the only remedy and curbing measure.

Classification Criteria

Here the fourth section of the criteria—close-end statements of Environmental Management Criteria is only studied to understand the adherences to RT classification scheme in the RT branded accommodation units. This includes hotels, resorts, homestays, and houseboats. Total points required for the three categories: Diamond, Gold, and Silver are given in Table 6.1 and the detailed environmental management criteria are given in Table 6.2. Those who qualified for the minimum of 500 points in all four criteria are eligible for RT Branding.

Table 6.1: Scores Required for Classifying the Unit (Hotel/Resort/Homestay/Houseboat)

	Criteria	**Maximum**	**Minimum**	**Classification Category Marks**	**Total Marks 1,000**
Section 1	Sustainable Management	200	100	Diamond	750-1,000
Section 2	Sociocultural	250	125	Gold	600-749
Section 3	Economic	250	150	Silver	500-599
Section 4	Environmental	300	125		
	Total	**1,000**	**500**		

Table 6.2: Environment Responsibility Criteria

Section	**Environment Responsibility Criteria**	**Score 300**	
1.1	**Sustainable Siting and Design**	**45 Marks**	**Marks**
1.1.1.	Buildings in conjunction with natural landscape (photos of landscape profile before and after construction)		
	1. Structures merge well with the existing landscape	1. All four 2. All three 3. Any two 4. Any one	1.20 Marks
	2. Contour designs have been used and earth movements minimized		2.15 marks
	3. Water courses have not been altered for construction		3.10
	4. Vegetation disturbance have been minimized and restored with native vegetation		4.5
1.1.2.	Gardens, green areas, golf courses, and sporting fields use native vegetation where possible or grasses that are adapted to the local climate	1. Yes 2. No	10 0
1.1.3.	New buildings reflect regional architectural vernacular and include regional art of crafts	1. Yes 10 2. No 0	10 marks
1.1.4	Existing structures have been adapted where possible	1. Yes 2. No	5 marks 0 mark

(*Contd.*)

Section	Environment Responsibility Criteria	Score 300	
1.2	**Locally appropriate principles of sustainable construction**	**45 Marks**	**Marks**
1.2.1	Buildings use regional construction materials, as long as these are obtained sustainably (which materials; sources indicted)	1. Yes 2. No	10 0
1.3.	**Code of conduct for visits to environmentally sensitive sites**	1. Yes 2. No	5 0
1.3.1.	Company policy includes established guideline or code of behaviour while visiting environmentally sensitive sites, and diligently adheres to it	1. Yes 2. No	5 0
1.4.	**Environment friendly purchasing policy**	40	
1.4.1.	Percentage of purchase of building materials from green or sustainable sources	1. >20% 2. 10 3. <10%	10 5 0
1.4.2.	Percentage of purchase of capital goods from green or sustainable sources	1. >20% 2. 10-20% 3. <10%	10 5 0
1.4.3.	Percentage of purchase of food items from green or sustainable sources	1. >20% 2. 10-20% 3. <10%	10 5 0
1.4.4.	Percentage of purchase of consumables from green or sustainable sources	1. >40% 2. 20-40% 3. <20%	10 5 0
1.5.	**Energy Conservation**		
1.5.1.	Percentage of total energy from renewable sources	1. >20% 2. 10-20% 3. 5-10% 4. <5%	10 7.5 5 0
1.5.2.	Percentage use of automated energy saving devices (keycards, sensors)	1. >60% 2. 40% 3. 40%	10 5 0
1.5.3.	Percentage use of CFL/LEDs	1. >60% 2. 40-60% 3. <40%	10 5 0
1.5.4.	Conduct of energy Audits	1. Yes 2. No	5 0

(*Contd.*)

Section	Environment Responsibility Criteria	Score 300	
1.5.5.	Average monetary investment in energy saving devices/technologies and renewable energies as a percentage of investments in energy equipments for the past three years	1. >20% 2. 15-20% 3. 10-15% 4. 5-10% 5. <5%	10 7.5 5 2.5 0
1.5.6.	Communication measures to conserve energy	1. Good 2. Average-2.5 marks 3. Poor-0 marks	5
1.6.	**Water Conservation**	**40 marks**	
1.6.1.	A water management and conservation programme exists	1. Yes 2. No	10 Marks 0 Marks
1.6.2.	Percentage of water-using equipment/activities that employ a water conservation technique	1. >50% 2. 25 3. 10 4. <10%	15 10 5 0
1.6.3.	Percentage of water recycled	1. >50% 2. 25-50% 3. 10-25 4. <10%	10 7.5 5 0
1.6.4.	Communication measures to conserve water	1. Good 2. Average 3. Poor	5 2.5 0
1.7	**Waste Management**	**40 marks**	
1.7.1.	Wastewater treatment plant exists and working properly	1. Yes 2. No	10 0
1.7.2.	Percentage of recycling and reuse of treated water	1. >50% 2. 25-50% 3. 10-25% 4. <10%	15 10 5 0
1.7.3.	Presence of an integrated solid waste management system that functions effectively—Description of the type of system 1. Segregation, recycle and reuse within the campus 2. Segregation and disposal through the local arrangement 3. Disposal through the local arrangement 4. No arrangement	1. Type 1 2. Type 2 3. Type 3 4. Type 4	15 10 5 0

(*Contd.*)

Section	Environment Responsibility Criteria	Score 300	
1.8	**Attempts to reduce Green House Gas emissions**	**70**	
1.8.1	An initiative was undertaken to reduce greenhouse gas emissions and creation of awareness		
	1. Tree planting within the compound	All six	30 marks
	2. Tree planting in nearby areas	All five	25 marks
	3. Participation in public environmental programme	All four	20 marks
	4. Publication of environmental booklets	All three	15 marks
	5. Availing carbon credit	Any two	10 marks
	6. Celebration of environment day	Anyone	5 marks
1.8.2	Eco-friendly practices		
	1. Prohibition of plastic bags and bottles	1. All eight	40
	2. Usage of Paper bag	2. All seven	35
	3. Practice on taking back the plastic bags/ bottles	3. All six	30
	4. Written policy in minimizing printing	4. All five	25
	5. Encouraging group travel	5. All four	20
	6. Promoting organic products	6. All three	15
	7. Use of soap, shampoo dispensers, etc. in the bathroom	7. Any two	10
	8. Promoting less water usage	8. Any one	5
Total			**300**

Source: www.keralatourism.org

Source: Adapted from Kerala Tourism, Government of Kerala.

Analysis of the Open-Ended Statements

Environmental Responsibility

Sustainable Siting and Design

Gardens, green areas, golf courses, and sporting fields use native vegetation where possible or grasses that are adapted to the local climate

The proportion of gardens, green areas, golf courses, and sporting fields use native vegetation where possible or grasses that are adapted to the local climate is found 1.00 which means all the respondents were informed about the plan. This proportion is found significant at a 5 per cent level of significance, i.e., a p-value less than 0.05. Table 6.3 depicts the results.

Table 6.3: Gardens, green areas, golf courses, and sporting fields use native vegetation where possible or grasses that are adapted to the local climate

Criteria 1.1.2.	Criteria Followed Yes/No	Total No. of Resp-onses	Observed Pro-portion	Test Pro-portion	Significance (Two-Tailed)
Gardens, green areas, golf courses, and sporting fields use native vegetation where possible or grasses that are adapted to the local climate	Yes	13	1.00	.50	000
	No	0	0		
	Total	13	1.00		

Source: Primary Data.

Existing structure has been adapted where possible

The proportion of the existing structure has been adapted where possible is found 1.00 which means all the respondents were informed about the plan. The remaining 15 per cent do not adhere to these criteria. This proportion is found significant at a 5 per cent level of significance, i.e., a p-value less than 0.05. Table 6.4 illustrates the result.

Table 6.4: The existing structure has been adapted where possible

Criteria 1.1.2.	Criteria Followed Yes/No	Total No. of Resp-onses	Observed Pro-portion	Test Pro-portion	Significance (Two-Tailed)
The existing structure has been adapted where possible	Yes	11	0.85	.50	0.022
	No	2	0.15		
	Total	**13**	**1.00**		

Source: Primary Data.

Locally appropriate Principles of Sustainable construction

Buildings use regional construction materials, as long as these are obtained sustainably (which materials; sources indicated)

The proportion of the buildings that use regional construction materials, as long as these are obtained sustainably (which materials; sources indicated), is found 1.00 which means all the respondents were informed and followed the plan. This proportion is found significant at a 5 per cent level of significance, i.e., a p-value less than 0.05.Table 6.5 shows the result.

Table 6.5: Buildings use regional construction materials, as long as these are obtained sustainably

Criteria 1.2.1	Criteria Followed Yes/No	Total No. of Resp-onses	Observed Pro-portion	Test Pro-portion	Significance (Two-Tailed)
Buildings use regional construction materials, as long as these are obtained sustainably (which materials; sources indicated)	Yes	13	1.00	.50	000
	No	0	0		
	Total	**13**	**1.00**		

Source: Primary Data.

Code of conduct for Visits to Environmentally Sensitive Sites

Company policy includes established guideline or code of behaviour while visiting environmentally sensitive sites, and diligently adheres to it

The proportion of the ecompany policy includes established guideline or code of behaviour while visiting environmentally sensitive sites, and diligently adheres to it is found 0.92 which means 92 per cent of the respondents were informed and followed the plan. The remaining 8 per cent do not adhere to this criterion. This proportion is found significant at a 5 per cent level of significance, i.e., a p-value less than 0.05. Table 6.6 gives the result.

Table 6.6: Company policy includes established guideline or code of behaviour while visiting environmentally sensitive sites, and diligently adheres to it

Criteria 1.3.1.	Criteria Followed Yes/No	Total No. of Resp-onses	Observed Pro-portion	Test Pro-portion	Significance (Two-Tailed)
The company policy includes established guideline or code of behaviour while visiting environmentally sensitive sites, and diligently adheres to it	Yes	12	0.92	.50	003
	No	1	0.08		
	Total	**13**	**1.00**		

Source: Primary Data.

Water Conservation

Water management and conservation programme exists

The proportion of the water management and conservation programme **exists,** is found 1.00 which means all the respondents were informed of the plan. This proportion is found significant at a 5 per cent level of significance, i.e., a p-value less than 0.05. The results are presented in Table 6.7.

Table 6.7: A water management and conservation programme exists

Criteria 1.6.1	Criteria Followed Yes/No	Total No. of Resp-onses	Observed Pro-portion	Test Pro-portion	Significance (Two-Tailed)
Water management and conservation programme **exists**	Yes	13	1.00	.50	000
	No	0	0		
	Total	**13**	**1.00**		

Source: Primary Data.

Waste Management

Wastewater treatment plant exists and working properly

The proportion of wastewater treatment plants that exist and working properly is found 0.92 which means 92 per cent of the respondents were informed and followed the plan. (The remaining 8 per cent does not adhere to this criterion.) This proportion is found significant at a 5 per cent level of significance, i.e., the p-value is less than 0.05. Table 6.8 gives the result.

Table 6.8: Wastewater treatment plant exists and working properly

Criteria 1.7.1	Criteria Followed Yes/No	Total No. of Resp-onses	Observed Pro-portion	Test Pro-portion	Significance (Two-Tailed)
Wastewater treatment plant exists and working properly	Yes	12	0.92	.50	003
	No	1	0.08		
	Total	**13**	**1.00**		

Source: Primary Data.

Post-COVID Scenario

The global pandemic affected the entire activity of the accommodation sector. In January-February months of 2021, the average tourist arrivals to the houseboat segment are 60-80 domestic tourists per day and this number is somewhat more in the pre-COVID scenario and no foreign tourist arrivals at all. There is a revival in the tourism sector after the global pandemic. But the unexpected second wave of the global pandemic forced all stakeholders to stop the business and are at the brink of sudden closure. At this juncture, the leading stakeholders of tourism in the State of Kerala call for a meeting on 4 May to think of an action plan on behalf of a "Tourism Protection Samithi" and to submit before the newly elected Government of Kerala under the leadership of C.S. Vinod and Boby Mathew Somatheeram. They identified the needs of the areas which should give priority and will soon submit before the government. In the current scenario, they are not in a position to remit the electricity and water bill together with the loans. They are willing to demand a moratorium in financial matters. Kerala is the first state who declared Tourism as an Industry in the year 1986. The stakeholders are not yet benefited from the output of this declaration. The first thing that they have to do to get the benefits of industry status. For the last 25 years why the policymakers are not looking into this matter or the stakeholders are not moving for industry benefits is a surprising one. When all the income from tourism is stopped then only they are bothered about such demand. But in the discussion, they pointed out the cases of states like Karnataka and Maharashtra have acclaimed the industry status with its benefits. While Kerala Tourism is shining in the World Tourism scenario with many unique initiatives like Responsible Tourism and PEPPER tourism initiatives all the stakeholders and their employers have to avail all of the benefits like other industry people get. Kumarakom is a small destination in Kottayam district. The contribution of income from the tourism sector at Kumarakom is an approximate amount of 115 crore. A premium resort's income in the year 2018 is 19 crore. Their electricity charge comes around 15 lakh per month. The majority of the customers are foreigners. In the year 2020, their annual income is around 65 lakh, because of domestic tourists. But they retained all their workforce with half salary.

The problem is that in all the areas of tourism employees have to look for other jobs for livelihood. It may affect the quality of the staff shortly. Government intervention is very very essential in this regard. The previous discussion forum was afraid of this kind of challenge too. Like other countries do—especially Austria, the UK—they already given a vaccination to majority of their citizens and controlled the pandemic and revived tourism segment. The protection forum also planning to give vaccination to all of their employees highlighting their survival issues.

The policymakers have to think of a new tourism policy giving due attention to domestic tourism and neighbourhood district travel schemes to retain the tourism industry. Premium resorts are forced to reduce their workforce by half or to reduce their salary/ perks by half. The majority of the medium properties hold their staff without salary. Just before the second wave, there are inquiries from the majority of the southern state for accommodation. Small level inquiries from the UK also reported. The only measure is to give vaccination to all and thereby improve the situation and regain the travel trend as in the pre-COVID time. Most of the owners have the opinion that it may take a minimum of two years to a maximum of four years.

Findings

- From the analysis, it is evident that the criteria discussed above are following successfully by the classified RT classified resorts of Kumarakom. The majority of the statement's adherence levels are maximum to 100 per cent to a minimum of 85 per cent. From at one can observe that environmental practices are essential for the existence of the industry thereby the accommodation sector can minimize the energy, water, and waste problems. Since the United Nations focuses on achieving sustainable development goals, through the RT classification scheme, the hotel sector can easily achieve all 17 goals. The responsible tourism practices are found useful in minimizing the negative issues and maximizing the positive benefits. The major advantage is that all stakeholders are equally benefited by this kind of classification criteria. Local community participation is another advantage.

- The post-COVID scenario discloses that domestic tourism should give priority to international tourism. A weekend travel and neighbourhood district travel scheme can also be promoted.
- Retain the employees in the respective industry is found to be a very big challenge.
- Ensure the safety and security of all in the industry.
- Even though Kerala is the first state who have declared tourism as an industry, more than the declaration no fruitful outcome can be seen like other industries enjoying. If it is implemented, the employees get some kind of consolation like others get during a pandemic. Massive job losses were reported in this area.

Suggestions

- For the promotion of sustainable tourism, this will be one of the future options. Policymakers could implement the classification scheme on an all-India basis. The practitioners of these people are recommending these practices in all kinds of hospitality segments.
- Global pandemic created more the gap between the haves and have not. The STEP project (Sustainable Tourism Eliminating Poverty) should be rejuvenated to help the marginalized people in the tourism sector after the pandemic.
- Government intervention is essential in sanctioning the benefits to the employees and employers of tourism like other industries benefited.
- To retain tourists special offers can be given like discounts in different components of the tourism segment.
- Vaccination to all is the only possible remedy now.

Conclusion

Of the total of 1,000 points, 500 points have been set as the eligibility criteria to become an RT classified hotel. Properties with scores between 750-1,000, 600-749, and 500-599 will be classified as platinum, gold, and silver respectively. In the hospitality sector, the major cause of concern is energy and water usage along with waste generation. The majority of the hotels can manage well this issue due to the RT classification scheme. Biodiversity conservation is an added advantage of this scheme. At the inception level, only 13 resorts are partnered with this classification. Today this scheme is revised and around 1,300 accommodation units follow successfully the scheme. Sustainable practices require the hour and this approach is an apt method for minimizing the negative environmental issues and maximize positives. So far the Government of India had given a vaccination to 20 crore of people. It may prevent the pandemic spread in the third level covid pandemic. It is hoped that by giving vaccination to all we can survive and can revive the tourism industry.

References

Knowles, T. *et al.* (1998). "The Development of Environmental Initiatives in Tourism: Responses from the London Hotel Subsector". *International Journal of Tourism Research, 1*: 225-65.

Kasim, A. (2006). "The Need for Business Environmental and Social Responsibility in the Tourism Industry", *International Journal of Hospitality & Tourism Administration, 7*(1): 1-22.

Musavegane, R. Nicolas S.J. (2013). "Responsible Tourism Practices in the Cape Town Subsector", *International Journal of Hospitality and Tourism System, 6*(2): 52-63.

Jones, P. David & Hillier Damphne Comfort (2017). *Athens Journal of Tourism*, The SDGs and the Tourism and Hospitality Industry, 2017-1-X-Y-Jones.Pdf

7

Issues, Challenges and Scope for Sustainable Tourism Development in Kumaun Region of Uttarakhand

Bhuwan Chandra Melkani and *Anil Kumar*

Introduction

Since time immemorial travel is a part of human life. Travel and tourism existed in different ways in different times. Early people travel to fulfil their different needs and motives, the first being those who travelled for the search of food. Food gatherers were considered to be the first travellers. This was followed by those who travelled with the motive of doing trade. Many kingdoms were evolved and battles were fought to extend the reign of the emperors of that time. Tourism has not evolved overnight and is not a new phenomenon, rather it took decades to evolve travel and tourism industry which we see today. Tourism is a diverse phenomenon, which has its social, economic, natural, political impacts that are positive as well as negative. Tourism being one of the fastest growing service sector industry if promoted by many countries as most of the economies are trying their best to capture major share in the tourism industry as a means of getting competitive edge over other countries of the world. Tourism has its testimonies in the earliest records of history and has undergone phenomenal rate of growth during the present century. Yet there is no universally accepted definition of tourism even now. Huniker and Krapf gave the first definition of tourism by defining it as "The sum of phenomenon and relationship arising from the travel and stay of non-resident in so far as it does not lead to permanent residence and is not connected to any earning activity" (Dileep, 2019). In general, tourism can be defined as a process involving a visit performed by a person from his place of residence to some far destination for more than one day and which does not anyhow related to motive of earning. With the advancement in accommodation and transportation facilities which are the two major elements of travel industry, it is very easy to go anywhere anytime to explore destination and to spend leisure time. This development took years and decades to transform the tourism industry, one of the major transformation that took place in the travel and tourism industry is after the world wars and especially the Second World War. Tourism sector holds strategic importance in the Indian economy providing several socio-economic benefits. Provision of employment, income and foreign exchange, development or expansion of other industries such as agriculture, construction, handicrafts, etc., are some of the important economic benefits provided by the tourism sector. In addition, investments in infrastructural facilities such as transportation, accommodation and other tourism related services lead to an overall development of infrastructure in the economy.

The State of Uttarakhand which is also known as "Abode of Gods", is one of the preferred tourist destinations across the globe. The state was formed as the 27th state on 9 November 2000. Uttarakhand, in spite of being a small state, has certain key features that make it distinct from other states of the country and highlights its potential for development. However, development has predominantly been in the plains, and the hill districts have been left behind. All the hill districts have subsistence farming as their main economic activity. Due to subsistence livelihood, migration and a remittance economy operate in the hill districts. They are land-locked with huge distances between the markets and resources. Because of these constraints, traditional agriculture cannot be the lead sector for development. Thus, the state faces the challenge of promoting livelihoods to minimize migration through local employment and income generation, and to enhance the quality of life of people living in villages. The positive features of these hill districts are that they have enormous potential for tourism, a suitable climate for high-value agriculture, and a pleasant environment due to 60 per cent forest cover. The tourism sector has been a major constituent of the service sector that already contributes almost half (49.6%) of the Gross State Domestic Product. Given the factor endowments, there is huge potential for growth in the tourism sector considering the demand from both the domestic and international markets in terms of content and standard of facilities and utilities. The state attracts tourists for pilgrimages, cultural tourism, nature tourism, adventure tourism, wildlife tourism, ecotourism, and amusement and leisure tourism. The approach to tourism development in Uttarakhand has to be based on the strengths of this state. Since Uttarakhand is rich in natural beauty with a unique mountain environment as well as rich historical and cultural assets, diverse products have to be designed for various categories of people who travel to this state for different motives.

There are two divisions of the state namely the Kumaun and the Garhwal region. The present study is concerned with the Kumaun Region of Uttarakhand and hence main focus will be on the tourism development in the region only. The name "Kumaun" is derived from "Kurmanchal". The word Kurmanchal is combination of two words "Kurm" which means tortoise and "Aanchal" which means mountain. The name is after Kurmanchal mountain which got corrupted with the passage of time and in local dialect called as Kumaun or Kumaon. According to mythological belief, the mountain is associated with Kurma incarnation of Lord Vishnu. There are many other legends which are associated with the Kumaun Region. In *Skanda Purana* the region lies in "Manaskhand". The tortoise reincarnation took place near Kali River. The area on the right side of Kali River is known as "Kumaun" in local dialect. There are six districts in the Kumaun Region namely Almora, Bageshwar, Champawat, Nainital, Pithoragarh and U.S. Nagar. Initially, there were only two districts in the Kumaun Region. Under the British rule, Kumaun was divided into Kumaun and British Garhwal. Blessed with flora and fauna the Kumaun Region is visited by tourists in large numbers throughout the year. The tourism industry is emerging as a major sector for the growth and development of the region and locals residing in the region. There are many tourist destinations in the region that are world famous. One of them is "Nainital" which is known as the lake district of India. In the Kumaun Region tourism of various forms have been developed and promoted like adventure tourism, leisure tourism, trekking, wildlife tourism. Being surrounded by majestic Himalayas the region offers splendid view of mesmerizing snow covered mountain peaks like Trishul, Panchachuli, Nanda Devi, the region attracts nature lovers. Nature lovers and wildlife lovers are majorly attracted by the Jim Corbett natural park and Askot wildlife sanctuary. Many beautiful hill stations such as Kausani, Nainital, Munsyari, Ranikhet are located in the Kumaun Region which are the best destinations for leisure and holiday tourists. Tourists can enjoy paragliding at Naukuchiyatal and can explore trekking also. The Kumaun Region attracts large number of pilgrimage tourists through its historic Hindu Temples such as Garjiya Temple, Haidakhan Temple, Kainchi Dham Mandir, Naina Devi Temple, Gairar Golu Devata Temple and many more. Nanakmatta Sahib Gurdwara is a famous Sikh pilgrimage centre situated in Udhamsingh Nagar district of the region. Many fairs and festivals held every year like the Kainchi Mela, Purnagiri Mela, Jauljebi fair, all these attract large number of tourists to the region.

Factors Influencing Tourist Inflow & Tourism Development

1. Strategic location: Tourism primarily depends on strategic location as well as its natural and historical attractiveness. A place that can easily be accessed by tourists becomes a prime destination to explore by the tourists across the globe. Geographical location includes its climate, landscape and terrains. Kumaun Region being blessed with flora and fauna, snow capped Himalayas, scenic view of mountains and many more attracts tourists in large numbers towards it.

2. Economic status indicator: Economic status is also major factor that helps it for sustaining balanced growth through tourism. The per capita income tells about the standard of living of the people living there. Tourists looking for business purposes consider this as a major element as their main motive while visiting as a tourist is trade, which is possible only if their vision matches with the potential of the destination they are looking to visit. In all these ways economic status indicator clearly defines whether it is a promising place for visit or not. The Government of Uttarakhand has considered this factor and has granted budgets for development of tourist destinations and tourism promotional schemes so that it would help in generation of employment opportunities and will help to raise the standard of living of people in Kumaun Region.

3. Attractiveness as a tourist destination: The historical and natural attractiveness attracts large numbers of tourists to visit. Whether it may be ancient man-made archaeological sites which attracts large numbers of tourists from across the globe who visit these places to see the beauty of nature. A region having rich cultural heritage and historical background also form a key factor to make it to be a favoured tourist destination. In 2019, leisure tourism accounted for 78.6 per cent of the total share as compared to 21.4 per cent from business spending. There are many famous and well-known tourist destinations that are famous not only in India but across the globe. Nainital is one of them which is famous as lake district of India.

4. Accommodation: Availability of quality accommodation facilities influence and affect the tourist inflow in the tourist destinations. Accommodation in hotels, lodges, homestays are available in most of the tourist destinations in the Kumaun Region. KMVN has established its own tourist rest houses to provide quality accommodation service at reasonable cost which act as a major tool in attracting tourists in large numbers. Whereas in some of the tourist destinations which are far from cities there is still need for development of quality accommodation services.

5. Accessibility: Accessibility of a particular destination influence the tourist inflow towards it. A destination which is easily accessible is preferred by majority of tourists. Road, rail and air connectivity are the three ways through which visitors can reach particular destination. The associated stakeholders should consider this factor in mind and frame policies as per considering this factor. Kumaon Region is well connected with motorable roads but during monsoon it becomes difficult to reach many destinations. Railway connectivity is not that much developed in the region and same is the scenario of air connectivity.

Literature Review

Bansal and Amit (2010) examined the perception of tourists visits in Uttarakhand. The study revealed that the prime purpose of visit is adventure, leisure. Most of the visitors were of young age for whom infrastructure and associated facilities are more essential. The study revealed that better infrastructure facilities should be provided to boost domestic tourists. Low cost airlines, railways should also be promoted to create new tourist destinations.

Joshi (2016) examined in his study the role of tourism industry in the economic development and the challenges faced. Tourism is growing gradually in the State of Uttarakhand and the tourism industry has great potential for employment generation for the local community residing nearby the tourist destinations. Ecotourism has potential for development of the region. Both the government and the private organisations have to work in cooperation to be actively engaged in the development of the tourism industry.

Rana and Anna (2016) examine the potential of tourism industry in the economy of Uttarakhand taking into consideration employment and revenue generation using secondary data. The results of the study revealed that there is untapped potential avenue in the state in respect of tourism sector for economic development and welfare of people. More attention needed to be paid by the policymakers in expenditure on travel and tourism to utilize the resources to their full capacity.

Jaiswal and Bisht (2017) assessed the growth of tourism in the State of Uttarakhand. The results of their study revealed that tourism has a great potential in the development of the state and tourism infrastructure should be focused by the government. There are new forms of tourism that are needed to be exploited such as rural tourism, ecotourism, water sports should also be developed to attract large number of tourists in the state.

Maheshwari and Sharma (2017) in their study analysed the role of community based tourism as a tool for developing the Garhwal region of Uttarakhand State. The results so obtained revealed that to attract more visitors to the tourist destinations there should be an appropriate arrangement of tourist facilities, service guide and accommodation is essential enhancement of tourism facilities is not easy task without participation of local community. The locals should be trained so that they can play their role in the development of tourism industry.

Kala and Bagri (2018) in their study examined the barriers for community participation which has direct impact on tourism development. The results of the study emphasized the need for both greater advocacy of community participation and the need to design particular strategies that can encourage local participation and are customized to emerging destination context.

Imran and Nguyen (2018) examined in their study the possibilities of home-stay programmes and the willingness of the residents in Uttarakhand on such programmes. The results show that the tourism industry has not brought economic benefits for the households involved in the industry; however, this could be owing to the community not being involved in tourism development. In addition, most of the villagers considered that the home-stay programme could create opportunities for jobs and improve the income of the local community, but the home-stay programme has not yet been developed.

Kumar and Rana (2018) in their study examined factors that impact tourism in Himalayan region of Uttarakhand. The results of the study revealed that tourism has both social and economic impact. They recommended that if information technology in various aspects of tourism industry is used to attract more tourists, foreign exchange earnings will rise which will help in regional development.

Research Methodology

The present study employs qualitative approach to analyse the issues and challenges of tourism industry in the Kumaun Region and to suggest policy measures to capitalize the new forms of tourism in the region. The study uses secondary source of data for which books, research papers, and government reports are used. The area of the present study is the Kumaun Region of Uttarakhand.

Objectives of the Study

1. To understand and examine the factors affecting tourism development in a particular region.
2. To examine the issues and challenges affecting tourism development in the Kumaun Region.
3. To identify the scope for tourism development in the Kumaun Region.
4. To suggest policy measures to overcome the issues and to capitalize the new forms of tourism for the development of tourism industry in the Kumaun Region.

Issues and Challenges Relating to Tourism Development in Kumaun Region

1. Unstructured Development: In the Kumaun Region of the Uttarakhand State, the major issue for the development of tourism industry is the unstructured development which has negatively impacted upon its growth and is necessary to be considered as a challenge by the associated stakeholders. The result of this unstructured development of tourist destination lead to the carrying capacity of these destinations which has been exploited which is a major threat in front of the tourism industry and its associated stakeholders. Due to lack of proper administrative planning some destinations which has potential to be developed as a tourist destination, these destinations have not been developed and exploited to their full potential.

2. Inefficient public transportation system: Transportation system plays an important role in development of tourism industry and that's why it is considered as one of the important element in the tourism industry. Due to inefficient public transport system in the Kumaun Region, the tourist destinations have not been explored to their full potential. It is often seen that tourists tend to prefer visit a destination by hiring private taxis as the public transport is somehow uncomfortable to them and in some cases there is no other means of transport than private taxis and cars.

3. Lack of coordination among government agencies: The lack of coordination among various government agencies is yet another issue that put problems in front of the development of tourism industry in the Kumaun Region. In most of the cases, government agencies work in isolation and plan their activities as per the benefit they presume from tourism. This results in creation of challenge in front of the tourism industry and it suffers from loss and face competition from other regions. The Garhwal Mandal or the Garhwal Region of the state shows a well coordination among the government agencies. For infrastructural development of destinations proper fund allocation is essential which can be possible if coordination among these agencies exists, but due to limited coordination among government agencies these infrastructural plans are not completed on time.

4. Limited level of community participation: It is essential to involve the local community in the tourism planning process in modern era of tourism as they get in close connection with the tourists and know about the destinations well. Tourism developmental activities can be well planned with proper community participation. Due to less focus and importance on this phenomenon in the Kumaun Region challenge in front of tourism industry arieses. Community-based tourism and village tourism can only be promoted when the local community will be aware about these forms of tourism.

5. Traditional mode of providing information: Due to change taking place in the environment, it is necessary to adopt the modern technology. Use of internet, modern advertising and promotion strategies play major role in the development of tourism industry around the globe. In the Kumaun Region either these modern amenities are less known to many of the associated stakeholders of tourism industry or their use is limited. Websites which have been developed to provide information to the tourists are not updated on regular basis. All this create a challenge for the development of tourism industry in the Kumaun Region.

Scope for Development of Tourism in Kumaun Region of Uttarakhand

1. Ecotourism: The Kumaun Region is showing great potential in ecotourism which is a new form of tourism that is not much explored in the region. Ecotourism refers to the form of tourism where the environment, local community and visitor all benefit. Ecotourism involves travel to destinations where flora, fauna, and cultural heritage are the primary attractions. One of the goals of promoting ecotourism is to offer tourists insight into the impact of human beings on the environment, and to foster a greater appreciation of our natural habitats. Being rich in flora, fauna and cultural heritage, the Kumaun Region has great potential in this form of tourism.

2. Village Tourism: Village Tourism, being a new concept in the Kumaun Region, introduced from the West is gaining popularity owing to the fact that a huge bulk of our population still resides in the villages and to know "India" in totality you have to know the Indian villages first. The reason being promotion of tourism by the Tourism Department is to give tourists the experience of way of living of the people residing there. Some major destinations in the Kumaun Region are Jeolikot, Martola, Kalimat Village, Sitalkhet which have the potential in village tourism with their serene beauty.

3. Community-based Tourism: Community-based tourism is a form of tourism in which local residents invite the tourists to visit their communities with the provision of overnight accommodation. This form of tourism enables the tourists to discover local habitats and wildlife, and celebrates and respects traditional cultures, rituals and wisdom. In the Kumaun Region there is a need to promote community-based tourism as the structural development of tourism industry is possible in the best manner through this. The community will be aware of the commercial and social value placed on their natural and cultural heritage through tourism, and this will foster community-based conservation of these resources.

4. Home-stay Tourism: Home-stay tourism has a great potential in the Kumaun Region of Uttarakhand. It is the best way of experiencing the famed Himalayan hospitality of Uttarakhand. As the name suggest home-stay is staying in someone's home as a paying guest for short time period where the guests are provided with budget friendly accommodation and services by individual family and the local community. There are many registered home-stays available in this heavenly state of India where one explores rural locality full of splendid natural surroundings, enjoy local culture and cuisine, explore hidden spots; all this with the help of native people. People of Uttarakhand are simple and warm and follow the ancient Vedic tradition of *atithi devo bhava* (Guests are God) and they welcome their guests with open arms and offer personalized care and services.

Suggestions

1. Planned development of tourist destination should be done in the Kumaun Region to promote inflow of tourists to the region which will enhance the revenue earning of the region and also to develop the destinations that have potential for development.

2. Efficient public transportation system should be developed which link tourist destinations with major cities, railway stations and airports.
3. Well coordinated system among the various governmental agencies should be developed and regularly monitored so that their coordination enable scope for tourism development.
4. Local community should be encouraged to take participation in the tourism planning for structural development of tourist destinations.
5. The use of modern amenities should be encouraged by the government among the associated stakeholders which will contribute in reducing the miscommunication and will provide useful information to the tourists on updated manner.

Conclusion

The tourism industry has evolved as one of the fastest growing sectors all across the globe and is playing huge role in development of economies with its immense potential by creating employment and revenue generation. Being blessed with rich flora and fauna, the Kumaun Region of Uttarakhand is visited by tourists throughout the year. The mesmerizing view of snow capped peaks, wildlife conservation parks, pilgrimage centres, fairs and festivals are some of the reasons that attracts tourists to the destinations in the region. The tourism industry in the region is facing issues which are needed to be solved and the government should consider the suggestive measures provided in this study. The region has vast potential in variety of form of tourism such as ecotourism, village tourism, home stay tourism and community-based tourism. The associated stakeholders should take necessary steps and should promote these forms of tourism in cooperation with government so that the tourism can be developed as a tool of economic development in the Kumaun Region.

References

Bagri, S.C. & Kala, D. (2018). "Barriers to Local Community Participation in Tourism Development: Evidence from Mountainous State Uttarakhand, India". *Tourism: An International Interdisciplinary Journal, 66* (3): 318-33. Retrieved from https://hrcak.srce.hr/index.php?show=clanak&id_clanak_jezik=303072

Bansal, S.P., and Gangotia, Amit (2010). "Perception of Tourist: A Case Study of Uttarakhand". *International Journal of Hospitality & Tourism Systems, 3*(1): 55-63. Retrieved from http://www.publishingindia.com/GetBrochure.aspx?query=UERGQnJvY2h1cmVzfC81NDMucGRmfC81NDMucGRm

Dileep, M.R. (2019). *Tourism: Concepts, Theory and Practice*, Dreamtech Press, New Delhi.

Imran, M. & Nguyen, NTB (2018). "A Community Response to Tourism, Focusing on the Home-stay Programme in K Village in Nainital, Uttarakhand, India". *Journal of Urban and Regional Studies on Contemporary India, 4*(2): 55-62. Retrieved from https://core.ac.uk/download/pdf/197310116.pdf

Jaiswal, B., & Bisht, Madhu (2019). "Tourism Sector in Uttarakhand: A Brief Overview after the State Formation". *International Journal of Research in Economics and Social Sciences (IJRESS), 7*(7): 277-95. Retrieved from https://www.academia.edu/34274775/Tourism_Sector_in_Uttarakhand_A_brief_Overview_after_the_State_Formation

Joshi, B. (2016, September). "Tourism Development in Uttarakhand: Scope and Challenges". *Uttarakhand Socio-Economic Mirror, Quarterly Bulletin, DES, GoUK, Theme: Uttarakhand Tourism, 1*: 20.

Maheshwari, A., and Sharma, P. (2017). "Community Based Tourism: A Tool for Sustainable Development in Garhwal Region, Uttarakhand". *International Journal of Scientific Research, 6*(4): 557-60. Retrieved from https://www.worldwidejournals.com/international-journal-of-scientific-research-(IJSR)/fileview.php?val=April_2017_1491832348__192.pdf

Rana, Gaurav & Kumar, Suneel & Mairaj, Hashir. (2015). "Status and Scenario of Tourism Industry in India: A Case Study of Uttarakhand". In S.P. Bansal, S. Kulshreshtha, & P.K. Gautam (Eds.). *Inclusive Growth and Sustainable Development,* Edition: 1st, Chapter 56, Bharti Publication. https://www.researchgate.net/publication/315101403_STATUS_AND_SCENARIO_OF_TOURISM_INDUSTRY_IN_INDIA_-_A_CASE_STUDY_OF_UTTARAKHAND/link/58ca53c0a6fdcc08b167f7a3/download

8
Issues in Leisure Travel Decisions During COVID-19 Pandemic

An Exploratory Study

Nilanjan Sengupta and *Mousumi Sengupta*

Introduction

The COVID-19 pandemic has had an unmatched influence on people's mobility, worldwide. As of 17 December 2020, there have been 7,28,51,747 confirmed cases of COVID-19, including 16,43,339 deaths, reported to WHO (https://covid19.who.int/). In India, as of 17 December 2020, total number of reported Coronavirus Cases is 99,79,447 (https://www.worldometers.info/coronavirus/country/india/). The travel and tourism sector has been realized as a crucial factor for the worldwide spread of the COVID-19 virus and the travel-related operations and procedures had been paused. It caused deep financial losses in the sector, due to lockdowns and stringent travel restrictions implemented to curtail the spread of the virus, worldwide (Arezki and Nguyen, 2020; Novellia *et al.*, 2018; Stezhko *et al.*, 2020; Yanga *et al.*, 2020). By the end of March 2020, a large number of countries had implemented movement restraints, ranging from full or partial compulsory quarantines (usually referred to as lockdowns) to nonbinding requests for activity restrictions, such as stay-at-home requests, closing certain types of trades, cancelling large gatherings and events, etc. (BBC, 2020). National governments typically announced rigorous measures to contain inward and outbound travel to manage the extent of disease during pandemics (Cahyanto *et al.*, 2016; Yanga *et al.*, 2020). Stringent actions have primarily included quarantining upon arrival (Folayan and Brown, 2015) and travel embargos (Mackenzie, 2014). In this given context, leisure tourism faces a multidimensional challenge from both the tourism demand (perceived health, social, psychological risk) and supply-side (massive fiscal deficits, job losses, business liquidation, human capital depletion), since, people's willingness to travel, concerns during the leisure travels, and resultant leisure travel decisions, have been drastically changed. The present chapter makes an attempt to investigate certain issues in the context of leisure travel decision, prevailing among the residents of cities of Bangalore and Mysore, in India.

Literature Review

Leisure is defined as the time when an individual is not occupied with work and is free to carry on activities of his/her personal likings. Travel is an expression of what leisure means to people and is quite a popular choice in any country or society. While personal values, choice of leisure activities, personality of individuals have been influencing the leisure activity and travel decisions, it is also noted that, human behaviour is influenced by social standards and endorsements (Van Bavel *et al.*, 2020). In this regard, researchers are trying to address the issue of social influence on travel behaviour, notwithstanding the usual environments (Kim *et al.*, 2018). These studies are motivated by the idea that the behavioural forms of people vary with the behaviour of the reference group (Manski, 1993). In addition, the frequency of optional activities such as leisure, have also been found to be related with social setup features (Carrasco and Miller, 2006; Parady *et al.*, 2019; Parady *et al.*, 2020).

Perceived risk about respiratory health issues in the context of leisure travel

Within the tourism context, perceived risk is associated with a tourist's opinion of ambiguity and possible adversarial consequences resulting from the consumption of travel and tourism offerings (Adam, 2015; Liu *et al.*, 2016). Opinions of ambiguity and adversarial consequences may be extracted into eight separate typologies, namely, health, psychological, physical, equipment, financial, satisfaction, time and social risk, respectively (Fuchs and Reichel, 2011; Qi *et al.*, 2009; Olya and Al-ansi, 2018; Reisinger and Mavondo, 2005; Wolff *et al.*, 2019).

Perceived risk as a multidimensional paradigm, may have diverse repercussions for tourists in their decision making, whereby one or more risk dimension(s) can modify a tourist's assessment of a location their intention to travel (Carballo *et al.*, 2017; Reisinger and Mavondo, 2005). Nugraha (2014) and Wolff *et al.* (2019) stated that the perceived risk aggravates worry and other adverse affective behaviour that may negatively impact a tourist's travel intent.

Respiratory health issues and leisure travel decisions

It has been noted that, SARS outbreak had played a major role in modifying people's lifestyle, work pattern, and leisure travel behavioural pattern, as a result of supposed hazards (internal motivational factor), and external actions, such as, travel bans and, stay-at-home rules (Wen *et al.*, 2005). Liu *et al.* (2010) found that, occurrence of air travel between the U.S. and three destinations (China, Hong Kong, and Taiwan) have been substantially decreased, as a result of the SARS outbreak.

After investigating more than1.7million flight records during the H1N1 pandemic in 2009, Fenichel *et al.* (2013) found that, the general anxieties over the H1N1 influenza (as measured by Google Trends) were responsible for 0.34 per cent of missed flights during the pandemic.

In the same line, Kim *et al.* (2017) found that, during f MERS outbreak in South Korea, the anxiety of getting exposed while travelling, impacted the travel behaviour, heavily. Supporting this, Hotle *et al.* (2020) proposed that, the perceived risk of exposure to ailments (such as influenza), during travel, had negative influence on travel decisions, and, individuals would prefer to travel to those destinations, where the risk exposure to the virus was comparatively less.

Leisure Travel Decisions and COVID-19 Pandemic

It has been noted that, change in travel patterns could help in controlling the spread of COVID-19, and, thus, individuals' behavioural change was desired, in the context of travelling (West *et al.*, 2020), resulting into stay-at-home policies, lock-downs, and so on.

Keeping this in mind, in the context of travel and tourism, studies have been conducted, investigating the impact of recent COVID-19 pandemic on the travel and tourism sector, though less in number as yet (e.g., Molloy *et al.*, 2020; De Vos, 2020; Lee and Lee, 2020; Sobieralski, 2020, Ito *et al.*, 2020).

For example, Sobieralski (2020) emphasized the high vulnerability of the airline industry in US, during COVID-19 pandemic, as it an uncertain period for the individuals to make travel decisions. Molloy *et al.* (2020), while conducting a study in Switzerland, identified certain behavioural changes among individuals during travel.

However, Slovic (1987) has argued that there might be a gap between actual risks and the perception of risks by individuals and, identified three key factors associated with risk perception: (i) dread, (ii) unknown (unfamiliarity), and (iii) number of people involved. In this line, Rogers (1983) argued that, the change in the travel behaviour during COVID-19, might be based on perceived risk and not the actual risk, which led to the decision to engage in protective behaviour and resultant travel decision.

Similarly, De Vos (2020) conducted a study on the possible consequences of social distancing on day-to-day travel patterns and, emphasized that people should be encouraged to change their behaviour while travelling, instead of a full-fledged stay-at-home situation (which might lead to undesired social isolation and limited physical activities).

Summarizing various research findings, three major type of risks can be identified as the perceived risks which might influence the leisure travel decisions, based on various researches: health, psychological, social risks.

Health risk is related with possible threats to the health and well-being of the traveller, during travel and tourism events (Olya and Al-ansi, 2018). This invariably acts as an influencer in the process of travel decision making (Huanga *et al.*, 2020). Not only the vulnerability to and degree of health hazard significantly affect the behaviour of tourists (Cahyanto *et al.*, 2016; Jonas *et al.*, 2011), during COVID-19 pandemic, the psychological and social risk also play a major role in modifying the tourists' behaviour. Adam (2015) argued that, psychological risk is related to the likelihood of damaging self-image and fear of getting exposed to unknown situations. Social risk is perceived based on how the travel decision would affect the tourist's social reference groups, such as, friends and family, in terms of their opinion of them (Wang, 2017). Therefore, all the three types of perceived risks might influence the travel decisions, in various ways.

However, there is a need to investigate the changes in travel patterns caused by the current COVID-19 pandemic, in more details.

Methodology and Data Collection

The present study has attempted to investigate the opinion of people residing in Bangalore and Mysore, about various issues in their decision making of leisure travel. The objectives of the study were as follows:

- To investigate whether the respondents' average willingness level for leisure travel vary, based on the change in the COVID-19 pandemic situation.
- To investigate whether the respondents' average agreement level for leisure travel decision vary, taking into consideration the various issues, such as, health, economic, social, psychological, and, work-related, in the context of COVID-19 pandemic situation.
- To investigate whether the respondents' average agreement level for leisure travel decision vary, based on their age, gender, occupation, education level, and, annual income, in the context of the COVID-19 pandemic situation.

A questionnaire was prepared with multiple choice questions, addressing the health, economic, social, psychological, and, work-related issues, which may have impact on the agreement level of the respondents to make leisure travel, each represented by certain items. (total items fot total 5 issues = 19). The items are as follows:

Items under health-related issues

1. Health infrastructure and facility at the destination.
2. Pollution level at the travel destination.
3. Health safety regulations.
4. Own general health concerns.
5. Co-traveller's general health concerns.
6. Travelling in own vehicle.

Items under economic issues

1. Discount in Air/Train/Bus/Taxi fare.
2. Availability of cancellation policy for travel or accommodation.
3. Available budget.

Items under social issues

1. Family pressure/expectation.
2. Social status.
3. Demonstration of travel by the friends and family.

Items under psychological issues

1. Boredom or monotony.
2. Need for connecting with people.
3. Depression and anxiety.
4. Choice of leisure activities.

Items under work-related issues

1. Availability of work vacation.
2. Expiry of vacation leave.
3. Reimbursement policy at work.

The sample for the study was the residents of Bangalore and Mysore, in the State of Karnataka. For the present study, conveneint sampling technique was used. The questionnaie was sent and the respodnents were requested to respond in terms of their agreement for each item. The questionnaire used a 5-point Likert scale for each item (Strongly agree = 5, Agree = 4, Undecided = 3, Disagree = 2, Strongly disagree =1). The questionnaire was sent to 193 residents. Responses were received from 105 residents (54%). The data has been collected between September and December 2020.

Keeping the objectives in mind, following hypotheses were tested in the present study:

Hypothesis 1

Hypothesis 1_0: The distribution of the average willingness level of making leisure travel decision, based on the change in the COVID-19 pandemic situation, is not significantly different across the respondents.

Hypothesis 1_a: The distribution of the average willingness level of making leisure travel decision, based on the change in the COVID-19 pandemic situation, is significantly different across the respondents.

Hypothesis 2

Hypothesis 2_0: The distribution of the average agreement level of the respondents, for making leisure travel decision, in the context of the COVID-19 pandemic situation, is not significantly different across all the 19 items.

Hypothesis 2_a: The distribution of the average agreement level of the respondents, for making leisure travel decision, in the context of the COVID-19 pandemic situation, is significantly different across all the 19 items.

Hypothesis 3

Hypothesis 3_0: The distribution of the average agreement level of the respondents, for making leisure travel decision, in the context of the COVID-19 pandemic situation, is not significantly different, across the 6 items under the health-related issues.

Hypothesis 3_a: The distribution of the average agreement level of the respondents, for making leisure travel decision, in the context of the COVID-19 pandemic situation, is significantly different, across the 6 items under the health-related issues.

Hypothesis 4

Hypothesis 4_0: The distribution of the average agreement level of the respondents, for making leisure travel decision, in the context of the COVID-19 pandemic situation, is not significantly different, across the 3 items under the economic issues.

Hypothesis 4_a: The distribution of the average agreement level of the respondents, for making leisure travel decision, in the context of the COVID-19 pandemic situation, is significantly different, across the 3 items under the economic issues.

Hypothesis 5

Hypothesis 5_0: The distribution of the average agreement level of the respondents, for making leisure travel decision, in the context of the COVID-19 pandemic situation, is not significantly different, across the 3 items under the social issues.

Hypothesis 5_a: The distribution of the average agreement level of the respondents for making leisure travel decision, in the context of the COVID-19 pandemic situation, is significantly different, across the 3 items under the social issues.

Hypothesis 6

Hypothesis 6_0: The distribution of the average agreement level of the respondents, for making leisure travel decision, in the context of the COVID-19 pandemic situation, is not significantly different, across the 4 items under the psychological issues.

Hypothesis 6_a: The distribution of the average agreement level of the respondents, for making leisure travel decision, in the context of the COVID-19 pandemic situation, is significantly different, across the 4 items under the psychological issues.

Hypothesis 7

Hypothesis 7_0: The distribution of the average agreement level of the respondents, for making leisure travel decision, in the context of the COVID-19 pandemic situation, is not significantly different, across the 3 items under the work-related issues.

Hypothesis 7_a: The distribution of the average agreement level of the respondents, for making leisure travel decision, in the context of the COVID-19 pandemic situation, is significantly different, across the 3 items under the work-related issues.

Hypothesis 8

Hypothesis 8_0: The distribution of the average willingness level of making leisure travel decision, based on the change in the COVID-19 pandemic situation, is not significantly different across the respondents, based on age, gender, occupation, education level, and, annual income.

Hypothesis 8_a: The distribution of the average willingness level of making leisure travel decision, based on the change in the COVID-19 pandemic situation, is significantly different across the respondents, based on at least one of the factors, such as, age, gender, occupation, education level, and, annual income.

Data analysis

Out of the total 105, 15 respondents were from the age group 18-25 years, 18 from the age group 26-33 years, 40 from the age group 34-41 years, 24 from the age group 42-49 years, and 8 from the age group 50 years and more. 73 respondents were male and 32 were female. 66 respondents passed graduation level education and 39 were postgraduate. Occupation-wise, 26 were self-employed, 45 were in service and 34 were engaged in their own business. Per annum, 1 respondent had income less than 5 lakh, 27 had income between 5-11.99 lakh, 46 had income between 12-18.99 lakh, 25 had income between 19-25.99 lakh, and 6 had income of 26 lakh and more.

To measure the opinion of the respondents, the questionnaire has got the required overall consistency level, in measuring the same (Cronbach alpha = .869). In order to understand the level of agreement assigned to each of the items, related to health, economic, social, psychological, and, work-related, the respective averages, assigned by the respondents, were computed. Taking into consideration the average score in the descriptive statistics (Table 8.1), one could note that the factor "travelling in own vehicle" has been assigned as the most crucial factor in leisure travel deicision (mean = 3.88 SD = .73), while the factor "reimbursement policy at work" has been assigned as the least crucial factor in leisure travel deicision (mean = 3.08, SD = .98). However, the average agreement level of the respondents, regarding the role of the all the items, while taking leisure travel decision, in the context of the COVID-19 pandemic situation, have been assigned a score of more than 3, thus, demonstrating that the respondents acknowledge the significance (more or less) of all the items while making leisure travel decisions (Table 8.1).

Table 8.1: Descriptive Statistics

Items	Mean	Standard Deviation
12. Health infrastructure and facility at the destination	3.342857	1.054556
13. Pollution level at the travel destination	3.571429	0.841897
14. Health safety regulations	3.219048	1.074002
15. My general health concerns	3.419048	0.97843
16. My co-travellers' general health concerns	3.514286	0.92106
17. Travelling in own vehicle	3.885714	0.737906
18. Discount in Air/Train/Bus/Taxi fare	3.666667	0.977307
19. Availability of cancellation policy for travel or accommodation	3.495238	1.020217
20. Available budget	3.619048	0.870245
21. Family pressure/expectation	3.638095	0.991539
22. Social status	3.342857	1.054556
23. Demonstration of travel by the friends and family	3.571429	0.841897
24. Boredom or monotony	3.571429	1.036425
25. Need for connecting with people	3.457143	0.990615
26. Depression and anxiety	3.647619	0.930064
27. Choice of leisure activities	3.52381	1.056984
28. Availability of work vacation	3.542857	1.009842
29. Expiry of vacation leave	3.704762	0.865179
30. Reimbursement policy at work	3.085714	0.981701

To test the Hypothesis 1, respondents have been asked to indicate their willingness to take decision for leisure travel in the present situation (scenario 1) and in case COVID virus was fully/nearly eradicated or controlled (scenario 2). Two-paired T-test revealed that the respondents' willingness for taking decision to go on leisure travel would be changed significantly, in case of the scenario changes from 1 to 2 (p value = .0000, α = 0.05). **Therefore, Hypothesis 1_0 has been rejected.**

The rest of the null hypotheses could be tested, using either ANOVA or Kruskal-Wallis Test, based on whether the assumption of normality for the sample was satisfied. In order to test the assumption of normality, Shapiro-Wilk Test was used. From the test, it was noted that, normality assumption was not satisfied by the data. Hence, Kruskal-Wallis Test (K-W Test) was used to investigate the proposed hypotheses.

Based on the above, to investigate whether the distribution of the average agreement level of the respondents, for making leisure travel decision, in the context of the COVID-19 pandemic situation, is significantly different across all the 19 items, Kruskal-Wallis Test was conducted. It was noted that, the *p-value* was significantly less than the level of significance (p-value = .0000, α = 0.05). Hence, it was concluded that, there were significant differences between average agreement levels assigned by the respondents, for all the items. **Therefore, Hypothesis 2_0 has been rejected.**

To investigate whether the distribution of the average agreement level of the respondents, for making leisure travel decision, in the context of the COVID-19 pandemic situation, was significantly different for the items under health-related, social, economic, psychological and work-related issues each, Kruskal-Wallis Test was conducted. From Table 8.2, it was noted that, for the items, under economic, social, and psychological issues, the *p-value* was more than .05. Therefore, there was no significant difference in the average agreement level of the respondents, for making leisure travel decision, in the context of the COVID-19 pandemic situation, for the items, under economic, social, and psychological issues. Hence **Therefore, Hypothesis $4_{0,}$ $5_{0,}$ $6_{0,}$ have been retained.**

Table 8.2: Kruskal-Wallis Test result for items under each issue

Issues	p-value	Significance
Health-related issues	**1.14E-05**	**yes**
Economic issues	0.412845	no
Social issues	0.082368	no
Psychological issues	0.60035	no
Work-related issues	**8.55E-06**	**yes**

However, for the items, under health-related and work-related issues, the p-value was significantly less than the level of significance (p-value = .0000, α = 0.05). Therefore, there was significant difference between average agreement levels assigned to the items by the respondents, for the items under the health-related and work-related issues. **Therefore, Hypothesis 3_0 and 7_0 has been rejected.**

Table 8.3: Tukey's HSD/Kramer Test

Group 1	Group 2	Mean	Std Err	q-Stat	Lower	Upper	p-value
Health-related issues							
12. Health infra-structure and facility at the destination	17. Travelling in own vehicle	0.54	0.09	5.9	0.17	0.91	00
14. Health safety regulations	17. Travelling in own vehicle	0.67	0.09	7.25	0.3	1.04	00
15. Own general health concerns	17. Travelling in own vehicle	0.47	0.09	5.08	0.1	0.84	00
Work-related issues							
28. Availa-bility of work vacation	30. Reimbur-sement policy at work	0.46	0.09	4.91	0.15	0.77	00
29. Expiry of vacation leave	30. Reimbur-sement policy at work	0.62	0.09	6.65	0.31	0.93	00

In order to identify, in which of the items respondents differed in their average agreement level, non-parametric post-hoc comparison test (Tukey's HSD/Kramer Test) was used. It was noted that, for the certain items under health-related and work-related issues, agreement level of the respodnents about the decision on the leisure travel differed significantly (p-value was less than .05). For example, respodnents's agreement level differed for health infrastructure and facility at the destination, health safety regulations and own general health concerns vis-à-vis travelling in own vehicle, as a part of their concern regarding health-related issues. Again, respodnents's agreement level differed for availability of work vacation vis-à-vis reimbursement policy at work, and, expiry of vacation leave vis-à-vis reimbursement policy at work, as a part of their concern regarding work-related issues (Table 8.3).

To investigate whether there was significant difference in the average agreement level of the respondents, for making leisure travel decision, depending on the change in the COVID-19 pandemic situation, based on their age, gender, occupation, education level, and, annual income, Kruskal-Wallis Test was conducted (Table 8.4). It was revealed that, respondents differed significantly on the taking leisure travel decision, depending on the change in the COVID-19 pandemic situation, based on their level of education (p-value is less than .05). **Therefore, Hypothesis 8_0 has been rejected**. However, the other factors, such as, age, gender, income and occupation did not have any such significance.

Table 8.4: Kruskal-Wallis Test result for change in the willingness to travel, based on COVID-19 situation

Factors	p-value	Significance
Age	0.614	No
Gender	0.447	No
Education level	**0.015**	**Yes**
Occupation	0.227	No
Income	0.05	No

Discussion

For the purpose of the present study, the data was collected from September to December 2020. Even before this time, the travel restrictions across India has begun to relax. Substantial number of cases of recovery from COVID-19 have been documented and testing procedures have been geared up. In general, awareness about the virus and the rules of social distancing has been repeatedly highlighted by various regulatory bodies, including the state and the central government of the country. In this context, the study revealed that, the respondents' willingness for taking decision to go on leisure travel would be changed significantly, in case improvement in the COVID-19 situation. This was expected since respondents did not want to expose themselves unnecessarily, while travelling. However, respondents' agreement in making travel decision, based on various issues, did vary across the items, mentioned in the questionnaire. This needed further study. The respondents' agreement level in leisure travel decision varied significantly only for the health-related and work-related issues, and not for the other issues, such as social, economic, and psychological. This depicted that respondents had different levels of concerns in ensuring safer travel, related to healthy and hygienic travel measures and accommodation, location-specific health facility, affordability, and own health concern. Also, workplace policies, such as policies related to vacation leave and reimbursement, acted as an influencing factor, towards deciding the nature, duration, and standard of travel. The study also revealed that respondents' leisure travel decision was significantly different, based on their level of education, and not on their age, gender, income, and occupation. This needs to be explored further. At the end, it is to be noted that, the study has been conducted in an uncertain time and with limited data. Further study in this regard is needed.

References

Adam, I. (2015). "Backpackers' Risk Perceptions and Risk Reduction Strategies in Ghana", *Tourism Management, 49*: 99-108.

Arezki, R. and Nguyen, H. (2020). "Novel Coronavirus Hurts the Middle East and North Africa Through many Channels", in Baldwin, R. and di Mauro, B.W. *Economics in the Time of COVID-19*, Centre for Economic Policy Research, London.

BBC (2020). "Coronavirus: The World in Lockdown", in *Maps and Charts*. https://www.bbc.com/news/world-52103747. (Accessed on 31 May 2020).

Cahyanto, I., Wiblishauser, M., Pennington-Gray, L. and Schroeder, A. (2016), "The Dynamics of Travel Avoidance: The Case of Ebola in the U.S.", *Tourism Management Perspectives, 20*: 195-203.

Carballo, R.R., Leon, C.J. and Carballo, M.M. (2017), "The Perception of Risk by International Travellers", *Worldwide Hospitality and Tourism Themes, 9*(5): 534-42.

Carrasco, J.A. and Miller, E.J. (2006) "Exploring the Propensity to Perform Social Activities: A Social Network Approach", *Transportation*. Springer, *33*(5): 463-80.

De Vos, J. (2020). "The effect of COVID-19 and Subsequent Social Distancing on Travel Behaviour". *Transp. Res. Interdiscip. Perspect, 5*: 100121. https://doi.org/10.1016/j.trip.2020.100121. edu.au/vital/access/services/Download/mq:44472/SOURCE1?view¼true (Accessed on 21 April 2020).

Fenichel, E.P., Kuminoff, N.V., Chowell, G. (2013). "Skip the Trip: Air Travellers' Behavioural Responses to Pandemic Influenza". *PLoS One,* 8. https://doi.org/10.1371/journal.

Folayan, M. and Brown, B. (2015). "Ebola and the Limited Effectiveness of Travel Restrictions", *Disaster Medicine and Public Health Preparedness*, p.1.

Frei, C., Mahmassani, H.S., Frei, A. (2015). "Making Time Count: Traveller Activity Engagement on Urban Transit." *Transp. Res. Part a Policy Pract, 76*: 58-70. https://doi.org/10.1016/J. TRA.2014.12.007.

Fuchs, G. and Reichel, A. (2011), "An Exploratory Inquiry into Destination Risk Perceptions and Risk Reduction Strategies of First Time vs. Repeat Visitors to a Highly Volatile Destination", *Tourism Management, 32*(2): 266-76.

Hotle, S., Murray-Tuite, P., Singh, K. (2020). "Influenza Risk Perception and Travel-related Health Protection Behaviour in the Us: Insights for the Aftermath of the COVID-19 Outbreak". *Transp. Res. Interdiscip. Perspect.* 5, 100127. https://doi.org/10.1016/j.trip.2020.100127

https://covid19.who.int/

https://www.worldometers.info/coronavirus/country/india/

Huanga, X., Daib, S. and Xub, H. (2020), "Predicting Tourists' Health Risk Preventative Behaviour and Travelling Satisfaction in Tibet: Combining the Theory of Planned Behaviour and Health Belief Model", *Tourism Management Perspectives*, *33*: 100589.

Ito, H., Hanaoka, S., Kawasaki, T. (2020). "The Cruise Industry and the COVID-19 Outbreak". *Transp. Res. Interdiscip. Perspect, 5*: 100136. https://doi.org/10.1016/j.trip.2020.100136.

Jonas, A., Mansfeld, Y., Paz, S. and Potasman, I. (2011), "Determinants of Health Risk Perception among Low Risk-Taking Tourists Travelling to Developing Countries", *Journal of Travel Research*, *50*(1): 87-99.

Kim, C., Cheon, H., Choi, K., Joh, C.H., Lee, H.J. (2017). "Exposure to Fear: Changes in Travel Behaviour During Mers Outbreak in Seoul". *KSCE J. Civ. Eng., 21*: 2888-2895. https://doi.org/10.1007/s12205-017-0821-5.

Kim, J., Rasouli, S., Timmermans, H.J. (2018). "Social Networks, Social Influence and Activity Travel Behaviour: A Review of Models and Empirical Evidence". *Transp. Rev., 38*(4): 499-523, Taylor & Francis.

Lee, D., Lee, J. (2020). "Testing on the Move: South Korea's Rapid Response to the COVID-19 Pandemic". *Transp. Res. Interdiscip. Perspect.* https://doi.org/10.1016/j.

Liu, B., Pennington-Gray, L. and Schroeder, A. (2013), "Images of Safe Tourism Destinations in the United States held by African Americans", PASOS. *Revista de Turismo y Patrimonio Cultural, 11*(3): 105-21.

Liu, B., Schroeder, A., Pennington-Gray, L. and Farajat, S.A.D. (2016). "Source Market Perceptions: How Risky is Jordan to Travel to?", *Journal of Destination Marketing & Management*, *5*(4): 294-304.

Liu, J., Moss, S., Zhang, J. (2010). "The Life Cycle of a Pandemic Crisis: SARS Impact on Air Travel", in *Allied Academies International Conference*, New Orleans, LA.

Mackenzie, D. (2014), "Ebola Travel Ban Will not Work", *New Scientist, 224*(2992): 4-5.

Manski, C.F. (1993). "Identification of Endogenous Social Effects: The Reflection Problem", *The Review of Economic Studies*. Wiley-Blackwell, *60*(3): 531-42.

Molloy, J., Tchervenkov, C., Hintermann, B., Axhausen, K.W. (2020). "Tracing the Sars-CoV-2 Impact: The First Month in Switzerland". *Transp. Find.* https://doi.org/10.32866/001c.12903.

Novellia, M., Burgessb, L.G., Jonesc, A., Ritchie, B.W. (2018), "'No Ebola. . . Still Doomed'—The Ebola Induced Tourism Crisis", *Annals of Tourism Research, 70*: 76-87.

Nugraha, A.K.N.A. (2014). "Consumers' Decision to Visit a Risky Destination Country: An Analysis of Tourists' Risk Taking", Doctoral dissertation. Macquarie University, available at: www.researchonline.mq.

Olya, H.G.T. and Al-Ansi, A. (2018). "Risk Assessment of Halal Products and Services: Implication For Tourism Industry", *Tourism Management, 65*: 279-91.

Parady, G.T., Katayama, G., Yamazaki, H., Yamanami, T., Takami, K. and Harata, N. (2019). "Analysis of Social Networks, Social Interactions, and Out-of-Home Leisure Activity Generation: Evidence from Japan", *Transportation*, Springer, *46*(3): 537-62.

Parady, G., Takami, K., Harata, N. (2020). "Egocentric Social Networks and Social Interactions in the Greater Tokyo Area". *Transportation*, 1-26. https://doi.org/10.1007/s11116-020-10079-y Springer, in press.

Qi, C.X., Gibson, H.J. and Zhang, J.J. (2009). "Perceptions of Risk and Travel Intentions: The Case of China and the Beijing Olympic Games", *Journal of Sport & Tourism, 14*(1): 43-67.

Reisinger, Y. and Mavondo, F. (2005), "Travel Anxiety and Intentions to Travel Internationally: Implications of Travel Risk Perception", *Journal of Travel Research, 43*(3): 212-25.

Rogers, R.W. (1983). "Cognitive and Psychological Processes In Fear Appeals and Attitude Change: A Revised Theory of Protection Motivation", *Social Psychophysiology: A Sourcebook*, Guilford Press, pp. 153-76.

Slovic, P. (1987). "Perception of Risk". *Science, 236*(4799): 280-85, American Association for the Advancement of Science.

Sobieralski, J.B. (2020). "COVID-19 and Airline Employment: Insights From Historical Uncertainty Shocks To The Industry". *Transp. Res. Interdiscip. Perspect, 5*: 100123. https://doi.org/10.1016/j.trip.2020.100123

Stezhko, N., Oliinyk, Y., Polishchuk, L., Tyshchuk, I., Parfinenko, A. and Markhonos, S. (2020). "International Tourism in the System of Modern Globalisation Processes", *International Journal of Management* (*IJM*), *11*(3): 97-106.

Van Bavel, J.J., Baicker, K., Boggio, P. S., Capraro, V., Cichocka, A., Cikara, M., Crockett, M.J., Crum, A.J., Douglas, K.M., Druckman, J.N. and others (2020). "Using Social and Behavioural Science to Support COVID-19 Pandemic Response", *Nat. Hum. Behav.* Nature Publishing Group, pp. 1-12.

Wang, H.Y. (2017). "Determinants Hindering the Intention of Tourists to Visit Disaster-hit Destinations", *Current Issues in Tourism, 20*(5): 459-79, doi: 10.1080/13683500.2015.1062471

Wen, Z., Huimin, G., Kavanaugh, R.R. (2005). "The Impacts of Sars on the Consumer Behaviour of Chinese Domestic Tourists". *Curr. Issues Tour, 8*: 22-38. https://doi.org/10.1080/13683500508668203.

West, R., Michie, S., Rubin, G.J., Amlôt, R. (2020). "Applying Principles of Behaviour Change to Reduce SARS-CoV-2 Transmission", *Nat. Hum. Behav*, 1-9, Nature Publishing Group.

Wolff, K. and Larsen, S. (2016), "Flux and Permanence of Risk Perceptions: Tourists' Perception of The Relative and Absolute Risk for Various Destinations", *Scandinavian Journal of Psychology, 57*(6): 584-90.

Wolff, K., Larsena, S. and Øgaard, T. (2019). "How to Define and Measure Risk Perceptions", *Annals of Tourism Research, 79*: 102759.

Yanga, Y., Zhang, H. and Chen, X. (2020), "Coronavirus Pandemic and Tourism: Dynamic Stochastic General Equilibrium Modelling of Infectious Disease Outbreak", *Annals of Tourism Research, 83*, doi:10.1016/j.annals.2020.102913 (Accessed on 21 April 2020).

Zhang, J., Litvinova, M., Liang, Y., Wang, Y., Wang, W., Zhao, S., Wu, Q., Merler, S., Viboud, C., Vespignani, A. and others (2020) "Changes in Contact Patterns Shape the Dynamics of the COVID-19 Outbreak in China", *Science*, American Association for the Advancement of Science.

9

Pandemics and Its Repercussions on Travel and Tourism Industry

A Case Study of COVID-19

Shan Eugene Palakkal

The Silent Scourge

The story of people and pathogens is that of a difficult evolutionary marriage. Pathogens want to live and prosper. Killing off humans—the hosts—would become a self-defeating exercise. Both parties therefore, try to work towards mutual survival. After a certain point of time, the two declare an uneasy truce and humans start to live with pathogens. This has been happening so many times before and will be the same with the novel Coronavirus.

By contrast, the Coronavirus is a relatively slow-moving pandemic. It gave ample notice to mankind from the time COVID-19, thought to have an animal origin, transmitted to humans in Wuhan, China last November.[1] In fact, long before the 8-12 weeks that COVID-19 took to make its presence felt around the globe—dinosaurs got only a 8-12 minutes heads-up—humankind had been warned by its precursor coronaviruses such as SARS and MERS.

For many years, the travel and tourism industry made the world go round. Airlines dominated the air and airports were bustling areas, until they became the vehicle of transfer of the nCOVID-19, then they became "ground zero". Borders had to be closed to all categories of travellers, social events curtailed to stem the tide of the disease. Global and local markets have all collapsed and governments around the world are in dire straits trying to strike a balance between keeping their market economies going, averting unemployment, and depriving the poor while trying to respond to public health essentials.

The History of Pandemics

Throughout history, as humans populated across continents, infectious diseases have been a constant companion. Let us browse through the history of deadly pandemics from Antonine Plague to the COVID-19[2]:

S. No.	Name	Period of Occurrence	Originated/ Place	Type
1	Antonine Plague (Plague of Galen)	165-80 AD	Roman empire	Either small pox or measles
2	Japanese Small pox Epidemic	735-37 AD	Dazaifu (Japan)	Variola virus
3	Plague of Justinian	541-42 AD	Egypt	Rats/Fleas/ Yersinia pestis bacteria
4	Black Death[3]	1347-51 AD	China	Rats/Fleas
5	New World Small pox	1520-onwards	Africa and Europe	Variola virus
6	Great Plague of London	1665	England	Rats/Fleas
7	Great Plague of Milan	1629-31	Northern and Central Italy	Rats/Fleas
8	Cholera Pandemic	1817-23	India	Cholera bacteria
9	Third Plague	1885	Yunnan (China)	Rats
10	Yellow Fever	1800	Georgia (US)	Virus/ Mosquitoes

(*Contd.*)

S. No.	Name	Period of Occurrence	Originated/ Place	Type
11	Russian Flu	1889-90	Bukhara (Russian Empire)	Could be H2N2
12	Spanish Flu[4]	1918-19	Canton (China)	H1N1 virus/ Pigs
13	Asian Flu	1957-58	Guizhou (Chinese province)	H2N2 virus
14	Hong Kong Flu	1968-70	Hong Kong	H3N2 virus
15	Swine Flu	2009-10	Mexico (North America)	H1N1 virus/ Pigs
16	SARS	2002-03	Guangdong (China)	Coronavirus/ Bats, Civets
17	Ebola	2014-16	Democratic Republic of Congo	Ebola virus/ Wild animals
18	MERS	2015-present	Jeddah (Saudi Arabia)	Coronavirus/ Bats, camels
19	COVID-19	2019-present	Wuhan (China)	Coronavirus/ Yet to find (maybe Pangolins)

There has been consistent trend overtime, in terms of mortality rate, despite the persistence of pandemics throughout history. In earlier societies, people believed in spirits and that gods inflicted deadly diseases upon those that deserved his wrath. This unscientific idea often led to uncounted and unnecessary deaths in millions.[5] Fortunately, humanity's understanding of the causes of deadly diseases has improved, resulting in drastic improvement in the response to pandemics.

SARS and MERS (Middle-East Respiratory Syndrome), two coronaviruses that led to the outbreaks in 2002 and 2012 respectively, did cause severe symptoms but their transmission rates were compared to COVID-19—the name given to the novel coronavirus by WHO. Wuhan outbreak is called novel coronavirus as it is a new strain that has not been previously identified in humans.[6] Although it is from the same family of viruses as SARS and MERS, it is not the same virus. Eating meat or not is not the issue. Viruses causing diseases in wild animals that act as their natural reservoirs, for example bats, can spread to intermediate species, the camels in the case of MERS, and then get transmitted to humans. It is also possible that humans may get it directly from the wild animals on direct contact while travelling to places where normally humans wouldn't have gone earlier.

Nipah virus, which struck Kerala in 2018, too arose from bats, but is not a coronavirus infection even though respiratory trouble is one of the symptoms. In fact, several viruses carried by bats can cause diseases in humans and the coronavirus is just one of them.

A public health emergency of international concern, or PHEIC, which is what the 2019-nCoV has been declared to be by WHO, is defined as "an extraordinary event which is determined to constitute a public health risk to other states through the international spread of disease and to potentially require a coordinated international response". While WHO notes that six times PHEIC declarations have been made were due to communicable diseases:

Name	Year
H1N1 influenza (Swine flu)	2009
Polio	2014
Ebola	2014 & 2019
Zika virus	2016
Novel coronavirus	2020

From hunter-gatherers to metropolitan living, humanity's reliance on one another has sparked opportunities for diseases to spread. Urbanisation also brings more and more rural people into denser neighbourhoods, at the same time population increase is also putting great pressure on the environment. Passenger air traffic too has doubled. These trends are directly or indirectly have a deep impact on the spread of such diseases.

Tourism and Hospitality in the Time of Pandemics!

Across the world, tourism and hospitality usually is badly affected by pandemics, because of the natures of the business, which is always related to travelling of people. History recaps that epidemics and pandemics have had an immediate impact on hotels, restaurants, airlines industries, travel and tour agencies due to international travel restrictions, social media and media coverage and government measures.

World economic had crippled with lost production and demand, devastating effects on families and communities in panic and follies by governments taking hasty decisions. Thereby countries take some time to recover. Global markets go into a tailspin, as investors, stampede out of stocks and commodities and flock to relative safety of government bonds, prompted by fears of a global recession due to the spread of pandemics. It is well-established that disease outbreaks have a slowing down effect on the economy.

If we analyse the previous pandemics that affected the world, the number of people affected and died was not many as compared to other tragedies, but just the fear about the panic among the society can produce a substantial impact on the global economy too.[7] As a result of this most of the people do not travel and choose other alternatives. This affects the tourism industry and in turn the country's economy.

The airline industry is the worst off, with losses crossing millions of dollars. Without government aid, carriers say they may shut shop. Hospitality depends on daily transactions to break even. Human resources and rentals are the highest costs. If the pandemic situation does not abate most of them look at closures and layoffs.

While people make decisions on whether or not to travel to a particular country, they are also concerned about health care systems at that place. On the other hand, there are chances to face a shortage of employees if they are affected, this might result in the organisational performance. Also multinational organisations limits their business executive travels to the affected countries, and this creates marginal decrease in the demand for hotel rooms and airlines. Most of the countries also tighten their securities especially at airports in times of pandemics.

Severe Acute Respiratory Syndrome (SARS) was the first real global health emergency experienced by countries in this century.[8] It broke out as an atypical pneumonia and spread rapidly throughout China and Southeast Asia. The World Health Organisation (WHO) declared certain places as high-risk tourist destinations and international tourists were warned not to visit and a number of other countries restricted Chinese travellers from entering their countries. A similar situation is arising with the 2019-nCoV.

Restaurant industries are seen as an upmarket, debauched drinking space reeking of prosperity, but they suffer from an image issue. No one realized that they have the highest failure rate 81 per cent restaurants do not last 30 months.[9]

During times of pandemics, certain governments are controlling outbound travellers who could be described as "close contact", i.e. one who has been within 2 meters of an infected person. They are not infected, but they could be vectors. Mandatory multi-step fever checks are done on all outbound passengers. Screenings are done strictly—three to four times at an airport—departure hall, security, checkpoint and boarding gates.

The bigger crisis seems to be "panic" during pandemics. People begin to stockpile food, groceries, hand sanitizers, masks, soap, etc. During the SARS epidemic, people did not have smart phones. Even though people were scared, the maximum precautions were facemasks and washing of hands. There were no lockdowns. It is sometimes the uncertainly created by the novelty of the virus, the universality of it and high levels of data connectivity leads pandemic acquiring epic proportions in the minds of the people around the world. Anxiety level shoots up. Also staying constantly in a stressed state takes a toll.

nCOVID-19 and Its Ill-Effects on Tourism

In December 2019, the WHO had declared an outbreak of the

febrile respiratory illness of unknown etiology from Wuhan, Hubei province of China[10]; the flu-like disease has infected 80,000 people and killed 3000 in China. Beyond mainland China, however, it has jumped to nearly 40 countries and territories, with many deaths. This is one of the biggest health crisis the world has faced in recent times. Stuart Siddell, an Emeritus professor at the University of Bristol, who has been researching on coronavirus for over 25 years says how increased contact between humans and wild animals have the potential to unleash more outbreaks caused by viruses previously restricted to animals.[11]

COVID-19 is a different beast. White guys, world leaders and rich and international travellers are getting it. Therefore, the implication, anyone can get it. You and I can get it! A surfeit of information is fuelling the panic around the disease. Movies and Documentaries were made about it. The universality or "it could happen to me" is why some news stories get enormous media attention, while others barely take a blip? If Boris Johnson and lakhs of Americans can get COVID-19, any Indian in any class can get it too. This has enabled COVID-19 to get media coverage like no other disease in the past, which obviously leads to higher anxiety levels. In China, COVID-19 remains largely contained in Hubei province,[12] next is Europe that is the worst affected.[13] Italy has most COVID-19 cases outside China as it has similar living conditions.[14]

This is usually the time of the year when schools slow down to a stop and plans are made for the annual great family exodus. But the COVID-19 pandemic has killed the romance of leaving on a jet plane.

Within a month, the first industry that was hit hard and seriously affected was "Tourism". Star hotels across major cities are shut for customers due to the country-wise lockdown too. While suspension of flights has led to no new bookings, the industry is staring at heavy losses as maintaining star hotels are expensive. Several hotels are offering takeaways through food delivery apps and keeping dine-in-facilities for guests who checked in before the lockdown came into effect. Such guests include long staying occupants on official assignments and those stranded due to curbs in movement. Changi Airport has shut one complete terminal for a year, as they don't expect traffic to grow for a year. At the moment, Chinese tourism industry is already "lifeless".

Travel and Trade restrictions in the wake of the outbreak have already caused big losses to businesses and Bloomberg reported that China may cut its economic growth expectations for 2020 due to the outbreak.

Africa has long been a source of concern, and a case in Nigeria raised fears that more infections might lurk there undetected. The pandemic has proliferated around the globe over the past week, emerging on every continent except Antarctica, prompting many governments and businesses to try to stop people travelling or gathering in crowded places.

Three-weeks after the first lockdown was announced, the rate of growth of new COVID-19 cases has come down in India. Across the states, while Kerala has led the country in containing the spread of the virus, others like Maharashtra and Madhya Pradesh have seen increases in the average daily new infections despite the lockdown.[15]

Now with all the shutdowns, another whole set of anxieties are emerging—what will happen to business, economy and jobs? At best, it will sink morale and motivation. At worst it could lead to serious mental health issues.

With hundreds of international tourists who had booked a trip to Tamil Nadu and Kerala in March and May, were forced to put off their plans due to the novel COVID-19 outbreak, has thrown the tourism sector into a crisis. With some foreign travellers could not make their trips to India due to travel restrictions from coronavirus-hit countries, many are cancelling their tour programmes due to fear and panic. There were six groups of Italian tourists each consisting of 25-27 individuals and 2 Japanese groups scheduled to visit Tamil Nadu and Kerala,[16] all of which were cancelled. Now several tour operators and hoteliers are suffering monetary losses. Due to the virus spreading across the world, the Union government had announced the people travelling from Korea, Iran, Italy, France,

Spain, United Kingdom besides North America or having a travel history to these countries since 10 February should be quarantined for 14 days on arrival in India.[17]

On an average, 8 million-plus tourists visit Goa each year; of which nearly a million are foreigners. A sizeable chunk of these foreign tourists visit casinos. The state government collected Rs. 411.44 crore as revenue in 2018-19 from offshore and onshore casinos. Due to the outbreak, the Goan government has banned locals from gambling in 14 casinos from 1 February 2020.[18] Even countries like Macau, South Korea and Vietnam have banned locals from entering casinos.

Some neighbours have closed borders and halted imports and exports. Iran had cancelled concerts and soccer matches nationwide and universities and schools closed in many countries. Airlines have restricted flights to Italy, Spain, while prices for masks and gels have skyrocketed.[19] For us, in India, air travel traffic is going to definitely take more than a month to start, and then it is going to take at least a couple of years to come back to at least 50 per cent of what we were.[20] and that depends on how many airlines survive. Once-busy airports with thousands of travellers arriving or departing are now ghost places with deserted hallways, empty parking lots and mostly blank screens showing arrivals and departures.

So much for keeping business rolling during coronavirus pandemic. The Council of Foreign Relations has cancelled a roundtable called "Doing Business Under Coronavirus" that was scheduled in New York due to the spread of the infection itself.[21]

This insidious virus has cast a pall of fear, panic and death throughout the world, catching countries without strategies to deal with and throwing international and national health organisations and governments into makeshift strategies, responding without any coordination at different rates of speed to the spread of COVID-19. In countries with large informal economies, government decrees exacerbate the crisis by introducing social distancing, lockdowns and self-isolation. Social distancing might be the best way to fight the virus, but it also means that businesses, big and small are feeling the coronavirus heat. The pandemic thus present the tourism sector with major and evolving challenges. Statistics on international air travel show that the industry has come to an abrupt halt. The cruise industry has been upended with media sources characterising ships as "ocean-going petri dishes" while showing the trauma and human tragedy of cruise ships like Ruby Princess, Zaandam and the Rotterdam.[22]

Kerala's hospitality industry is also badly struck. With business conferences, retreats and B2B meetings cancelled, room occupancy is as low as 20 per cent. Operational costs are not met.[23] Bengaluru's restaurants have seen a staggering 70 per cent decline in footfall—be it fine dining or the small *darshinis*.[24] Most hotel chains are talking of 15-30 per cent pay cuts for upper management and unpaid leave for junior staffs. It is these lower rungs who might suffer the most. Ironically now Kerala is seen as a role model in India in containing the highly pathogenic outbreak.

Pandemics have changed people to pray. Mosques are asking the faithful to pray from home; while some worshippers are coming to prayer in masks. March is festival season in Kerala but temples, including Sabarimala, have cancelled cultural programmes and feasts, holding only rituals.[25] Even the hugely popular Venkateshwara Temple in Tirupati (Tamil Nadu) had been shut down.

It was Lent, but many in Kerala parishes had cancelled daily prayers and religious heads had asked their devotees to pray from home. Even some churches had cancelled confessions and blessings by hand. In Mumbai, hugely popular Siddhivinayak and the Mumbadevi temples have shut their doors. Meanwhile, the forest department has banned tourists entry to all ecotourism destinations and national parks in Kerala. The ban will be applicable to all programmes within forests, including nature camps.[26]

For tour operators, the virus that emerged out of the blue has proved to be a double-whammy as thousands of Indians have put off their foreign trips for the summer vacation. Southeast Asian countries are the worst hit for the tourism industry while European countries are putting up travel restrictions.[27]

"It is too soon to know, but the WTTC has made a preliminary calculation in collaboration with (research firm) Oxford Economics which estimates that the crisis will cost the tourism sector at least $22 billion".[28] This calculation was based on the experience of previous crises such as SARS or H1N1, and was based on losses deriving from Chinese tourists who have not been travelling in recent weeks. Actually, the Chinese are the tourists who spend the most when they travel. The economies most likely to suffer would be those much dependent on Chinese tourism, such as Hong Kong and Macau, Thailand, Cambodia and the Philippines.[29] Cases of novel coronavirus in the Middle East have raised concern among travellers and travel agents. UAE, Kuwait, Qatar, Oman and Saudi are popular destinations for leisure travellers for summer holidays in April and May.[30] Travel and Tour operators are worried that if not contained well, travel to the Middle East could suffer like it happened to Southeast Asian destinations. Middle East is the most popular transit hub for travellers flying to Europe and the US, as people do not wait to fly via Singapore, because of the spread of the COVID-19 there. Travel to regions of Europe like Italy, Spain has been affected as students have to be told to leave.

The outbreak across the globe may impact the Everest climbing season in Nepal beginning from March with many trekkers from counties like China, South Korea, Italy and Japan cancelling their expeditions.[31] It is to be noticed that pandemics like COVID-19 would have a deeper impact than natural disasters, as people cannot predict when the pandemic would be totally over.

If the lockdown is lifted then, and flights allowed to resume, a few domestic ones could be the first to take to the skies and international flights would follow later, as and when travel restrictions ease globally on a country-by-country basis. Some airlines instead of refunding for the cancelled flights are offering vouchers for future travel within a year for the amount booked.[32] Passengers insisting on refunds face a steep cancellation fee.

Reeling from the lockdown blow, stock indices of all major stock markets have fallen because of the slowdown. Two-fifths of total passenger traffic and almost half of revenues will be wiped out in 2020, estimates the Airports council International; 20-30 per cent fewer international tourist arrivals are predicted in 2020 and will amount to losses up to $450 billion; the cancellation of all major sporting events means the entire ecosystem—sportsperson, managers, staff, broadcast crews—are staring at pay losses. According to IATA, annual loss is expected to be approximately $113-260 billion for the airline industry which will not be bearable by the airlines.

Coronavirus is spreading at a rapid pace across the world, particularly in Europe, prompting governments to mandate home quarantining. Quarantines are not particularly easy to implement—they require sacrifices and trust in the government, but also adequate infrastructure so people can safely quarantine themselves.[33]

Most shops, restaurants and tourist sites in the world's most visited country (France) are already shuttered. This April, Passover, Easter and Ramzan—touch-stone-holidays of three major religions—had collided for the first time in two decades. The Tower of David Museum has been collaboration with two virtual reality production houses—Blimey and Occupied VR—to create an immersive augmented reality experience for the crowds expected at the medieval stone citadel. But unfortunately, the pandemic shut everything down. Israel closed its borders to foreign visitors. A virtual reality experience "The Holy City" was started online for free from 9 April 2020.[34] "The Holy City", a documentary shot in stereoscopic, 360 degree virtual reality takes viewers to some of Jerusalem's most important religious events : the holy fire ceremony; the Ramzan prayers at Al Aqsa Mosque and the priestly blessings for Passover at the Western Wall.[35] The documentary consists of footage from the 2019 ceremonies as well. Also Experience Mecca used 3D modelling to give views a first-hand walk-through of Islam's holiest city and the rhythmic circumambulation of the Tawaf ritual that bookends each annual Hajj. Those who wish to drop in to Vatican City virtually can do so via Vatican's website, where a number of landmarks can be visited in 360-degree immersive panoramas produced in collaboration with Vatican and the Villanova University.

From live-streamed opera performances to 360-degree tours of tourist destinations, here is how to virtually travel during pandemics—

1. In response to New York City's ban on public gatherings, New York's Metropolitan Opera has suspended shows and live streaming past performances for free on its website every night.
2. Broadway stars have partnered with Boradway World to produce a series of virtual mini-performances. These are filmed by stars in their living rooms and posted on BroadwayWorld.com. e.g. the Indian Film Industry too has done something similar, with Amitabh Bachchan in the lead, to raise a fund to help the daily wage earners to support them in this hard times and spreading awareness of "stay home, stay safe".
3. Explore.org has hundreds of webcams set up in national parks and wildlife sanctuaries around the world and aggregates their live-streams on its website. These include Underwater Channel Islands Kelp Forest cam, Manatee cam at Florida's Blue Spring Park and the Decorah Eagles cam.
4. Google Arts and Culture, thanks to its 360-degree mapping technology,[36] offers an inside look at some of the world's most iconic attractions like Bogd Khaan Palace Museum in Mongolia, Milan Cathedral in Italy, Pyramids of Egypt, Stonehenge, Machu Picchu, Taj Mahal, etc.
5. In addition to iconic attractions, Google Arts and Culture allows users to tour the world's foremost museums in 360-degree and browse hi-res images of their collections.

6. The China Guide, a Beijing based travel agency, has developed a virtual tour of one of the great Wall of China's most iconic sections, Jinshanling to Simatai.
7. A number of zoos and aquariums around US have set up webcams in their most popular enclosures. The Houston Zoo, Monterey Aquarium and San Diego Zoo each run multiple webcams.

Now airline and travel planners are offering credit notes to customers whose travel plans have been cancelled due to the pandemic, as full refund is becoming a stretch on their finances. There is no expiry date for this credit, so one can use it for their next travel. Some are pushing their vacation to September and beyond. Some customers are willing to reschedule holiday trips post October for countries like New Zealand, Australia, Bali, Singapore; but most of them want to cancel their trips to Europe.

Right now none of the global brand hotels are ready to give guidance.[37] They expect businesses to decline 60-70 per cent.

Starting from a wet market in China's Wuhan, the novel coronavirus has reached the remote countries of the world. While many industrialized countries have managed to slow down the spread, it is the developing world that is witnessing the fastest rate of spread at present.[38] The Middle East countries are more vulnerable at present.[39] In such a scenario, the short-to medium-term outlook for the tourism industry, appears dire and demands an examination of possible effective solutions.

Some conspiracy theorists suggest "an accidental leak of a biological weapon in making could have triggered the transmission rate" which are totally false.[40] The COVID-19 pandemic has unleashed hostilities against Southeast Asians, South Asians, Blacks and Hispanics in the US and Europe. A very visible aspect of public shaming is the name attached to the disease. Everyone panics in a pandemic; but when fear grips elites and they overreact with all the resources and power at their command, it can dramatically distort the situation. Coercion and suspicion of others on the basis of religion or appearance destroys social trust, the magic potion of basic goodwill and cooperation that makes societies work.

Kerala is relatively resilient not because they have superheroes—with all due applause for its CM and health minister—but because the state has better capacities and a tradition of collective action. Its public health care is better than most, its grassroots institutional work, its communities are a strong weave. Kerala took early action, when the catastrophe striked, like sealing borders and thoroughly screening contacts and used media to show where infected people had gone, so others know if they were in danger and could ask for tests themselves. Solidarity in a crisis like pandemic or a flood is a natural response. The UNWTO and the WHO met at Geneva to coordinate response to COVID-19. UNWTO called for solid international leadership and for tourism to be included as a priority in future recovery efforts. World Health Organisation (WHO) also committed to ensure solidarity, forbearance and cooperation continue to be among the region's key weapons in the battle against COVID-19.[41]

Lessons to Learn and the Road to Recovery

We are still in the Stage II[42] of the pandemic. It is urgent that countries which have yet to experience the full brunt of the disease should observe and learn from those who have been impacted, notably China, Italy, Iran and the Republic of Korea. For future, when COVID-19 is brought under control, the government must plan on pandemics being a regular feature of national and international life. We can identify the following key factors: human populations expanding into erstwhile animal habitats; lifestyle changes including the desire for meat proteins and consuming exotic meats; spread of urbanisation; expansion of temperature controlled living environments and the frequency and volume of domestic and international travel. In sum, India must expect and prepare itself for a perfect storm. COVID-19 is a dire threat, but it can also be a trigger for cleaning up India's public health system.

During the recovery period, unlike other business sectors, tourism will take a longer time to return to normalcy because tourists need to ensure that the situation is really safe and secure before they travel again.

Three areas of reform are urgent:

1. India must ramp up public health expenditures, aiming to at least double our spending to 2.5 per cent GDP. Going by this nothing less than this will build capacity at every level of health care.
2. We need change in the relationship between caregivers and care seekers. Abusive caregivers and care seekers diminish the empathy and trust that sustain a positive health system.[43] We also need caregivers and care seekers alike to cooperate fully.
3. Reform in institutional design at every level is now essential. A whole of government approach is vital. It means jurisdictions between central, state and municipal authorities are clearly defined and simultaneously that interagency cooperative mechanisms are developed. Suasion and coordination rather than overbearing and buccaneering leadership have to steer public health within and across jurisdictions, so that buy-ins are acheieved at every level.

With the usage of appropriate safety measures and action plans one can prevent the spread of such diseases. The personnel working in the hospitality and tourism industry should be aware of this because they always need to have contact with guests from across the world. They should be provided with Personal Protective Equipment (PPE) like masks, gloves, aprons, etc. and also they should allow the employees to work from home (telecommuting) to reduce the risk of contaminating the disease.[44]

Stigma produced in the churn of a pandemic has a long afterlife. Science was supposed to liberate people from irrational beliefs by providing that pathogens don't look for a particular race or place—all they need is a human body, warm, moist and nutrient rich. Unfortunately, even the scientific understanding of hosts, vectors and carriers has been appropriated to reinforce social prejudices. The aim is to efficiently control potential mayhem.

Unfortunately, many startups will not survive the impact of the COVID-19, as we see tons of layoffs and startups have switched their full-time employees to part-time jobs.[45] At times startups quickly develop additional solutions for COVID-19 applications in the areas of prevention, detection, disruption management and operational efficiency. Sitata is another company working in disruption management. They offer mobile-based platform that provides travellers with pre-trip health and safety advice, real-time monitoring of travel disruptions and automated safety check-ins with real-time assistance. Thus airlines can learn a lot about how to better manage trip disruptions and help improve their service.

Learning from earlier pandemics, various tourism researchers have called for a proactive crisis response and management planning. Unfortunately, coordinated crisis management and communication plans are rarely implemented effectively. Pandemics have also resulted in social distancing, discrimination and misinformation among countries central to outbreaks. Even movies based on the killer viruses theme could not jolt the world.

The Indian government should also have begun a media engagement strategy, along with a multi-lingual, information campaign on every aspect of the crisis. It should revise its media and communication strategy around the COVID-19 crisis to build an atmosphere of trust, social cohesion and purpose—where the media and people are participants.

Completely shutting down everything is the only way to prevent certain outbreaks into a catastrophe. With educational institutions, and offices shut, people are trying to "reinvent family time". People gather in fours and fives for *yoga* or dance or music classes, while parents struggle to keep young kids engaged. Streaming services are in high demand, as are online schooling resources, virtual museums and operas and free online Ivy League courses.

Few business that survive will take time to recover—restaurants, transport and tourism, logistics, entertainment, automobile, real estates and consumer durable will at least take 12-24 months.[46]

The pandemic will eventually ebb. Some might look back and wonder if we overreacted. But one thing is certain: Life will never be the same again—for young and for old; for countries and for ethnicities. Lessons will be drawn both at the individual and global level. People and nations will be more circumspect and wary of each other. Some barriers and biases—both physical and mental—that have emerged during the crisis may become entrenched. Globalist and isolationists will argue more fiercely about the nature of international relations, trade and emigration.

As one prepares to hunker down and wait for such pandemics to reach its expiry date, perhaps people might turn to books, writing and old-fashioned friendships. Who knows this sense of ending might also herald a year of magical thinking!

Here are few tips to deal with pandemic anxiety:

1. Do not watch the news or read articles constantly.
2. Realise that the virus will pass.
3. Focus on what you can do productive in the lockdown days and think what you can plan to do when things get back to normal.
4. After taking all precautions, Trust God, accept His will and hope for the best.
5. StayHome #Travel Tomorrow.

Researchers across the world are racing to find a cure to the new coronavirus that has killed many. The battle is to find a vaccine that will make us immune to SARS-CoV-2, the novel coronavirus that causes COVID-19. But that can take time—maybe a year or more. It is very difficult for the world to remain in lockdown for that long. China, US and Europe have all begun clinical trials, but the global effort is underlined by the fierce competition between countries and companies to be the first to not only win the scientific accolades, the patents and the revenues, but also the first to secure a vaccine in the interest of the national security.

Whether it is aviation, or all travel-related, tourism-related industries, it is going to be in shambles for the next two years.

The stakeholders will have to "hasten slowly" to try and revive the industry.

International tourism will experience a slump and will slowly pick up pace eventually. In the long term, domestic and regional tourism will have to be our first point of call. Tourism and leisure can play a role in helping people recover and rediscover nature. To keep India's name on the tourism map we need to organise virtual events to showcase cultural and heritage resources. The Museums and the ASI can lead this process. Vested organisations, graphic designers, IT experts, film makers and photographers need to work collaboratively to digitize all these resources. We much create electronic and virtual tourism options. In this cause, small enterprises in the tourism value chain will need to be supported by state governments as they are the driving force behind the industry's recovery. Therefore to embrace digital change and to grow, the tourism sector must be "social, local and mobile". This approach can emerge as a result of the growth of smartphones and the greater local precision they provide.

Leaders in the tourism industry must take feedback and consult with their stakeholders including the final consumer. Government leadership in terms of economic policies and packages to support the aviation industry and SMEs during lockdown period is necessary to keep them on the run, till the crisis subsides or else there will be no industry to go back to post-COVID-19.

In the coming days tourism academics need to step-in and contribute to research-based, data-driven ideas and solutions to support what will be left of the tourism industry. They need to support new creativity and new opportunities that will lead to recovery. Tourism education will have to be changed entirely to reflect new realities.

Tourism depends on the environment and people. One lesson we learnt from this crisis is, it is the earth that will fight back if we do not protect it. We must reimagine what sustainable tourism is for India. Communities of people are important, as without them there is no travel and tourism too. Tourism futures must take cognizance of the fact that the earth has enough to support everyone's need if we are sustainable, but not enough to support corporate greed.

As a response to the need for sustainable and socially innovative tourism, the trend of "staycation" and "slow tourism" is growing.[47] More and more destinations are promoting regional tourism. For example, France is leading the way in establishing visitors' programmes such as #ExploreParis, Loire a Velo and Un air de Bordeaux.[48] Slow tourism seems to offer an alternative to both the hurried traveller and to the sun, sand and sea mass tourists. Slow tourism requires acceptance of a slow pace, and greater personal interaction with the locals and their culture. Advocates of this type of tourism promise a more authentic travel experience, a greater consumption of local products, preservation of heritage, use of clean energy, an ethical vision of tourism and a deeper concern for the ecology and for the quality of life of locals and visitors. This new approach to tourism could generate new businesses such as artisan and zero-kilometer markets; new micro-museums.

One thing we all do know is travel, hospitality and tourism will never be the same. It is time to "reinvent" travel and tourism for the sake of the people and planet earth. Nature has given us a change to rethink our trajectory. Work and recreation should be restructured and leisure reconfigured to prioritise well-being and equity and the long-term sustainability of the world rather than just profit and ambition. In the meantime, let us all stay at home today and dream of travel tomorrow.[49]

To conclude, such pandemics reminds us that crisis is danger and opportunity. The dangers are here; the opportunities must be seized.

Notes

1. *The Times of India*, 12 March 2020, p. 11.
2. *Sunday Times of India*, 1 March 2020, p. 1.
3. The outbreaks reached Crimea in 1345. Once the pestilence reached the major ports in Europe, it proceeded along overland routes to major cities, felling one after the other. The famous trading route that

had once brought prosperity to European cities was transferred into a highway of death that travelled in the shape of furry black rats. Thus for a period, trade almost came to a halt. Nayan Chanda, "Invisible Danger from Afar", *The Times of India*, 16 April 2020, p. 8.

4. During the First World War , Chinese labourers travelled to camps in France to dig trenches for the Allies and may have carried the virus strain that set off the pandemic. One of the major impacts of the outbreak was on the result of the war. Though the flu hit both sides, Austrians and Germans were affected so badly that the outbreak derailed their offensives.
5. One of such case was that of the Justinian's plague, the Byzantine historian Procopius of Caesarea traced the origins of the plague (the Yersinia pestis bacteria) to China and north-east India, via land and sea trade routes to Egypt where it entered the Byzantine Empire through Mediterranean ports. Even though he knew that trade played a role in the spread, he blamed the outbreak on Emperor Justinian, declaring him to be either cursed or invoking God's punishment for his evil deeds.
6. Kenneth Mohanty, "How Wuhan outbreak became 6th Global Health Emergency in 10 Years". *Sunday Times of India*, 16 February 2020, p. 2.
7. *Times of India*, 25 March 2020, p. 16.
8. SARS broke out in Guangdong Province in southern China in November 2002.
9. *The Times of India*, 3 April 2020, p. 12.
10. The first case was confirmed on 31 December 2019. The outbreak was epidemiologically linked to the Wuhan Seafood Wholesale Market involving the sale of seafood and live animals.
11. Durgesh Nandan Jha, "Conspiracy Therorists are Wrong—Coronavirus Exists in Nature..." *The Times of India*, 21 February 2020, p. 16.
12. 84 per cent of the total 80,924 confirmed cases of coronavirus in China are confined to Hubei as of 10 March 2020, the date for which WHOs latest situation report is available. *The Times of India*, 12 March 2020, p. 2.
13. 46 per cent were reported in Europe, 26 per cent were reported in Western Pacific region (from Japan to New Zealand) and 23 per cent were reported in Eastern Mediterranean.
14. Also Iran and Spain.
15. The lockdown in India came into effect from 23 March and has now extended to 3 May 2020.

16. Yogesh Kabirdas, "COVID-19 Proves a Body Blow for Inbound Tourism in State", *The Times of India*, 29 February 2020, p. 2.
17. *Ibid.*
18. *The Times of India*, 16 February 2020, p. 2.
19. Reuters, "WHO Warns of Pandemic Risk", *The Hindu*, 26 February 2020, p. 12.
20. As said by Aviation safety expert and retired airline Instructor pilot Mohan Ranganathan on 17 April 2020.
21. *The Times of India*, 12 March 2020, p. 11.
22. *The Times of India*, 19 April 2020, p. 16.
23. As said by Sooraj Ramakrishnan (Senior Sales Manager) Zuri Kumarakom.
24. Anuradha Ramam, "Hard Times", *The Hindu—Magazine*, 22 March 2020, p. 3.
25. *Ibid.*
26. In Idukki district, the CWW has directed the closure of all tourism programmes in Periyar Tiger Reserve, boating activity in Thekkady, Gavi safari and tourist accommodations. The ban is applicable to other tourism centres including Kaprikkadu Abhayaranyam, Paanamkuzhi, Nedumbarachira, Nedumbaserry Suvarnodhyanam and Ernakulam Mangalavanam. *The Times of India*, 11 March 2020.
27. Yogesh Kabirdas, "COVID-19 Proves a Body Blow for Inbound Tourism in State", *The Times of India*, 29 February 2020, p. 2.
28. *The Times of India*, 28 February 2020, p.18.
29. *Ibid.*
30. *The Times of India*, 26 February 2020, p. 2.
31. *The Times of India*, 29 February 2020, p. 2.
32. *The Times of India*, 15 April 2020, p. 8.
33. Self-quarantining possible in only 15 per cent of India's homes. *The Times of India*, 19 March 2020, p. 2.
34. Debra Kamin, "For Shut-in Pilgrims, Holiest Sites are a Click Away", *The Times of India*, 1 April 2020, p. 11.
35. *Ibid.*
36. *The Times of India*, ET Panache, 4 April 2020, p. 4.
37. Trip.com Group is the only OTA that has issued some sort of guidance.
38. US and Canada after leading the growth rates, saw considerable declines (from 26 March to 5 April), Atul Thakur, "7 Weeks that Rest the World", *The Times of India,* 14 April 2020, p. 8.
39. *Ibid.*

40. Durgesh Nandan Jha, "Conspiracy Therorists are Wrong: Coronavirus Exists in Nature..." *The Times of India*, 21 February 2020, p. 16.
41. Poonam Ketrapal Singh, "The Battle against Coronavirus", *The Times of India*, 27 February 2020, p. 12.
42. Stage 1—the first cases are reported. Several nations are still in this phase. Stage II—early containment efforts have failed to keep up with the rapid spread of the disease, by travelling. Stage III—either everyone is infected or the outbreak is brought under control with a vaccination.
43. Kanti Bajpai, "Danger and Opportunity", *The Times of India*, 21 March 2020, p. 12.
44. *Ibid.*
45. RubiQ is a Tel-Aviv based startup that helps airlines reduce significant overload on call centers and streamline passengers' rebooking and refund processes. In the current situation, process automation is key.
46. *The Times of India*, 17 April 2020, p. 1.
47. These high-end hotels are offering stay to only the local population and large discounts for overnight stays. This form of staycation offers a new and local experience to area residents offering prized services and activities that allow area travellers to maximize vacation time. *Ibid.*
48. *The Times of India*, 17 April 2020, p. 2.
49. StayHome#TravelTommorrow, WHO Initiative.

10

Terra Incognita

The Itineraries of Theyyam and Its Impact on Ecotourism in Kerala

Mallika A. Nair

Terra Incognita or *terra ignota* is a Latin term which means "unknown land" and is used in cartography to refer to regions that have not been mapped or documented. The term is used here in a connotative sense to emphasize upon those permutations and combinations of human existence with nature in eco-criticism that are yet to be mapped. The unending dominions of discrimination and power politics obdurately blur the significance of nature thereby jeopardizing all existence. The present chapter as the title indicates seeks to map new ways of perception and thought through an extensive enquiry into the ritualistic art form of Theyyam and its evolution into its present status as the most vibrant façade of Cultural Tourism in North Malabar.

Theyyam, the cultural art form of North Malabar region of Kerala has carved out a very special niche for itself in the vast annals of Kerala's tryst with ecotourism. It coalesce the different strains of Dravidian and tribal culture along with Classicism thereby transcending the narrow terrains of a mere ritualistic art form and evolving itself into its present status as an eco-critical narrative.

As Bhawani Cheerath says in her book titled *Theyyam: The Other Gods* (2012).

> ".. The warp and weft of Kerala's society is tethered to ritualistic worship and an agrarian community's organic bonding with nature. Nowhere is it as pronounced as in Theyyam." (Cheerath, 2012)

It has, in many ways, contributed towards the growth and expansion of the tourism industry in North Malabar. A closer look at the life and people of North Malabar would help us decipher the many ways in which Theyyam as an art form has integrated itself into the social fabric of the region. The ritualistic art form of Theyyam forms the cultural matrix of North Malabar and is often performed in temple premises and ancient homesteads. The performers of this folk art form belong to the lower castes and tribes of the hilly regions of Kasargode, Kannur and Waynad.

The Concept of *Kaavu* and Its Association with Theyyam

Theyyam nurtures the dance of Mother Earth through the preservation of ***Kaavu.***The Theyyam performance happens within the sanctums of the ***Kaavu*** signifying the deep ecological bonding between the two. The community of Theyyam artisans and performers proclaim themselves as living deities of this religious Humanism. Thus, a study of the ritualistic art form of Theyyam takes us to the imminent issue of protecting the sacred groves called ***Kaavu*** that gives it its sustenance, thereby attempting to redeem the dangerously tilting balance of biodiversity in the Western Ghats. Madhav Gadgil in his report to the Ministry of Environment and Forests, Government of India, says,

> "...The Western slopes of the Ghats have a natural cover of evergreen forest ... and the vegetation reaches its highest diversity towards the southern tip in Kerala with its high saturated, rich tropical rain forests." (Report of the WGEEP, 2011)

The scared groves scattered across the region are fragments of forests distributed across vast areas of land. These sacred groves are known as ***Kaavu*** in the state of Kerala and are communally protected zones of biodiversity. They are also culturally significant as they connote the religious and spiritual sentiments of the community where they exist. These sacred groves have a very important role in maintaining the environmental balance in the region. They operate as the lungs of the Western Ghats that border many of the Southern states of the country like Kerala, Karnataka and Tamil Nadu. The Western Ghats play a very important role in regulating the climate of the region thereby bringing monsoon rains to these states. These sacred groves which are approximately 500 in number soak up the rain thereby feeding the water bodies in the region and making it a treasure trove of biodiversity. The state of Kerala has witnessed some of the most devastating floods in its history since 2018. Environmentalists proclaim these to be the direct impact of the depletion and destruction of the Western Ghats, making it one of the most ecologically sensitive locales on earth.

The preface of the report of the Western Ghats Ecology Expert Panel submitted to the Ministry of Environment and Forests, Government of India, says,

> "... The Western Ghats are naturally an important focus of sustainable development efforts. The protector of the Indian peninsula, the Mother of the Godavari, Krishna, Netravathi, Kaveri, Kunthi, Vaigai and a myriad other rivers, Kalidasa likens the Western Ghats to a charming Maiden; Agastyamalai is her head, Annamalai and Nilgiri the breasts, her hips the broad ranges of Kanara and Goa, her legs the northern Sahyadris. Once the lady was adorned by a sari of rich green hues; today her mantel lies in shreds and tatters. It has been torn asunder by the greed of the elite and gnawed at by the poor, striving to eke out a subsistence. This is a great tragedy, for this hill range is the backbone of the ecology and economy of South India." (Preface to WGEEP, 2011)

The report calls for immediate action against the depletion of ecosystem in the Western Ghats.

The *Kaavu* as an Ecologically Sensitive Zone

Illegal land mining and increased human interference in the eco-sensitive zones have taken away much of the sacred groves that compliment the Western Ghats in the districts of Kannur and Kasargode in North Malabar. If culture and community are notions that compliment and complete one another, an enquiry into the various cultural nuances of the people inhabiting the area would help in deciphering the need of sustenance with the problems and necessities of real life. The sacred groves of Kerala demonstrate how the concept of environment and ecology can be comprehended in an indigenous space while evolving into a proper understanding of the climatic changes happening in the region. So, what role does ecological tourism have in the area? and how can tourism help sustain the sensitive biodiversity and environment of the region? These questions take us to a significant report on the Western Ghats, published in 2011 that calls for a participatory method of ecological conservation wherein the responsibility of sustaining the environment falls equally upon the common public, the governments at the grassroots level, complimented by the state and central governments.

As the WGEEP report states,

> "It is imperative that we involve local people and promote proper public awareness through encouragements offered to social and cultural practices that preserve and enhance biodiversity." (WGEEP, 2011)

The North Malabar regions of Kannur and Kasargode is home to more than 500 such sacred groves, out of which approximately 250 of these cover an area of more than three acres of land. These extensive expanse of forest cover assists in controlling soil erosion. They act as natural sponges in absorbing water and helps meet the water requirements of the region. The ***Kaavu*** helps rejuvenate groundwater resources as they harbour many water bodies like streams and ponds. They also act as hotspots of biodiversity wherein the flaura and fauna take refuge from vanishing ecosystems. Thus, preservation of the Sacred Groves of North Malabar becomes all the more urgent.

Role of Theyyam in Ecological Sustenance

It is here that the ritualistic art form of Theyyam gains importance in the regional context of North Malabar. Theyyam can well be stated as a cultural performance/phenomenon that in the contemporary age have also become a means of economic sustenance to its performers. But the commercialisation of this ritualistic art form does not seem to be doing justice to the sustenance of biodiversity of the region. The vast forest areas are today vanquished and destroyed to create structures out of cements that in no way compliments the art form itself. The *Kaavu* or sacred groves are fast vanishing from sight and what remains are just residues of a few spruce trees. The efforts of cultural tourism in the area should be to reconnect this ancient art form to its primitive roots thereby encouraging a return to its primal and pristine past. This means that Theyyam performances taking place within the sanctum of a *Kaavu* would help regenerate within the spectator awe for Supreme Nature. It is this deep ecological sentiment that cultural tourism should foreground through ritualistic art forms like Theyyam. Each Theyyam performance is a gentle reminder of man's intimate connection with his roots and the soil that sustains his life. Theyyam narratives like the *Muchilottu Bhagavathy* Theyyam signify the regeneration of life through earth's seasonal cycles. The Theyyam returns each year to bless the soil and its children with the bounties of a good crop yield and health and happiness to the people. The very essence of ritualistic folk art forms like Theyyam lies in its ability to address the core of man's existence on earth and his beliefs that govern his life. Narratives like Theyyam are born out of the myths of a region. Theorists like Ruthven remarks, "The term 'Myth' has gained acceptance as standing for an elusive, almost unanalysable, amalgam of beliefs, attitudes and feelings." (*Myth,* 1976). The very idea of a *Kaavu* or sacred grove implies a group or collective of 9 to 15 trees, which were considered divine for their life saving medicinal purposes. These huge trees in their own power sustain a subsystem of flora and fauna, thereby creating a cumulative forest cover. So, the very idea of divinity associated with a sacred grove could have been one of environmental sustenance and preservation of biodiversity. The great forefathers of a community abstained human interference within these groves by indulging the human mind in beliefs and fears associated with the divine presence of wrathful deities within its deep and mysterious sanctum sanctorum. The intricacies of the human mind that harboured the ancient fear of the unknown must have contributed to his reverence of these dense forests. It is from these sacred groves that thousands of rivulets emerge to form the rich water bodies of rivers and the life line of a community.

Conclusion: Ecology and Ecotourism

Thus, although recent trends in tourism industry believe in the demystification of rituals associated with folk art forms like Theyyam, it could indeed contribute towards a more meaningful communication between a culture and its people by emphatically rooting the performer and his performance in its natural space. Rather, in more simple terms, to try not to remove Theyyam from its original locales and move it to the sophisticated quadrangles of theatrical performance. Theyyam has from time immemorial been the façade of North Malabar and its identity to the world. Ecotourism and exercises that indulge in nature treks as well as measures such as documentary/film festivals to showcase and spread profound awareness of the biodiversity of the Western Ghats will, no doubt, help one of the most vibrant natural resources of the Indian subcontinent from being extinct. Demarcating areas close to the sacred groves as plastic free zones and preservation of natural water bodies will also go a long way in preserving the environment. Tourism can definitely help in the economic as well as ecological sustenance of the local community. and a regeneration of ritualistic art forms like Theyyam can indeed, return man to a more pristine future. Environmental policies of the world are best implemented locally and in short span of time. It is indeed the need of the hour that the Western Ghats and its signature of Sacred Groves be preserved as a model on how local measures for the conservation of ecology can be applied globally to curb environmental issues like global warming. An icon like the young Environmentalist Greta Thunberg reminds us that the end is not far.

The Western Ghats needs us to preserve it even as we need the Western Ghats for our own survival. Theyyam and tourism might as well be the means of charting a route map to attain this sublime goal.

References

Cheerath, Bhavani & Rajesh Komath (2012). *Theyyam: The Other Gods*. Banglore: Stark World Publishing, Print.

Dorairaj, A. Joseph (2003). *Myth and Literature*. Folklore Resources and Research Centre (FRRC), Palayamkottai, Print.

Gadgil, Madhav (2011). *Report of the Western Ghats Ecology Expert Panel*. Submitted to the Ministry of Environment and Forests, Government of India.

Nair, Mallika (2018). *Component* (2), Stride UGC Major Research Project Proposal.

Narayanan, Aju. (2006). "Theyyam Padanathinu Our Naveena Vazhy", *Kelyi*. Vol. 110, October-November.

Ruthven, K.K. *Myth*. London: Methuen and Co. Ltd., 1976. Print.

11
Factors Affecting the Sustainable Ecotourism Development amongst the Tourism Service Providers in São Paulo, Brazil

Bijith George Abraham, Glen T. Hvenegaard, Varghese Manaloor and *Hugo Narumiya*

Introduction

Brazil is the fifth largest country in the world and has abundant natural and cultural heritage resources. As the ninth wealthiest economy in the world, the country has experienced significant economic growth, especially in the service sectors (UNCTAD, 2016). Tourism in Brazil has become a significant contributor to economic development and employment generation (OECD, 2018). After hosting the 2014 FIFA World Cup, Paralympic Games, and the Rio 2016 Olympics, the country experienced a significant increase in tourist arrivals. The country witnessed 6.62 million international tourist arrivals in the year 2018, which was the largest in its history (UNWTO, 2019). São Paulo and Rio de Janeiro are the two destinations most visited by tourists (Brazil's Ministry of Tourism, 2019). In 2017, the Brazilian tourism industry placed 16th worldwide in terms of tourism spenders (UNWTO, 2018). Considering the significance of the tourism industry, Brazil has opportunities in sustainable tourism development involving local communities, service providers, and businesses.

The tourism industry of the country is growing because of its comparative advantage in natural habitats that provide opportunities for ecotourism, adventure travel, cultural-historic tourism, and sun and beach tourism. According to UNESCO, Brazil has the richest biodiversities in the world, which provide ample options for biodiversity conservations and implementing large-scale reforms as enacted in the Sustainable Development Goals of the United Nations 2030 Agenda (UNESCO, 2018). Consequently, the Brazilian government is making efforts to facilitate the situation by implementing legal instruments for best practices. The approaches will help keep checks and balances and encourage community participation in decision making that will help with conservation of natural environments.

As a community participatory approach for nurturing tourism, ecotourism is a viable option (TIES, 2015). Ecotourism is one of the strongest growing subsectors of the tourism industry emerging extensively in the natural areas, is dependent on protected areas and is also a critical source of income for many countries (Hakim, 2017). This subsector of tourism is built on the goals of sustainability, environmental protection, and education (TIES, 2015; McCool, 1995). With abundant naturally endowed tourist locations and year round pleasant weather, the Brazilian tourism industry has great potential to increase the level of ecotourism, and to support the goals of ecotourism.

The ecotourism destinations require more attention in addition to the natural acquisitions and resource endowments. It is very important to understand the role of small entrepreneurs as service providers (or the tour companies) for providing ample options for tourist preferences. These entrepreneurs can help in ensuring the protection of environment, revenue generation, conservation education, and community development (Jones and Spadafora, 2016). The local community helps provide and facilitate destination management through their involvement in decision making and park management activities (Mequanint and Gebremedhin, 2015). These efforts invariably support environmental conservation, increases community participation in management and enables social entrepreneurs to simplify tourism and its development to become more sustainable (Drăgoi, *et al.*, 2017).

The role of the tourism service providers (tour companies) is critical in promoting the tourism network of Brazil. However, one of the greatest challenges for these service providers is to incentivize sustainable development in practice. To attain this objective, the service facilitators should practice the norms and regulations associated with ecotourism. These sustainability practices may eventually result in nature protection, visitor enjoyment and support to local communities through income and employment. Tourism marketing alliances can also play a crucial role in facilitating sustainability policies and practices of ecotourism service providers.

The integration of Information Communication Technologies (ICTs) have resulted in advancement in the tourism industry and the provision of tailored experiences to the tourists. The interest of customers is matched and customised, as ICT provides instant information about the tourism destination and tourism products. Marketing through such media also plays a significant role in facilitating sustainability policies and practices of ecotourism. The sustainability goals of the ecotourism programme led by these web-based service providers could be advanced by joint initiatives between the government and the industry to implement standards to certify the ecotourism industry as protected areas. The cooperative programmes between the government and the private sector could incentivize education, information, and marketing for service providers. However, the pace of change will depend on improvements in governance, enforcement of laws, and certification of the programmes to regulate environmental damage of Brazilian ecosystems from tourism exploration and associated issues. The chapter attempts to examine the characteristics, outcomes, conservation goals, certification standards and quality of the web-based ecotourism service providers to meet sustainability practices in the State of São Paulo, Brazil.

Review of Literature

Ecotourism focuses on nature-based tourism-related activities that result in minimum damage to the environment, educate tourists, and helps local communities (McCool, 1995). In general, it has a significant association to conservation and sustainability development "that meets the needs of the present without compromising the ability of future generations to meet their own needs" (World Commission on Environment and Development, 1987). The concept of sustainable development is important as it provides environmental protection (Sharpley, 2010), greater priority to community participation, avenues for employment, methods to alleviate poverty (Neto, 2003), and also opportunities to increases export revenues (UNEP, 2013). It is therefore associated with the impacts included in the "triple bottom line" elements (i.e., economic, social and environmental aspects) in addressing the needs of the visitor, industry, and the local community (UNWTO, 2015). As sustainable tourism minimises the negative externalities to the environment and culture and also generates local income (UNEP, 2013).

To enhance the sustainability of ecotourism destinations, it is essential to understand the travel behaviour of the tourists, including their tour activities, satisfaction levels, and the decision to revisit (Rajasenan, Manaloor and Abraham, 2012). Each tourism destination should strive to protect natural resources, preserve nature through local community involvement, and educate tourists about nature (TIES, 2015). This is because the tourism industry is often blamed for environmental and sociocultural damages (McCool and Moisey, 2008). Ecotourists, thus motivated to learn about nature and their decisions are determined primarily by their special interests (Hall and Weiler, 1992). Such practices should be beneficial to the local community for ensuring environmental protection (UNEP, 2013).

Given the need for sustainability of resources and the potential for considerable achievements to environmentally conscious tourists to avoid negative impacts, many tourism stakeholders are proposing or implementing certification schemes (Spenceley, 2019). Such certification systems assure customers that the practices rendered by the service providers adhere to minimum standards (Toth, 2002). Honey and Rome (2001) define certification as "a voluntary procedure that assesses, audits, and gives written assurance that a facility, product, process, or service meets specific standards. It awards a marketable logo to those that meet or exceed baseline standards".

Ideally, ecotourism operators voluntarily conform to the standards agreed upon by the industry or an independent body. The goal of an ecotourism certification programme is to enhance sustainability practices, provide consumers information about sustainability practices, support marketing practices of companies, and to create opportunities for education and networking (Mazilu, Marinescu, & Gheorgheci, 2017; Font 2007; Issaverdis 2001). The benefit of certification is to ensure sustainability of ecotourism marketing through service providers (Medina, 2005) and to establish responsibility between the various stakeholders (McGahey, 2012). However, there are diverging objectives between the certified and non-certified service providers in tourism promotions (Bustam, Buta and Stein, 2012). Many countries and ecotourism sectors have implemented certification programmes with varying levels of success (Font, 2007).

The UNWTO (2004) suggests that indicators for ecotourism certification should focus on environmental conservation, preservation of local communities and their assets, reduction of negative impacts, education and interpretation, marketing and management, and safety. There are many issues to consider in any certification system, including the establishment of a body to administer the system, industry or government leadership, selection of indicators, measure and implement improvements apply standards to a wide variety of settings and operations (Issaverdis, 2001). In addition, there are real costs of administering a certification system, which requires certain degree of self-regulatory monitoring.

There are several opportunities and challenges for the ecotourism industry (GEC, 2007). The recent growth of the tourism sector is the result of significant advancement in information technology for marketing (Lai and Shafer, 2005). Tourists use information available on Internet sites to learn about the place and service providers. The web-based connectivity and multidimensional information available online has helped promote tourism destinations much more than a single-dimensioned promotion with traditional leaflets or brochures (Donohoe and Needham, 2008). Given the fact that information needs to be up to date, it is important to improve online marketing and publicity to meet the needs of nature tourists and the host community's expectations on a continuous basis (Sangpikul, 2010).

Despite widespread interest in ecotourism certification systems, there are several operational limitations. These limitations include the slow implementation by the private sector, lack of resources related to the marketing of certification programmes, lack of recognition for high-achieving operators, costs of becoming a member of the programme, lack of ongoing benefits for certified operators, the abundance of certification programmes leading to confusion among consumers, fake certification, and the institutionalisation of certification programmes (Font *et al.*, 2003; Medina, 2005; Jamal *et al.*, 2006; Spenceley and Bien, 2013). Moreover, there are concerns regarding the perceptions of certification programmes that are fully and regularly monitored (Font, 2007), which can lead to the successful implementation of guiding practices seeking consistent approaches from the government for tourism development (Fogle and Duffy, 2018).

Several researchers have looked at the perceptions of tourists about the certification programmes. Esparon *et al.* (2014), examined the importance of certification programmes and the performance of certified operators. Conaghan, Hanrahan, and Sligo (2010), reviewed the awareness and perception of a sustainable eco-certification programme on the importance of an international accreditation body for ensuring credibility and confidence in the system. The perception of the stakeholders also highlights the need for a globally recognized label for certification. Margaryan and Stenstad (2017) found that adoption of eco-certification by nature-based tourism companies in Scandinavia depended on their beliefs in the positive outcomes of certification, along with lifestyle, orientation towards sustainability, and organisational context.

Overall, there remains a research need to demonstrate the impact of certification schemes among the service providers related to sustainable ecotourism development. This study proposes that an eco-certification scheme, as represented by membership in an ecotourism organisation, will produce greater number of sustainability practices for members than non-members. The research question motivating this study was: How do ecotourism operators in the State of São Paulo promote their businesses through web-based marketing? More specifically, how do ecotourism operators emphasize sustainability practices?

Materials and Methods

We chose the State of São Paulo as a case study because this state is a central hub for ecotourism activities in Brazil. In addition, the city of São Paulo attracts a large number of national and international visitors. By 2017, the number of international visits to the city rose to 2.7 million foreign tourists, which is 17 per cent of the country's overseas tourists (São Paulo Turismo, 2018). of the 65 national tourism destinations, 12 are located in the state of São Paulo (Brazilian Ministry of Tourism, 2009). Beaches were the most visited destinations, followed by interior and historical cities (Government of São Paulo State Division of Tourism, 2011).

For analysis, we used the web pages of ecotourism operators operating in the state of São Paulo. We searched through various tourism and ecotourism portals as well as operator lists provided by the state government, national government, several tourism and natural history organisations. We initially used the keywords "ecotourism", "sustainable tourism", "operators", "firm" and "São Paulo". Keywords such as ecotourism and sustainable tourism proved to be too broad for the search, so the study collected an additional list of tourism operators certified by the Brazilian Association of Ecotourism Firms and Adventure Tourism (ABETA).

ABETA is the largest certification body in Brazil in nature and adventure tourism with 140 tourism enterprises as members (ABETA, 2015). In total, we found web pages from 110 ecotourism operators which had indicated that their firm was located in the State of São Paulo.

We used content analysis (Weber, 1990) of the entire text on each web page to maintain the semantic consistency of texts as units. Segments of each web page were classified using dichotomous questions based on:

- Certification in ABETA (yes/no)
- Activities offered (yes/no for each activity)
- Sustainability (yes/no for each item)
  - ❖ **Educational:** provide guides, provide pre-tour information provided, address conservation issues, provide an area map, and connect with local curricula,
  - ❖ **Environmental:** provide a mission statement, donate to sustainability causes, provide opportunities for tourists to donate, indicate water conservation programmes, indicate recycling programmes, indicate wildlife and agricultural conservation programmes, indicate research programmes, and use eco-friendly buildings,
  - ❖ **Social:** describe history and culture, indicate family connections, discuss benefits for community, highlight identity and culture,
  - ❖ **Economic:** indicate local ownership and local employment.
- Other: awards won, limit on the number of tourists in each group (yes/no)
- Location of activities (natural/artificial)

We used factor analysis to identify the underlying factors. Eighteen variables (Recycling programmes, Energy conservation programmes, Water conservation programmes, Wildlife/ Agricultural/Conservation programmes, Eco-friendly buildings, Identity & Culture, History & Culture, Tourist interaction, Local Ownership, Benefits & Community, Mission Statement, Etiquette, Research programmes, Donations to society, Opportunity for Tourist to donate, Provides Guides, Eco-Tour Information,

Activities/Training/Guides) were used in the factor analysis to identify the factors that illustrate the specific goals of the service providers. We also used a logistic regression model to ascertain the pertinent factors associated in the certification aspect of the ecotourism operators/service providers. Instead of a classical multiple regression model, a logistic regression model is used because of the nature of the dependent variable (dichotomous variable, binary variable). The dependent variable is non-linearly linked to independent variables while its logit is linear. The regression model helps ascertain the strength of relationship between the dependent and independent variables.

Results and Discussion

Out of the 110 ecotourism service providers, 69 were certified (62.7%) and 41 were non-certified (37.3%). Altogether, 44 ecotourism activities were identified from the selected 110 service providers. of these activities, 13 were offered by the certified operators, 8 activities were offered only by non-certified operators, and 23 were common for both certified and non-certified operators

Fig.11.1: Ecotourism activities offered by certified and non-certified tourism operators in São Paulo State, Brazil.

Source: Compiled from the Data.

(Fig. 11.1). Regarding the location of the ecotourism programme, 21 activities were offered in natural zones, 7 activities were offered in artificial zones, and 16 activities were offered in both zones (Fig. 11.2).

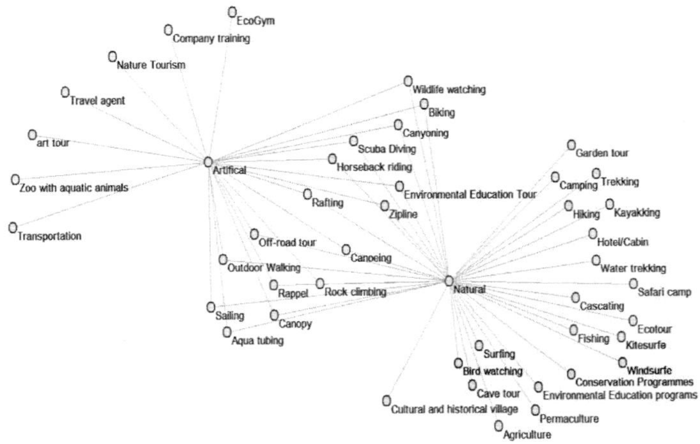

Fig. 11.2: Ecotourism activities by location type in São Paulo State, Brazil. *Source*: Compiled from the Data.

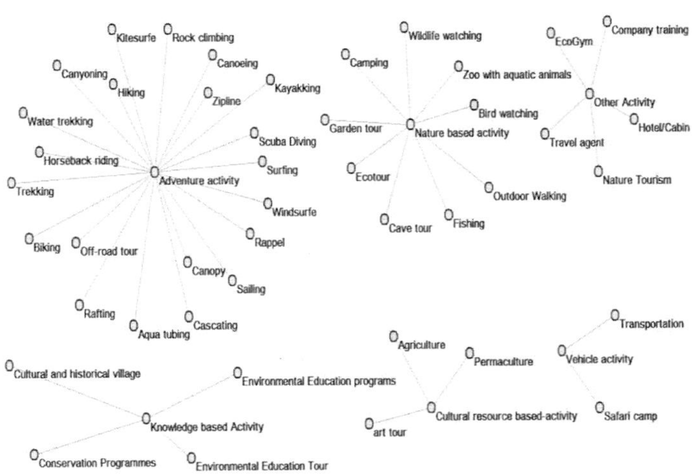

Fig. 11.3: Categories of ecotourism activities at São Paulo, Brazil. *Source*: Compiled from the Data.

We classified the information regarding the activities offered by the service providers (372 in total) into six categories (Fig. 11.3). of these categories, the adventure category had the most activities, followed by nature-based activities, knowledge-based, vehicle-based, cultural-based, and other activities. The dominance of adventure-based and nature-based activities is not surprising given that these activities occur in ecosystems and landscapes that are rich and diverse.

We also used CHAID (Chi-square Automatic Interaction Detector) tree diagram to understand interaction between variables. CHAID is a visual decision tree technique that can be used for prediction, classification, as well as to determine interaction between variables. It allows to predict how responses to some variables affect other variables. In the CHAID tree diagram (Fig. 11.4), there is no significant difference between the types of activities and whether or not that activities are offered by a certified operator (p = 0.210, chi-square = 7.145). In total, certified operators offer 69.4 per cent of the overall activities, compared to only 30.6 per cent for the non-certified operators. Figure 11.4 also shows the range of activities offered by certified and non-certified operators.

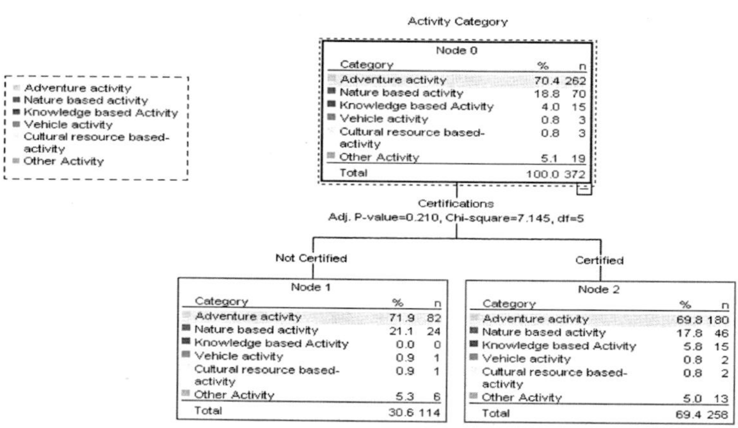

Fig. 11.4: Activity category by certification status.

There were significant differences in the kinds of activities by location (natural or artificial). About 21 activities are offered only in natural locations, 7 activities are offered only in artificial locations and 16 activities are offered in both locations. Table 11.1 shows that 86.8 per cent of the programmes were conducted in the natural settings. There were significant differences in the kind of activities by zones (natural or artificial). The adventure-based activities constituted 74.9 per cent of the total natural zone activities and only 40.9 per cent of the artificial zone activities.

Table 11.1: Activity and zone area of ecotourism destinations in São Paulo, Brazil

Activity Category	Number	Zone (Number)		Zone (%)	
		Natural	Artificial	Natural	Artificial
Adventure activity	262	242	20	74.9	40.8
Nature-based activity	70	62	8	19.2	16.3
Knowledge-based Activity	15	14	1	4.3	2
Vehicle activity	3	1	2	0.3	4.1
Cultural resource-based activity	3	2	1	0.6	2
Other Activity	19	2	17	0.6	34.7
Total	372	323	49	86.80	13.20
Chi-Square Tests—Activity category and Zone			Sig.		0.000
			Chi-Square		113.059

Source: Compiled from the Data.

Overall 86.8 per cent of ecotourism destinations were located in natural settings compared to 13.2 per cent in artificial locations (Table 11.1). Table 11.2 indicates that 67.8 per cent (219 activities out of 323 programmes) of the natural zone activities located in natural areas were certified. However, 79.6 per cent, (i.e. 39 activities out of 49) of activities in the artificial zone were certified. This highlights the significance of certified activities like hotel/

cabin, travel agents, parks, zoos, and gardens in sustainability practices. Altogether, 258 out of the total 372 activities were offered by certified operators.

Table 11.2: Certifications by zone preference

Certifi-cation	Zone					
	Natural		Artificial		Total Number	Total in %
	Number	Per cent	Number	Per cent		
Not Certified	104	32.2	10	20.4	114	30.6
Certified	219	67.8	39	79.6	258	69.4
Total	**323**	**100.0**	**49**	**100.0**	**372**	**100.0**
	86.8		**13.2**		**100.0**	

Source: Compiled from the Data.

The data further highlights the significance of the certification and zone preference based on the activities of the service providers (Fig. 11.5). Fig. 11.5a shows activity category by certification status (certified and non-certified) and Fig. 11.5b shows activity category by location of the activities (natural and artificial zones). The majority of the operators are certified and offer activities conducted in natural settings.

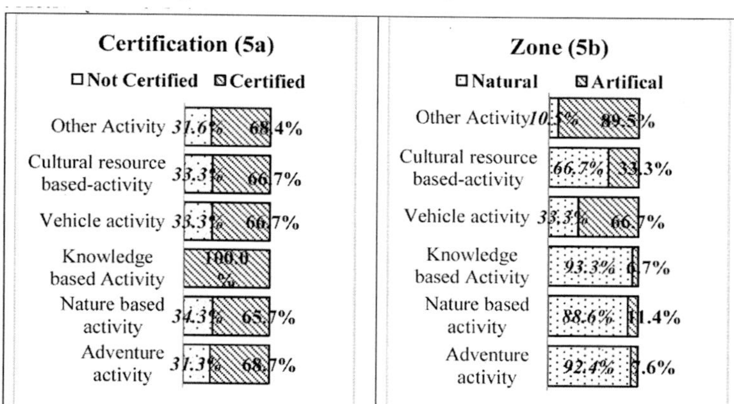

Fig. 11.5: Activity, certification and zone area of the destinations in São Paulo, Brazil.

Source: Compiled from the Data.

Table 11.3: Total variance explained with factor analysis

Component	Initial Eigen values			Extraction Sums of Squared Loadings			Rotation Sums of Squared Loadings		
	Total	% of Variance	Cumulative %	Total	% of Variance	Cumulative %	Total	% of Variance	Cumulative %
1	5.539	30.770	30.770	5.539	30.770	30.770	3.241	18.008	18.008
2	2.295	12.752	43.522	2.295	12.752	43.522	2.873	15.962	33.970
3	1.568	8.712	52.234	1.568	8.712	52.234	2.155	11.973	45.943
4	1.360	7.557	59.791	1.360	7.557	59.791	1.961	10.895	56.837
5	1.197	6.651	66.442	1.197	6.651	66.442	1.729	9.605	66.442

Ecotourism goals of the Service Providers

In order to understand the main factors that nurture the ecotourism goals of the service providers in São Paulo, Brazil, 18 statements were included in a factor analysis. The Cronbach's alpha coefficient of the selected variable was 0.861, which indicates high reliability since it exceeded the minimum standard of 0.70 (Tavakol and Dennick, 2011). To measure the strength of the relationship among variables, the Kaiser-Meyer-Olkin measure of sampling adequacy was 0.778, which is greater than the generally accepted minimum of 0.50 (Burns and Burns, 2008). The Bartlett's test was significant (approximate Chi-Square of 847.112, df = 153, $p < 0.001$). Therefore, it was appropriate to perform a factor analysis on these data.

The factor analysis revealed five factors with Eigen value greater than 1; these factors accounted for 66.4 per cent of the total variance (Table 11.3). Initially in the extracted sum of squared loadings, the first factor explained about 30.8 per cent, the second factor explained about 12.8 per cent, the third factor explained 8.7 per cent, the fourth factor explained 7.5 per cent, and the last factor explained about 6.7 per cent of the total variance. Later, the total amount of variance accounted in the extracted solution was redistributed over to the five extracted factors in the rotated sum of

Table 11.4: Rotated Component Matrix[a]—Factor Analysis

	Component				
	1	**2**	**3**	**4**	**5**
Recycling programmes	**.798**	.082	.005	.135	.196
Energy conservation programmes	**.776**	.169	.162	.234	.029
Water conservation programmes	**.708**	.176	.390	.025	-.124
Wildlife/Agricultural/ Conservation programmes	**.692**	.319	.016	.065	-.218
Eco-friendly buildings	**.621**	-.060	-.148	.317	.248
Identity & Culture	.098	**.874**	.234	.060	.146
History & Culture	.113	**.831**	.221	.057	.039
Tourist interaction	.129	**.735**	.019	.048	.238

(*Contd.*)

	Component				
	1	**2**	**3**	**4**	**5**
Local Ownership	.251	**.609**	.175	.361	.131
Benefits & Community	.078	.201	**.728**	.062	-.056
Mission Statement	-.198	.069	**.691**	.187	.160
Etiquette	.282	.176	**.630**	-.031	.287
Research programmes	.453	.125	**.554**	-.023	.097
Donations to society	.218	.108	-.012	**.896**	-.034
Opportunity for Tourist to donate	.206	.139	.218	**.859**	-.067
Provides Guides	-.071	.079	.055	-.017	**.839**
Eco-Tour Information	.067	.253	.238	.038	**.606**
Activities/Training/Guides	.324	.377	.028	-.244	**.519**

Extraction Method: Principal Component Analysis.
Rotation Method: Varimax with Kaiser Normalisation.
a. Rotation converged in 6 iterations.

squared loadings with the percentage of variance for the first factor at 18.0 per cent, the second factor at 16.0 per cent, the third factor at 12.0 per cent, the fourth factor at 10.9 per cent, and the last factor at 9.6 per cent of the total explained (cumulative) variance of 66.4 per cent.

The rotated component matrix (Table 11.4) represented the rotated factor loading which shows the weight and correlation between the variables and the factor. In the rotated component matrix of the factor analysis, the factors were explained based on the factor loadings of 0.5 and above. The first factor was labelled "Environmental sustainability" since it included variables relevant to the conservation of waste, energy, water, wildlife, and more. The second factor was labelled "Sociocultural sustainability" since it included variables such as identity and culture, history, tourist interaction, and local ownership, which shows the assurance of promoting and preserving the sociocultural aspect of the community. The third factor was labelled "Conduct and ethical operations", since it included variables such as benefits to the community, mission statement, etiquette, and research programmes. The fourth factor was "Economic contributions", since the variables such as operator donations and opportunity for tourists to donate clearly depict another important aspect of ecotourism which promote and generate revenue from tourist visits to benefit the community. The last factor was "Education and Interpretation" which included variables such as guides, eco-tour information, and guide training.

Certification Criteria of the Ecotourism Programme

To further understand the variables associated with ecotourism certification amongst the service providers, a logistic regression model was used to estimate the predicted dependent variable "ecotourism certification" using the pertinent independent variables. The model predicted the logit that was the rate of change in the "log odds" as X changes. The calculated exp (B) was the expected effect of the independent variable on the "odds ratio", which was the probability of the event divided by the probability of the non-event and they were in log-odds units.

The prediction equation was:

$$\log (p/(1-p)) = b_0 + b_1 \times x_1 + b_2 \times x_2 + b_3 \times x_3 + b_4 \times x_4 + b_5 \times x_5 + b_6 \times x_6 \quad \dots (1)$$

In this model, p was the predicted probability of being included in an ecotourism certification programme, and each x was a predictor variable included in the model (i.e. "type of destinations for ecotourism", "criteria for environmental conservation", "sociocultural assets for the community", "provision for education and interpretations", "conduct and ethical operations of the firm"; and "economic contributions from the tourist as donations").

Table 11.5: Variables in the Equation

		B	S.E.	Wald	df	Sig.	Exp (B)
Step 0	Constant	.521	.197	6.968	1	.008	1.683

As a precondition to use the logistic regression model for model prediction, it was important to test the hypothesis whether the constant term is significantly different from zero. The Wald Chi-square test in Table 11.5 examines the null hypothesis that "the constant is equal to 0". From the test it was evident that the constant in the equation was significant with p-value <0.008 and thus we rejected the null hypothesis.

Table 11.6: Hosmer and Lemeshow Test: Ecotourism Certification

Step	Chi-square	df	Sig.
1	10.175	8	.253

Next, we determined the overall fit of the model using the Hosmer and Lemeshow test (Table 11.6). As per the condition of "non-significance" for a favourable outcome, the p-value (0.253) was higher than the significance level (0.05). We concluded than the model fit the observed dataset. Hence, the model predictions could be determined with the given variables.

Table 11.7: Classification Table[a,b]: Ecotourism Certification

<table>
<tr><th colspan="3" rowspan="3">Observed</th><th colspan="3">Predicted</th></tr>
<tr><th colspan="2">Ecotourism Certification</th><th rowspan="2">Percentage Correct</th></tr>
<tr><th>no</th><th>yes</th></tr>
<tr><td rowspan="3">Step 0[a,b]</td><td rowspan="2">Ecotourism Certification</td><td>No</td><td>0</td><td>41</td><td>.0</td></tr>
<tr><td>Yes</td><td>0</td><td>69</td><td>100.0</td></tr>
<tr><td>Overall Percentage</td><td></td><td></td><td></td><td>62.7</td></tr>
<tr><td rowspan="3">Step 1[b]</td><td rowspan="2">Ecotourism Certification</td><td>No</td><td>13</td><td>28</td><td>31.7</td></tr>
<tr><td>Yes</td><td>4</td><td>65</td><td>94.2</td></tr>
<tr><td>Overall Percentage</td><td></td><td></td><td></td><td>70.9</td></tr>
</table>

a. Constant is included in the model.
b. The cut-off value is 0.500.

Table 11.7 shows the per cent of cases that were correctly predicted by the model increased from 62.7 per cent in the constant model to 70.9 per cent in the full model.

Table 11.8: Variables in the Equation

		B	S.E.	Wald	df	Sig.	Exp (B)
Step 1[a]	Type of Destination	.060	.533	.013	1	.910	1.062
	Education/ Interpretation	.527	.267	3.891	1	.049	1.693
	Environment/ Conservation	.417	.194	4.627	1	.031	1.517
	Sociocultural	.238	.223	1.132	1	.287	1.268
	Conduct/ Ethics	-.584	.273	4.579	1	.032	.558
	Economic contributions	-.105	.639	.027	1	.869	.900
	Constant	-.409	.818	.250	1	.617	.664

a. Variable(s) entered on step 1: Type of Destination, Education/Interpretation, Environment/Conservation, Sociocultural, Conduct/Ethics, Economic contributions.

We assumed a desired significance level less than 0.05. In Table 11.8, the variables of education/interpretation, and environment conservation positively contributed the model, whereas conduct and ethical operations of the company were less important in the model. The coefficient for education/interpretation says that, holding the type of destination, environmental conservation, sociocultural, conduct and ethics, and economic contributions at a fixed value, we will see a 84.46 per cent increase in the odds of being included in an ecotourism certification programme, for a one-unit increase in education/certification score since exp (0.527) = 1.693. Similarly, keeping type of destination, education/interpretation, sociocultural, conduct and ethics, and economic contributions at a fixed level, we would see a 63.59 per cent increase in the odds of being included in an ecotourism certification programme, for a one-unit increase in environmental conservation score since exp (0.417)=1.517. However, a 1 per cent increase in conduct/ethics predictor variable, while keeping all other predicator variables at a fixed level, would lead to a 82.01 per cent decrease in the odds of being included in an ecotourism certification since exp (-0.584)

= 0.558. All, the remaining predictor variables were statistically insignificant in the model. Hence, the model establishes that the service providers were giving prior importance to the sustainability aspects of ecotourism.

The fitted logistic regression equation was:

$$\log(p/(1-p)) = -0.409 + 0.060 \times \text{type of destinations} + 0.527 \times \text{education and interpretations} + 0.417 \times \text{environmental conservation} + 0.238 \times \text{sociocultural assets} - 0.584 \times \text{conduct and ethical} - 0.105 \times \text{economic contributions} \quad \ldots (2)$$

The activities of the ecotourism service providers were prioritised based on the certification and the location of the programmes. This eco-certification system presumed a well-planned ecotourism network. This will ultimately result in standardised eco-labelling, improved tourist value, facilitate education and interpretation, enhance local communities, identify sociocultural and environmental impacts, and promote sustainable use of natural environments (McCool, 1995; TIES, 2015). Hence, we demonstrate that the ecotourism certification is related to the sustainability efforts vis-à-vis providing conservation goals to the environment and educating ecotourists.

Limitations and Future Research

The study's limitations include the method of collecting data from the service providers' websites. No efforts were made to verify the accuracy of the information that service providers posted on their website. Nor, did we try to find out if the website was being updated on a regular basis. The study focused only on information available on the websites. No surveys of service providers or tourists were conducted to determine accuracy of information on websites. Also, most websites from which information was collected and analysed were in Portuguese. We depended on our Research Intern (HN) who was fluent in Portuguese. A survey-based research could be of help for future research.

The results in this study are based on information related to certification provided by service providers' websites. A survey based future research could help verify and determine satisfaction among ecotourists. Potential focus could be on questions such as: (1) Does certification lead to an increase in number of visitors wanting to experience ecotourism opportunities? (2) What impact does the certification have on biophysical characteristics of the ecotourism sites? and (3) How do service provider's and visitors perceive certification programmes? (4) Are customers satisfied with the experiences based on information they found on the websites?

Conclusion

The study illustrates the main characteristics that link ecotourism certification, sustainability activities, and ecotourism service providers in São Paulo, Brazil. We offer two main conclusions. First, the activities associated with the ecotourism programme were strongly related to certification. The majority of ecotourism operators, 62.7 per cent, were certified service providers, and 69.4 per cent of the total activities of the service providers were certified activities; in addition, 86 per cent of the ecotourism activities occurred in natural settings. Out of the total 44 activities, 13 were offered only by certified providers.

Second, the results from the factor analysis showed that environmental conservation was the foremost goal of the service providers followed by the sociocultural, conduct and ethics, economic contributions, and education and interpretation. The factor analysis also identified the pertinent factors by making use of a model for certification criteria of the service providers. The variables of environmental conservation and provision of education and interpretation positively contributed the model, highlighting the importance of sustainability aspects of ecotourism, rather than just profit motivations. Based on the factor loading results, eco-tourist service providers gave importance to "Environmental sustainability", "Sociocultural sustainability", "Conduct and ethical operations", "Economic contributions", and "Education and Interpretation".

Certification for ecotourism operators can help promote sustainability of ecotourism destinations. The logistic regression results suggest that a 1-unit increase in the education/interpretation score and environmental conservation score led to a 69 per cent and 51 per cent increase, respectively, in the odds of being included in an ecotourism certification programme. Thus, a policy intervention that can lead to more certified ecotourism providers will help safeguard the destination and meet the sustainability criterion.

References

ABETA (2015). *Brazilian Association of Ecotourism Firms and Adventure Tourism*. Retrieved from http://www.abeta.tur.br/index.php/explore-menu/conheca-os-associados

Brazilian Ministry of Tourism (2009). *Hábitos de Consumos do Turismo Brasileiro*. Retrieved from http://www.turismo.gov.br/sites/default/turismo/noticias/todas_noticias/Noticias_download/13.11.09_Pesquisa_Hxbitos_2009.pdf

Brazil's Ministry of Tourism (2019). *Tourism Statistical Yearbook 2019*, Ministry of Tourism, Vol. 46, December 2019.

Burns, R.P., & Burns, R. (2008). *Business Research Methods and Statistics Using SPSS*, Sage Publications.

Bustam, T.D., Buta, N., & Stein, T.V. (2012). "The Role of Certification in International Ecotourism Operators' Internet Promotion of Education". *Journal of Ecotourism*, *11*(2): 85-101.

Conaghan, A., Hanrahan, J., & Sligo, I.T. (2010). *Demand for and Perceptions of Sustainable Tourism Certification in Ireland*, Institute of Technology of Sligo.

Donohoe, H.M. & Needham, R.D. (2008). "Internet-based Ecotourism Marketing: Evaluating Canadian Sensitivity to Ecotourism Tenets". *Journal of Ecotourism*, *7*(1): 15-43.

Drăgoi, M., Iamandi, I.E., Munteanu, S., Ciobanu, R., & Lădaru, R. (2017). "Incentives for Developing Resilient Agritourism Entrepreneurship in Rural Communities in Romania in a European Context". *Sustainability*, *9*(12): 2205.

Esparon, M., Gyuris, E. & Stoeckl. N. (2014). "Does ECO Certification Deliver Benefits?: An Empirical Investigation of Visitors' Perceptions of the Importance of ECO certification's Attributes and of Operators' Performance". *Journal of Sustainable Tourism*, *22*(1): 148-69.

Fogle, E.L.V., & Duffy, L.N. (2018). "Guiding Practices for Implementing an Eco-certification Programme: A Case Study of Ecotourism Australia". *E-review of Tourism Research*, 15.

Font, X. (2007). "Ecotourism Certification: Potential and Challenges", pp. 386-405, in J. Higham (ed.), *Critical Issues in Ecotourism: Understanding a Complex Tourism Phenomenon*, Elsevier, Ltd, Oxford, UK.

Font, X., Sanabria, R., and Skinner, E. (2003). "Sustainable Tourism and Ecotourism Certification: Raising Standards and Benefits", *Journal of Ecotourism, 2*(3): 213-18.

GEC (2007). "Oslo Statement of Ecotourism", in *The International Ecotourism Society*, Retrieved from https://www.ecotourism.org/oslo-statement-on-ecotourism

Government of São Paulo State, Division of Tourism (2011). "Secretaria de Turismo. Companhia Paulista de Turismo e Eventos". *Turismo Paulista: Highlights*. São Paulo, p. 12.

Hakim, L. (2017). "Managing Biodiversity for a Competitive Ecotourism Industry in Tropical Developing Countries: New Opportunities in Biological Fields". *Conference Proceedings, 1908*(1): 030008, AIP Publishing.

Hall, B. & Weiler, C. (1992). "Introduction What's Special about Special Interest Tourism?", in Weiler, *Special Interest Tourism*, p. 5.

Honey, M., and Rome, A. (2001). "Protecting Paradise: Certification Programmes for Sustainable Tourism and Ecotourism". October, Institute for Policy Studies, Washington, DC.

Issaverdis, J.P. (2001). "The Pursuit of Excellence: Benchmarking, Accreditation, Best Practice and Auditing", pp. 579-94 in D.B. Weaver (Ed.), *The Encyclopedia of Ecotourism*, CAB International, Cambridge, MA.

Jamal, T., Borges, M., and Stronza, A. (2006). "The Institutionalisation of Ecotourism: Certification, Cultural Equity and Praxis", *Journal of Ecotourism, 5*(3): 145-75.

Jones, G.G., & Spadafora, A. (2016). "Entrepreneurs and the Co-creation of Ecotourism in Costa Rica", *Harvard Business School General Management Unit Working Paper*, pp. 16-136.

Lai, P., & Shafer, S. (2005). "Marketing Ecotourism through the Internet: An Evaluation of Selected Ecolodges in Latin America and the Caribbean". *Journal of Ecotourism*, *4*(3): 143-60.

Margaryan, L, and Stenstad, S. (2017). "Sustainable by Nature?: The Case of (Non) adoption of Eco-certification among the Nature-based Tourism Companies in Scandinavia". *Journal of Cleaner Production, 162*: 559-567.

Mazilu, M., Marinescu, R., & Gheorgheci, S. (2017). "Aspects Regarding the Romanian Certification in Ecotourism Destinations", *Annals of the Constantin Brancusi*, University ofTargu Jiu, Economy Series, (3), 109-17

McCool, S. (1995). "Linking Tourism, the Environment, and Concepts of Sustainability: Setting the Stage", In S. McCool & A. Watson (Eds.), *Linking Tourism, the Environment, and Concepts of Sustainability: Setting the Stage*, General Technical Report -Intermountain Research Station, USDA Forest Service 1995 No. INT-323, pp. 3-7.

McCool, S.F., & Moisey, R.N. (2008). "Introduction: Pathways and Pitfalls in the Search for Sustainable Tourism", *Tourism, Recreation and Sustainability*, 1-16.

McGahey, S. (2012). "The Ethics, Obligations, and Stakeholders of Ecotourism Marketing", *Intelektinëekonomika*, *6*(2): 75-88.

Medina, L.K. (2005). "Ecotourism and Certification: Confronting the Principles and Pragmatics of Socially Responsible Tourism". *Journal of Sustainable Tourism, 13*(3): 281-95.

Mequanint, F., & Gebremedhin, S. (2015). "Contribution of Local Community for Ecotourism Development in and around Abijata Shalla Lakes National Park with Emphasis to Women's Role, Ethiopia". *Australasian Journal of Social Science, 1*(1): 1-19.

Neto, F. (2003). "A New Approach to Sustainable Tourism Development: Moving beyond Environmental Protection", In *Natural Resources Forum 27*(3): 212-22, Blackwell Publishing Ltd.

OECD (2018). "OECD Economic Surveys-Brazil", Retrieved http://www.oecd.org/economy/surveys/Brazil-2018-OECD-economic-survey-overview.pdf

Rajasenan, D., Manaloor, V., & Abraham, B.G. (2012). "Tourist Profiles and Characteristics vis-à-vis Market Segmentation of Ecotourism Destinations in Kerala", *Journal of Economics and Sustainable Development*, *3*(14), IISTE, New York.

Sangpikul, A. (2010). "Marketing Ecotourism through the Internet: A Case of Ecotourism Business in Thailand", *International Journal of Hospitality & Tourism Administration*, *11*(2): 107-37.

São Paulo Turismo (2018). "São Paulo: City of the World. Facts and Figures of Business, Events, Travel and Tourism in the City of São Paulo". Retrieved http://www.observatoriodoturismo.com.br/pdf/DADOS_FATOS_2018_ING.pdf

Sharpley, R. (2010). "The Myth of Sustainable Tourism", Centre of Sustainable Development, *Working Papers Series*, (4) 2009.

Spenceley, A. (2019), "Sustainable Tourism Certification in the African Hotel Sector", *Tourism Review, 74*(2): 179-93. https://doi.org/10.1108/TR-09-2017-0145

Spenceley, A. and Bien, A. (2013). "Ecotourism Standards: International Accreditation and Local Certification and Indicators", pp. 404-17 in R. Ballantyne and J. Packer (eds.), *International Handbook on Ecotourism*. Edward Elgar, Cheltenham, UK.

Tavakol, M., & Dennick, R. (2011). "Making Sense of Cronbach's Alpha". *International Journal of Medical Education, 2*: 53.

TIES (2015). *The International Ecotourism Society*, Retrieved https://www.ecotourism.org/what-is-ecotourism.

Toth, Robert (2002). "Exploring the Concepts Underlying Certification", in *Ecotourism and Certification: Setting Standards in Practice*, Edited by Martha Honey, Island Press, Washington, DC, p. 73.

UNCTAD (2016). "Country Paper: Overview of the Services Sector in Brazil, Multi-year Expert Meeting on Trade, Services and Development Geneva", 18-20 May, Ministry of Development, Industry and Foreign Trade, Brazil and ILO Research Department.

UNEP (2013). *Green Economy and Trade*, Retrieved http://www.unep.org/greeneconomy/Portals/88/GETReport/pdf/Chapitre%207%20Tourism.pdf.

UNESCO (2018). *Brasilia-Education for Sustainable Development*, Retrieved http://www.unesco.org/new/en/brasilia/naturalsciences/environment/education-for-sustainable-development/

UNWTO (2004). "Indicators of Sustainable Development for Tourism Destinations: A Guidebook", World Tourism Organisation, Madrid, Spain.

UNWTO (2015). *Sustainable Development of Tourism*. Retrieved http://sdt.unwto.org/content/about-us-5.

UNWTO (2017). *UNWTO Tourism Highlights*.

UNWTO (2018). *Tourism Barometer*, March-April, Vol. 16.

UNWTO (2019). *International Tourism Highlights*. Retrieved https://www.e-unwto.org/doi/pdf/10.18111/9789284421152

WCED (1987). *World Commission on Environment and Development: Our Common Future*. Retrieved https://sustainabledevelopment.un.org/content/documents/5987our-common-future.pdf

Weber, R.P. (1990). *Basic Content Analysis*, No. 49, Sage.

World Bank (2005). *CSR in the Tourism Industry?: The Status of and Potential for Certification, Codes of Conduct and Guidelines*, World Bank, Washington, DC, Retrieved http://www.ifc.org/ifcest/economics.nsf/Content/CSR-Research.

12

Panel Autoregressive Distributed Lag (ARDL) Approach for Investigating the Tourism Driven Growth

New Evidence from the Context of South Asia

A. Sankaran

Introduction

Tourism is a modern industry, which involves vast amounts of human, monetary and physical resources worldwide. Due to its multifold benefits and fastest-growing nature, it has been recognized as a dynamic industry both in developed and developing countries. In recent decades, due to increased global integration and disposable income coupled with the knowledge economy, this sector is marching towards sustainable growth with a large-scale expansion (UNCTAD, 2006). At different levels, the travel and tourism industry occupies a predominant place globally and recognized in international trade as the largest service segment (Place *et al.*, 1998). In the Internet-driven world, the tourism sector increases the income of the people living in and around the tourism sport, and the international agencies' revenue directly or indirectly who are facilitating the tourists (Tang & Tan, 2013). The global economy moves towards the fastest economic growth creates some repercussion effects, including environmental damage. The tourism industry's importance can be mentioned from the environmental aspect that according to UNWTO (2008), this sector is responsible for only a shallow level of environmental degradation than that of the industrial sector.

Tourism has become one of the main drives of socio-economic development in a nation. Both developed and developing countries are using this sector as a piece of powerful equipment to attain perceptible growth at an increasing rate. Another highlight of the tourism sector is its forward and backward linkages with other ancillary industries such as hotels, restaurants, transportation, local markets, furniture, etc. In this connection, Grosso *et al.* (2007) articulated that the strength of forwarding and backward linkages for the tourism industry is more substantial than that of other sectors. Further, the statistical evidence provided by Ashley *et al.* (2007) revealed that this intersectoral connection of the tourism sector with other areas creates approximately 60 per cent extra impact in an economy. In the contemporary world, interestingly, tourism promotes even human development. The existing evidence provided by the ranking of the United Nations Development Programme (UNDP) demonstrated that there is a close association between international tourism and human development index. Further, in developing nations, the foreign exchange derived from international tourism is used for financing developmental projects such as micro, small & medium enterprises, infrastructural development, and, other sectors which are closely connected with the socio-economic development of these nations and more so in poverty alleviation programmes.

Owing to its upsurging contribution in all walks of developments in the past few decades, it attracts the attention of policymakers, researchers and academicians (Tang & Tan, 2013). Under such circumstance, though many studies pursued on different dimensions of the tourism sector, a scientific research examining the tourism-led growth hypothesis in the South Asian context in general and the impact of tourism in employment generation, in particular, is scanty. Hence, the present study addresses this issue and adds a piece of knowledge to the existing literature body through meticulous assessment using the time-series data for the recent decade by applying panel ARDL model. The result of the attempt revealed that (a) the impact of international tourist flow on the economic development is positive and significant and interestingly, (b) the global tourist flow also significantly generated employment opportunities in the South Asian countries over the study period.

Previous Studies

Tourism and Economic Growth

In the modern world, it is generally accepted that the tourism industry significantly contributes to the socio-economic development of a nation. Once, the former Secretary-General of *WTO Mr. Francesco Frangialli* uttered that the world nations' sustainable growth and economic acceleration is due to the dynamic and durable tourism sector's appreciable performance. The tourism-led growth theory put-forwarded by social scientists explicates that tourism sector can increase the economic development at more extensive rate (Balaguer and Cantavella-Jordà, 2002; Durbarry, 2004; Alegre, 2006; Nowak *et al.*, 2007; Brida *et al.*, 2008; Sakai, 2006; Kadir and Jusoff, 2010; Perez-Dacal *et al.*, 2014; Ridderstaat, Croes, & Nijkamp, 2016).

In the seminal research, a group of scholars pursued country-specific studies to re-examine the validity of the tourism-led growth. Among the available country-specific studies, Eugenio Martin *et al.* (2004) for twenty-one Latin America countries, Lee & Chang, (2008) for fifty-five OECD and non-OECD countries, Narayan *et al.* (2010) for four Pacific nations and Cárdenas-García *et al.* (2015) for one hundred and forty-four developing and developed nations found a long-run and positive relationship between tourism and economic growth. This result was consistent with the research findings of Balaguer & Cantavella-Jorda (2002) for Spain, Dritsakis (2004) in the case of Greece, Gundog & Hatemi-J. (2005); and

Demiroz & Ongan (2005) in Turkey, and Massidda and Mattana (2013) for Italy. Besides, few studies (see Oh, 2005; Katircioglu, 2009; Cai & Wang, 2010; Ghosh, 2011; and Arslanturk *et al.*, 2011) supported the growth-led tourism expansion in different parts of the world.

Benefit specific studies also conducted by scholars to assess the impact of tourism. In a historical research Kim & Chen (1964) mentioned that expansion to tourism is a unique channel for obtaining the foreign exchange. Hence, a few developing nations could be able to import machines and equipment to augment economic growth. Further, the available studies are focusing on the impact of tourism in earning foreign exchange. For instance, Bhatia (1971), Dube (1987), Vellas and Becherel (1995), Kumar (1998), Zulfikar (1998), and Narayanan & George (2001) found that there is a substantial positive impact of tourism in foreign exchange earnings. Further, a few of the studies, above-mentioned, revealed that in developing nations, the income generated by tourism is a capital to enhance the local and national economic layers.

Tourism and Employment

Both in developed and developing countries, the employment generation is necessary for the economy' smooth function. Tourism sector creates a considerable volume of employment opportunities at different levels. In this regard, Hjalager and Andersen (2001) mentioned that this sector's contribution for economic growth and employment generation is appreciable. Further, Mill and Morrison (1984) reported that tourism is one of the labour-intensive sectors and can accommodate the maximum number of persons for their benefits. In a comprehensive assessment, Ashley *et al.* (2007) revealed that tourism is basically a labour-intensive sector than that of the agricultural sector, and it accommodates both skilled and unskilled labours. The Econometric exercise of Onder, K., & Durgun, A. (2008) found a long run connection between tourism and growth of employment. Shukla & Ansari (2013) differ from others and they argue that the tourism industry is well-connected with other ancillary industry in both informal and formal sectors. Hence, it creates a sizeable number of employment opportunities.

In their analytical research, Mathieson and Wall (1982) classified the employment opportunities created by the tourism sector into three broad categories such as direct employment, indirect employment and induced employment. All these employment opportunities are increasing over the course of development. According to Icoz and Kozak (2002), there is a higher level of employment in tourism sector due to labour intensity, the existence of many part-time and temporary jobs, the availability of many low-paying employment opportunity and seasonal intensity. The statistical evidence offered by Goodwin (1999) depicted that interestingly tourism sector creates employment opportunities for women in many layers. The percentage of women employed in the tourism sector is ranging from 10 to 60 per cent, in some Muslim countries, approximately 10 per cent of the women labour is accommodated by tourism sector. The existing statistical evidence revealed that around 60 per cent in the employment created by the tourism sector is filled by women in Bolivia. Further, studies conducted by Belisle & Hoy (1980); Davis *et al.* (1988); Khan *et al.* (1990); West (1993); Uysal & Gitelson (1994); Archer (1995) and Durbarry & Sinclair (2002) concluded that tourism sector created a good number of job opportunities in different nations.

Estimation Procedure

The study proposed to estimate the functional relationship between tourism and economic development. More specifically, the chief objectives of the present study are to re-examine the validity of the *tourism-led growth hypothesis* and also to find out the effect of the tourism sector in creating employment opportunities in the South Asian region. The South Asian region is encompassed by eight nations such as Afghanistan, Bangladesh, Bhutan, India, Maldives, Nepal, Pakistan and Sri Lanka. Among those nations, the accurate time-series dataset is available only for six countries. Hence, we included these six nations such as Bangladesh, India, Maldives,

Nepal, Pakistan and Sri Lanka for our study as they reflect nearly 80 per cent of the tourism picture of South Asian region. The study area has been deliberately selected because of the remarkable progress of this region in the past few decades in the tourism sector. Further, this is a comfortable zone for Europeans and Americans due to a considerable exchange rate advantage, low cost and protected law for international tourists. The study has been conducted based on the secondary data, which are sourced from international level organisations such as World Development Indicator, World Travel and Tourism Council, World Tourism Organisation, the Statistics and Facts of Global Travel and Tourism Industry and OECD for the period spanning from 2000 to 2020. The variables included in the study are the total number of tourist flow, the total amount of many spent by tourists, GDP of the respective nations and employment generated by the tourism sector. Based on the objectives of the study, in the first estimation, GDP is the dependent variable and in the second estimation employment generated through tourism is the dependent variable in our model. To find out the nexus between variables, we used the panel ARDL model, which social scientists in tourism-related research very rarely use. The general form of panel ARDL procedure as follows:

$$Y_{1t} = \alpha_i Y_{i-1} + \sum_{j=0}^{1} \beta_{ij} X_{i,t-j} + \mu_i + \epsilon_{it} \qquad \text{.... (1)}$$

$X_{i,t-j}$ is an n×k vector of all independent variables (tourist arrival (LTARR), expenditure on tourist places (LTEXP), employment generation (LTEMP) in tourist sectors and economic development (LTGDP), and receipt (LTREC)), β_{ij} is k ×1 coefficient vector, μ_i country-specific effect $\in_{it}$ and is white noise term. Equation no. (1) can be transformed as an error correction term as;

$$\Delta Y_{it} = \delta_{1,i}(Y_{i,t-1} - \pi'_{1,i} X_{i,t-1}) + \pi^{*\prime}_{1,i} \Delta X_{it} + \mu_i + \epsilon_{it} \qquad \text{... (2)}$$

Where, $\delta_{1,i}$= -(1-α_i) and $\theta_{1.ji} = \frac{\sum_{j-0}^{1} \pi_{ij}}{1-\alpha_i}$

Results and Discussion

Tourism is one of the fastest-growing industries in most of the nations. In the recent study of Tugcu (2014) reported that tourism came as the fourth predominant industry after fuels, chemical and food. The horizontal and vertical expansion of this industry attract the attention of governments, and policymakers at length. The existing statistical evidence revealed that the total international tourist flow experienced a perceptible growth from 25 million in 1950 to 940 million in 2010 (UNCTAD, 2013). Further, it attained significant growth in the present decade. Additionally, this sector generates approximately 12 per cent of the global GDP, and it is 40 per cent in the case of the developing world. Against this empirical magnitude, the present study attempts to re-examine the tourism-led growth and the tourism sector's contribution towards employment generation in selected South Asian regions.

To check the data set's stationarity, we have performed Im, Pesaran and Shin (IPS, 1997) and Levin, Lin and Chu unit root test (LLC, 2002) presented the output in Table 12.1. The result shows that all variables are non-stationary in level but turns into stationary after taking their first difference in IPS unit root test. At the same time, LLC test reveals that except log value of employment, all variables are stationary at the first difference and employment is stationary at level.

Table 12.1: Panel Unit Root Test Result

Variables	IPS		Levin, Lin & chu	
	Level	1st difference	Level	1st difference
LTGDP	5.73	-5.11***	3.24	-4.29***
LTARR	2.56	-4.07***	1.86	-3.75***
LTEMP	-0.78	-6.11***	-3.22***	-
LTEXP	1.93	-4.54***	1.93	-4.54***
LTREC	3.26	-4.87***	0.89	-4.75***

***indicates statistically significant at 1 per cent level.

Hence, from the unit root test result, we conclude that our data series under study is mixed of *I (0)* and *I (1)*. Therefore, in this dilemma, Pesaran and Pesaran (2001) suggested panel ARDL method to identify cointegration among the variables. This seems to be more appropriate to test the short and long-run relationships among the variables.

Estimated Results

Tourism activities and its impact on GDP in South Asian countries such as Bangladesh, India, Maldives, Nepal, Pakistan and Sri Lanka are explored. Both short-run and long-run coefficients are discussed. The tourism sector's role and its potential can be enquired in the light of short-run and long-run estimates.

Table 12.2: Model 1

Maximum dependent lags: 4 (Automatic selection)
Model selection method: Akaike Information Criteria (AIC)
Selected model: ARDL (1, 2, 2, 2, 2)
Short run and long run elasticities
Dependent variable: LTGDP

Long-run result		Short-run result				
		Lags				
Variables	**Coefficient**	**Variables**	**0**	**1**	**2**	**3**
LTARR	0.14***	ΔLTGDP	-	0.42*	-0.05	-0.01
LTEMP	-0.22***	ΔLTARR	-0.05	-0.05*	-0.07	-
LTEXP	0.02***	ΔLTEXP	0.188**	0.177**	0.10	-
Constant	2.05**	ΔEXP	-0.02***	-0.01	-0.00	-
ECM	-1.02**					

*, ** and *** indicates significant at 10 per cent, 5 per cent & 1 per cent level, respectively ECM is error correction term.

Table 12.2 indicates the cointegrating panel relation between tourism components such as tourist arrivals, employment, and economic development (GDP). The long-run positive associations from tourists' arrival and tourism expenditure to GDP is highly significant. A one per cent change in tourist arrival contributes to 0.14 per cent increase in GDP in south Asian countries considered. South Asian countries have the potential to create tourism industry a well-flourished sector, which can contribute even larger outcome.

Tourism expenditure is very weakly influencing GDP. Only 0.02 percentage change is observable for a one per cent change in tourism expenditure. Hence, it could be mentioned that the tourism industry is a less explored activity in South Asian countries. So, the changes in these sectors are too low to influence the aggregate output of the economy.

Table 12.3: Model 2

Maximum dependent lags: 4 (Automatic selection)
Model selection method: Akaike Information Criteria (AIC)
Selected model: ARDL (4, 3, 3, 3)
Short-run and long-run elasticities
Dependent variable: LTEMP

Long-run result		Short-run result				
			Lags			
Variables	**Coefficient**	**Variables**	**0**	**1**	**2**	**3**
LTGDP	-2.99***	ΔLTGDP	-0.25	0.81***	-	-
LTARR	0.32***	ΔLTARR	0.30	0.13	-	-
LTEXP	-0.15**	ΔLTEXP	0.15	0.09	-	-
LTREC	0.46***	ΔLTREC	-0.01	-0.14	-	-
ECM	-0.50***					

*, ** and *** indicates significant at 10 per cent, 5 per cent & 1 per cent level, respectively ECM is error correction term.

The employment has a negative influence on the dependent variable that is moderately influencing GDP. Precisely, a 0.22 per cent of negative impact is stemming from a one per cent change in employment. Clearly, employment penetration in tourism is very less explored activity. The major portion of service sector employment is percolated in sectors other than tourism. Undoubtedly, tourism is yet to be taken-up as a vibrant economic activity by the people in these regions.

Error-correction term explains that there is a disequilibrium in the short-run, and there is a process of adjustment takes from short-run disequilibrium to long-run equilibrium at a speed of 102 per cent. The impact of employment is positive in the short-run, implying that there is no positive level effect as it becomes negative in the long-run. Also, the lagged value of GDP is positive. The one-year lagged impact of tourists' arrival is negligibly producing negative impact at 0.05 per cent.

Short-run, Long-run and Joint Causality

The causality can be inferred from the coefficients. The joint causal influence of the independent variables on GDP can be explained from the error-correction coefficient. The error-correction coefficient is negative and significant, implying the collective causality is escalating from independent variables to GDP.

So, short-run causality is understood to be flowing from the past values of GDP, tourist arrival, employment and expenditure, implying that these variables can influence GDP. While employment is positively influencing, tourist arrival and expenditure have a positive causal influence on GDP in the long-run, while employment has a negative causal impact on GDP.

Employment and Tourism: A Panel investigation

As discussed early, in the second model employed, the dependent variable is employment representing tourism sector activity. The impacts of other tourism-related variables on employment, along with GDP, is explored. The long-run influence of GDP is found to be negative on employment. A one per cent rise in GDP leads to a three per cent reduction in employment. The economic activities, constructing aggregate GDP, is not favourable to tourism-related activities to percolate. As a result, tourism generating activities are heavily lacking in this region. Tourism expenditure is also negatively influencing employment opportunities. For 1 per cent change of spending, a negative 0.15 per cent change is reflected in employment generation. What prevents employment generation in the tourism industry in South Asia is an important question to be probed into.

Tourist arrival and tourism receipts have positively contributed to employment generation. A one per cent rise in tourist arrival promotes 0.32 per cent change in employment. This indicates that tourism revenue attracts more job. Tourist arrival brings in 0.42 per cent change in employment. The direct proportional relationship between these variables highlights the potential of tourism sector in employment generation.

The negative error correction term implies that there is an adjustment process occurring from short-run disequilibrium situations back to equilibrium in the long-run at a speed of 50 per cent. A one-year lagged value of GDP has a positive impact on employment in the short-run.

Short-run and Long-run Joint Causality

As in the previous session, joint causality, short-run, and long-run causality can be interpreted from the error correction term and short-run coefficients. The independent variables have a joint causal impact on employment as the error correction term is negative and highly significant. Short-run causality is escalating from the one period lagged value of GDP as it is the only variable with a significant coefficient. The causal relation escalating from GDP and expenditure to employment generation is negative. With respect to tourists' arrival and receipts, positive causal relations are percolating from them.

Conclusion and Policy Implications

The entire work revolves around the relation between tourism components such as employment, receipts, expenditure, tourist arrival and GDP. The result has been classified into twofold: tourism influencing GDP and secondly tourism employment and its determining factors including GDP. In order to understand the dynamics, we used PMG technique in the umbrella model of panel ARDL approach for cointegration in the context of the South Asian region for the period from 2000-2020.

In the case of GDP, tourist arrival and tourist expenditure have a positive causal impact, but coefficients are weak. The tourist expenditure is negligibly low, but as the causality inferred from coefficients and error correction, there is the existence of ***tourism-led growth*** in South Asia and its potential remain untapped. The employment generation is positively influenced by tourist arrival and tourism receipts signifying expansion of tourism activity can absorb a lot of unemployed youth, which can drive economic growth.

The potential of tourism to contribute to aggregate output is not subjected to heated policy analysis. The diversification of the tourism sector is much needed to accomplish this task. Tourism should be considered as an essential sector of earnings. Then only it will bring effective policy decisions into work. The employment opportunity is very sluggish, and once given proper care, it can absorb a lot of unemployed youth. The policymakers should have a direction and a plan to tap the potential of tourism-led growth experience.

References

Alegre, J., & Pou, L. (2006). "The Length of Stay in the Demand for Tourism." *Tourism Management, 27* (6): 1343-55.

Arslanturk, Y., Balcilar, M., & Ozdemir, Z.A. (2011). "Time-varying Linkages between Tourism Receipts and Economic Growth in a Small Open Economy." *Economic Modelling, 28*(1-2): 664-71.

Kumar, Ajith M.K. (1998). "Psychographic and Demographic Profiles of Foreign Tourists Visiting Kerala with Special Reference to Spending Patterns". Unpublished Ph.D Thesis, Cochin University of Science and Technology (CUSAT), Kochi, Kerala.

Archer, B. (1995). "Importance of Tourism for the Economy of Bermuda". *Annals of Tourism Research, 22*(4): 918-30.

Ashley, C., De Brine, P., Lehr, A. & Wilde, H. (2007). *The Role of the Tourism Sector in Expanding Economic Opportunity.* Cambridge: John F. Kennedy School of Government, Harvard University.

Balaguer, J. & Cantavella-Jorda, M. (2002). "Tourism as a Long-run Economic Growth Factor: The Spanish Case." *Applied Economics, 34*(7), 877-84.

Belisle, F.J., & Hoy, D.R. (1980). "The Perceived Impact of Tourism by Residents A Case Study in Santa Marta," Colombia. *Annals of Tourism Research, 7*(1): 83-101.

Bhatia. (1971). *International Tourism: Fundamentals and Practices,* Sterling Publications, New Delhi.

Brida, J.G., Lanzilotta, B. & Risso, W.A. (2008). "Turismo y crecimiento económico: el caso de Uruguay. PASOS". *Revista de Turismo y Patrimonio Cultural, 6*(3): 481-92.

Cai, M., & Wang, Y.M. (2010). "Low-carbon Tourism: A New Mode of Tourism Development [J]". *Tourism Tribune, 1*(5): 13-17.

Cárdenas-García, P. J., Sánchez-Rivero, M. & Pulido-Fernández, J.I. (2015). "Does Tourism Growth Influence Economic Development?", *Journal of Travel Research, 54*(2): 206-221.

Davis, D., Allen, J., & Cosenza, R.M. (1988). "Segmenting Local Residents by Their Attitudes, Interests, and Opinions toward Tourism." *Journal of Travel Research, 27*(2): 2-8.

Demiroz, D.M., & Ongan, S. (2005). "The Contribution of Tourism to the Long-Run Turkish Economic Growth." *Ekonomický èasopis, 9*: 880-94.

Dritsakis, N. (2004). "Tourism as a Long-Run Economic Growth Factor: An Empirical Investigation for Greece Using Causality Analysis." *Tourism Economics, 10*(3): 305-16.

Dube, R. (1987). *Tourism in the Economy of Madhya Pradesh.* Daya Books.

Durbarry, R. (2004). "Tourism and Economic Growth: The Case of Mauritius." *Tourism Economics, 10*(4): 389-401.

Durbarry, R., & Sinclair, M.T. (2002). *The Price Sensitivity of Tourism Demand in Malta: a Report for the Malta Tourism Authority.* Nottingham University Business School, Nottingham.

Eugenio-Martin, J.L., Martín Morales, N. & Scarpa, R. (2004). "Tourism and Economic Growth in Latin American Countries: A Panel Data Approach", *FEEM Working Paper,* No. 26.

Ghosh, S. (2011). "Examining Tourism-led Growth Hypothesis for India." *International Journal of Indian Culture and Business Management, 4*(3): 347-55.

Goodwin, H. (1998, October). "Sustainable Tourism and Poverty Elimination." In *DFID/DETR Workshop on Sustainable Tourism and Poverty* (Vol. 13). London: Department for International Development.

Grosso, M.G., Lesher, M. & Pinali, E. (2007). "Services Trade Liberalisation and Tourism Development." *OECD Trade Policy Papers,* No. 57, OECD Publishing, Paris.

Gundog, L. & Hatemi-J., A. (2005). "Is the Tourism-led Growth Hypothesis Valid for Turkey?" *Applied Economics Letters, 12*(8): 499-504.

Hjalager, A.M. & Andersen, S. (2001). "Tourism Employment: Contingent Work or Professional Career?", *Employee Relations.*

İçöz, O. & Kozak, M. (2002). "Turizm ekonomisi: Turizmin makro ve mikro ekonomik etkileri. 2." *Baski, Ankara, Türkiye: Turhan Kitabevi Yayinlari.*

Im, K.S., Pesaran, M.H. & Shin, Y. (1997). "Testing for Unit Roots in Heterogeneous Panels." *Journal of Econometrics, 115*(1): 53-74.

Kadir, N. & Jusoff, K. (2010). "The Cointegration and Causality Tests for Tourism and Trade in Malaysia." *International Research Journal of Finance and Economics, 2*(1): 138-43.

Katircioglu, S.T. (2009). "Revisiting the Tourism-led-growth Hypothesis for Turkey Using the Bounds Test and Johansen Approach for Cointegration." *Tourism Management, 30*(1): 17-20.

Khan, H., Seng, C.F., & Cheong, W.K. (1990). "Tourism Multiplier Effects on Singapore." *Annals of Tourism Research, 17*(3): 408-18.

Kim, H.J. & Chen, M.H. (2006). "Tourism Expansion and Economic Development: The Case of Taiwan." *Tourism Management, 27*(5): 925-33.

Lee, C.C. & Chang, C.P. (2008). "Tourism Development and Economic Growth: A Closer Look at Panels." *Tourism Management, 29*(1): 180-92.

Levin, A., Lin, C.F. & Chu, C.S.J. (2002). "Unit Root Tests in Panel Data: Asymptotic and Finite-sample Properties." *Journal of Econometrics, 108*(1): 1-24.

Massidda, C., & Mattana, P. (2013). "A SVECM Analysis of the Relationship Between International Tourism Arrivals, GDP and Trade in Italy." *Journal of Travel Research, 52*(1): 93-105.

Mathieson, A. & Wall, G. (1982). *Tourism, Economic, Physical and Social Impacts.* Longman.

Narayan, P.K., Narayan, S., Prasad, A. & Prasad, B.C. (2010). "Tourism and Economic Growth: A Panel Data Analysis for Pacific Island Countries." *Tourism Economics, 16*(1): 169-83.

Narayanan & George (2001). *Tourism Management: A Global Perspective.*

Nowak, J.J., Sahli, M. & Cortés-Jiménez, I. (2007). "Tourism, Capital Goods Imports and Economic Growth: Theory and Evidence for Spain." *Tourism Economics, 13*(4): 515-36.

Oh, C.O. (2005). "The Contribution of Tourism Development to Economic Growth in the Korean Economy." *Tourism Management, 26*(1): 39-44.

Onder, K. & Durgun, A. (2008). *Effects of Tourism Sector on the Employment in Turkey: An Econometric Application.* Ministry of National Defence, Turkey, 365-73.

Pesaran, M.H. & Pesaran, B. (2001). *Working with Microfit 4.0: Interactive Econometric Analysis.*

Pérez-Dacal, D., Pena-Boquete, Y. & Fernández, M. (2014). "A Measuring Tourism Specialisation: A Composite Indicator for the Spanish Regions." Almatourism, *Journal of Tourism, Culture and Territorial Development*, *5*(9): 35-73.

Place, S., Hall, C.M. & Lew, A.A. (1998). *Sustainable Tourism: A Geographical Perspective*, 107-18.

Ridderstaat, J., Croes, R. & Nijkamp, P. (2016). "The Tourism Development–Quality of Life Nexus in a Small Island Destination." *Journal of Travel Research*, *55*(1): 79-94.

Mill, R.C., & Alastire, M. Morrison. (1984). *The Tourism System*, Prentice Hall International, USA.

Sakai, M. (2006). "12 Public Sector Investment in Tourism Infrastructure. *International Handbook on the Economics of Tourism*, 266.

Shukla, P. K. & Ansari, A.A. (2013). "Role of Tourism Industry in Employment Generation in Gujarat: A Geographic Assessment." *International Journal of Research in humanities, Arts and Literature*, *1*(2): 1-8.

Tang, C.F. & Tan, E.C. (2015). "Tourism-led Growth Hypothesis in Malaysia: Evidence based upon Regime Shift Cointegration and Time-varying Granger Causality Techniques." *Asia Pacific Journal of Tourism Research*, *20*(sup. 1): 1430-50.

Tugcu, C.T. (2014). "Tourism and Economic Growth Nexus Revisited: A Panel Causality Analysis for the Case of the Mediterranean Region." *Tourism management*, *42*: 207-12.

UNCTAD, G. (2006). "World Investment Report." *FDI from Developing and Transition Economies: Implications for Development.*

Uysal, M., & Gitelson, R. (1994). "Assessment of Economic Impacts: Festivals and Special Events." *Festival Management and Event Tourism*, *2*(1): 3-9.

Vellas & Becherel. (1995). *International Tourism*, MacMillan, London.

West, G.R. (1993). "Economic Significance of Tourism in Queensland." *Annals of Tourism Research*, *20*(3): 490-504

Zulfikar, M. (1998). *Introduction to the Tourism and Hotel Industry with Special focus on Front Office Management.* Pisces Publications, the Nature Conservation Bureau Ltd.

Web search

https://www.e-unwto.org/doi/epdf/10.18111/9789284413560

Index